THIS IS METAPHYSICS

THIS IS PHILOSOPHY

Series editor: Steven D. Hales

Reading philosophy can be like trying to ride a bucking bronco—you hold on for dear life while "transcendental deduction" twists you to one side, "causa sui" throws you to the other, and a 300-word, 300-year-old sentence comes down on you like an iron-shod hoof the size of a dinner plate. *This Is Philosophy* is the riding academy that solves these problems. Each book in the series is written by an expert who knows how to gently guide students into the subject regardless of the reader's ability or previous level of knowledge. Their reader-friendly prose is designed to help students find their way into the fascinating, challenging ideas that compose philosophy without simply sticking the hapless novice on the back of the bronco, as so many texts do. All the books in the series provide ample pedagogical aids, including links to free online primary sources. When students are ready to take the next step in their philosophical education, *This Is Philosophy* is right there with them to help them along the way.

This Is Philosophy: An Introduction
Steven D. Hales

This Is Philosophy of Mind: An Introduction
Pete Mandik

This Is Ethics: An Introduction
Jussi Suikkanen

This Is Political Philosophy: An Introduction
Alex Tuckness and Clark Wolf

This Is Business Ethics: An Introduction
Tobey Scharding

This Is Metaphysics
Kris McDaniel

Forthcoming:

This Is Early Modern Philosophy
Kurt Smith

This Is Environmental Ethics
Wendy Lee

This Is Epistemology
Clayton Littlejohn and Adam Carter

This Is Bioethics: An Introduction
Udo Schuklenk

THIS IS
METAPHYSICS
AN INTRODUCTION

KRIS McDANIEL

WILEY Blackwell

Registered Office
John Wiley & Sons, Inc., 111 River Street, Hoboken, NJ 07030, USA

Editorial Office
111 River Street, Hoboken, NJ 07030, USA

For details of our global editorial offices, customer services, and more information about Wiley products visit us at www.wiley.com.

Wiley also publishes its books in a variety of electronic formats and by print-on-demand. Some content that appears in standard print versions of this book may not be available in other formats.

Library of Congress Cataloging-in-Publication Data

Names: McDaniel, Kris, 1976– author.
Title: This is metaphysics : an introduction / Kris McDaniel.
Description: Hoboken, NJ, USA : Wiley-Blackwell, 2020. | Series: This is philosophy | Includes bibliographical references and index.
Identifiers: LCCN 2019056737 (print) | LCCN 2019056738 (ebook) | ISBN 9781118400777 (paperback) | ISBN 9781118400807 (ePDF) | ISBN 9781118400784 (epub)
Subjects: LCSH: Metaphysics.
Classification: LCC BD111 .M464 2020 (print) | LCC BD111 (ebook) | DDC 110–dc23
LC record available at https://lccn.loc.gov/2019056737
LC ebook record available at https://lccn.loc.gov/2019056738

Cover design: Wiley

Set in 10/12pt Minion Pro by SPi Global, Pondicherry, India

Printed in the United States of America

10 9 8 7 6 5 4 3 2 1

Dedicated to Safira, Ranger, Nina, and Leneah, with love.

THIS IS METAPHYSICS

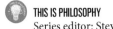 THIS IS PHILOSOPHY
Series editor: Steven D. Hales

Reading philosophy can be like trying to ride a bucking bronco—you hold on for dear life while "transcendental deduction" twists you to one side, "causa sui" throws you to the other, and a 300-word, 300-year-old sentence comes down on you like an iron-shod hoof the size of a dinner plate. *This Is Philosophy* is the riding academy that solves these problems. Each book in the series is written by an expert who knows how to gently guide students into the subject regardless of the reader's ability or previous level of knowledge. Their reader-friendly prose is designed to help students find their way into the fascinating, challenging ideas that compose philosophy without simply sticking the hapless novice on the back of the bronco, as so many texts do. All the books in the series provide ample pedagogical aids, including links to free online primary sources. When students are ready to take the next step in their philosophical education, *This Is Philosophy* is right there with them to help them along the way.

This Is Philosophy: An Introduction
Steven D. Hales

This Is Philosophy of Mind: An Introduction
Pete Mandik

This Is Ethics: An Introduction
Jussi Suikkanen

This Is Political Philosophy: An Introduction
Alex Tuckness and Clark Wolf

This Is Business Ethics: An Introduction
Tobey Scharding

This Is Metaphysics
Kris McDaniel

Forthcoming:

This Is Early Modern Philosophy
Kurt Smith

This Is Environmental Ethics
Wendy Lee

This Is Epistemology
Clayton Littlejohn and Adam Carter

This Is Bioethics: An Introduction
Udo Schuklenk

THIS IS
METAPHYSICS
AN INTRODUCTION

KRIS McDANIEL

WILEY Blackwell

The right of Kris McDaniel to be identified as the author of this work has been asserted in accordance with law.

Registered Office
John Wiley & Sons, Inc., 111 River Street, Hoboken, NJ 07030, USA

Editorial Office
111 River Street, Hoboken, NJ 07030, USA

For details of our global editorial offices, customer services, and more information about Wiley products visit us at www.wiley.com.

Wiley also publishes its books in a variety of electronic formats and by print-on-demand. Some content that appears in standard print versions of this book may not be available in other formats.

Limit of Liability/Disclaimer of Warranty
While the publisher and authors have used their best efforts in preparing this work, they make no representations or warranties with respect to the accuracy or completeness of the contents of this work and specifically disclaim all warranties, including without limitation any implied warranties of merchantability or fitness for a particular purpose. No warranty may be created or extended by sales representatives, written sales materials or promotional statements for this work. The fact that an organization, website, or product is referred to in this work as a citation and/or potential source of further information does not mean that the publisher and authors endorse the information or services the organization, website, or product may provide or recommendations it may make. This work is sold with the understanding that the publisher is not engaged in rendering professional services. The advice and strategies contained herein may not be suitable for your situation. You should consult with a specialist where appropriate. Further, readers should be aware that websites listed in this work may have changed or disappeared between when this work was written and when it is read. Neither the publisher nor authors shall be liable for any loss of profit or any other commercial damages, including but not limited to special, incidental, consequential, or other damages.

Library of Congress Cataloging-in-Publication Data

Names: McDaniel, Kris, 1976– author.
Title: This is metaphysics : an introduction / Kris McDaniel.
Description: Hoboken, NJ, USA : Wiley-Blackwell, 2020. | Series: This is
    philosophy | Includes bibliographical references and index.
Identifiers: LCCN 2019056737 (print) | LCCN 2019056738 (ebook) | ISBN
    9781118400777 (paperback) | ISBN 9781118400807 (ePDF) |
    ISBN 9781118400784 (epub)
Subjects: LCSH: Metaphysics.
Classification: LCC BD111 .M464 2020 (print) | LCC BD111 (ebook) | DDC
    110–dc23
LC record available at https://lccn.loc.gov/2019056737
LC ebook record available at https://lccn.loc.gov/2019056738

Cover design: Wiley

Set in 10/12pt Minion Pro by SPi Global, Pondicherry, India

Printed and bound by CPI Group (UK) Ltd, Croydon, CR0 4YY

10 9 8 7 6 5 4 3 2 1

Dedicated to Safira, Ranger, Nina, and Leneah, with love.

CONTENTS

AN INTRODUCTION TO *THIS IS METAPHYSICS*

0.1 Who is This Book for?

I wrote this book with three possible audiences in mind: philosophy majors 0.1
who are taking an upper-division metaphysics class, students in an entry-
level introduction to philosophy course, and members of the general public
who are curious about philosophy and willing to work through this book
outside of a classroom.

I expect that members of the first audience are going to have the easiest 0.2
time with this book because they already have some philosophy under their
belt and so are familiar with philosophical modes of questioning and reasoning. They will also have the guidance of a professional philosopher to
help address their questions, clarify what they might be confused about,
and suggest further things to think about beyond what I have the space to
deal with in this book. But I have done my best to make this book as accessible as possible to budding philosophers and the general public. I have
tried to present what is objectively very difficult material in an easy and
comfortable way by using down to earth language and a conversational
style, and by employing familiar examples to illustrate the theories and
arguments discussed. I have also included links to stuff that is online that is
relevant or useful to consider as you read through the book.

Even so, you should expect to work hard as you read this book. Philosophy 0.3
is not easy, and that is one reason that people have been wrestling with
philosophical problems for thousands of years. You can't expect to read a
philosophy book like you would read a *Harry Potter* novel. Instead, you

This Is Metaphysics: An Introduction, First Edition. Kris McDaniel.

should plan on periodically pausing after reading a section of the book—maybe even after reading a single paragraph—and then really thinking hard about what you've just read. When you pause, ask yourself the following questions:

What is the author trying to prove here?
That is, what conclusion is the author arguing for?
What are the premises he is using to reach this conclusion?
Do the premises really support the author's conclusion?
That is, if the premises are true, is the author's conclusion also likely to be true?
Are the premises of the author's argument true?
If the author's argument is not a good argument, is there a better argument for the same conclusion?
Are there good arguments *against* the author's conclusion?

In short, when working through a book of philosophy you must be a critical reader. You have to be an active participant, rather than a passive absorber of words and ideas. I've tried to make things as easy as possible, but I can't make an intrinsically difficult subject easy. If you aren't willing to do the work to think through the problems, puzzles, and arguments that will be discussed in the chapters to follow, you should put the book back on the shelf. I sincerely hope you won't though. The primary value of philosophy can only be seen by someone who has really worked through a philosophical problem.

0.4   Here is a suggestion for how to read this book critically. Read each chapter at least three times, but with deeper critical engagement each time. The first time you read the chapter, read it all the way through so that you get a feeling for the territory it covers. The second time you read the chapter, read it slowly, and pause at the end of each section so that you can write down any questions you might have about what is going on. If there is something that you don't understand while reading the chapter on this second reading, write down what you think you don't understand—and also guess what might be going on, and write your guess down too. If you have objections to an argument discussed, jot those down too. The third time you read the chapter, read it with the goal of finding answers to the questions you wrote down. Check to see whether any guesses you made have been confirmed or refuted. There is no guarantee that you will have all of these answers by the third read, but you should have a much clearer understanding of the issues discussed. In short, my recommendation is that you read through this book at three least times: first as a tourist, second as a detective, and third as a judge who compels the witnesses to answer your questions.

I will occasionally raise questions that I do not attempt to immediately 0.5 answer. When this happens, I invite you to pause and consider these questions before reading further. How might answering them one way rather than another affect the arguments you are considering?

I have tried to make this book as accessible as I can. This is why I have 0.6 made an effort to minimize the use technical jargon. But occasionally the introduction of technical terminology is important, and so sometimes I introduce some. My view on technical jargon is this: in every field, whenever it is feasible to avoid using technical phrases and stick instead to ordinary words, this is what you should do. Technical jargon should be viewed as a necessary evil, and like all necessary evils, it should be tolerated only when genuinely necessary, or at the very least, only when it is too cumbersome or annoying to do without it.

There are three situations in which it is a good idea to introduce techni- 0.7 cal jargon. First, sometimes using technical terminology lets you avoid writing out the same complicated sentences over and over again. In short, when you need an abbreviation, a bit of technical jargon can be useful. Here's a paragraph in which the introduction of some technical terminology would have been very helpful:

A lot of people want to know what makes a life worth living. Some people think that a person's life is worth living if and only if that person experiences a greater amount of pleasure than pain throughout the course of her life, and that a life is better or worse to the extent that the balance of pleasure over pain is higher or lower. But I think that the theory that a person's life is worth living if and only if that person experiences throughout her life a greater amount of pleasure than pain, and that a life is a better or worse life to the extent that the balance of pleasure minus pain in that life is higher or lower, is a false theory. Here is an argument against the theory that a person's life is worth living if and only if that person experiences throughout her life a greater amount of pleasure than pain, and that a life is a better or worse life to the extent that the balance of pleasure minus pain in that life is higher or lower. Suppose there is a person who spends the entirety of his life isolated from other human beings, acquires no interesting knowledge, and participates in no worthwhile activities, but derives a lot of pleasure from scratching himself. This person never experiences any pain. This person has a life that is barely worth living—few of us would switch places with him because we correctly think that our life is a better life. But the theory that a person's life is worth living if and only if that person experiences a greater amount of pleasure than pain throughout the course of her life, and that a life is better or worse to the extent that the balance of pleasure over pain is higher or lower, implies that this person has a great life. So, the theory that that a person's life is worth living if and only if that person experiences throughout her life a greater amount of pleasure than pain, and that a life is a better or worse life to the extent that the balance of pleasure minus pain in that life is higher or lower is false.

What a cumbersome paragraph to read! (It wasn't much fun to write either.) Even if the argument contained in this paragraph is a great argument, it is really hard to figure out what that argument is because you have to keep reading the same long chunk of words. Some way of abbreviating that long chunk would help. To see this, check out this paragraph:

> A lot of people want to know what makes a life worth living. Some people think that a person's life is worth living if and only if that person experiences a greater amount of pleasure than pain throughout the course of her life, and that a life is better or worse to the extent that the balance of pleasure over pain is higher or lower. Let's call this theory *hedonism*. I think that hedonism is a false theory. Here is an argument against hedonism. Suppose there is a person who spends the entirety of his life isolated from other human beings, acquires no interesting knowledge, and participates in no worthwhile activities, but derives a lot of pleasure from scratching himself. This person never experiences any pain. This person has a life that is barely worth living—few of us would switch places with him because we correctly think that our life is a better life. But hedonism implies that this person has a great life. So, hedonism is false.

I trust that you see that the second paragraph is much easier to read and understand *because* I introduced a bit of technical jargon, specifically, the word "hedonism." So sometimes technical terminology is necessary (or at least extremely helpful!) because it serves to abbreviate. But the jargon will be useful only if you also commit to remembering what that jargon abbreviates. So, when you come across any technical jargon, please commit yourself to remembering what it means! It will make your trek through this book more straightforward. (That said, there is a glossary at the end of the book that you may consult if you forget.)

0.8   A second reason to introduce technical terminology is that sometimes there isn't an unambiguous word or phrase in ordinary language to use, and it can be really annoying to have to constantly use an ambiguous word and then continually remind the reader which meaning you intend. A lot of words in English have more than one meaning. Most of the time this is harmless. Sometimes it is even humorous. Suppose I say to you, "I left most of my clothes at the bank." You might be really weirded out, at least until I clarify that I meant "river bank." Suppose I then say to you, "I put most of my money in the bank." You might think that I am not too bright—who buries their wallet before swimming in the river?—until I clarify that I meant "financial institution where one can deposit and withdraw money." "Bank" is ambiguous and so you had to exert some mental energy to figure out what it meant each time it was used. I'd prefer that your mental resources don't get used up, because you'll want to use them thinking about philosophy instead of about what words mean. Of course, the example I just gave was kind of silly, but technical words can be useful when ambiguity is important to avoid. (We'll see this lesson in action in Section 7.3).

There's a third reason to introduce technical jargon, but I am going to ask 0.9 that you wait until Section 2.10 to think about it. I promise I will talk about it there.

In general, when I introduce a word or phrase that is being used in a 0.10 technical sense, I will italicize the first use of that word and then provide an explicit technical definition. And, as I mentioned earlier, it's a good idea to memorize the technical jargon when it first appears so you don't waste precious brain power remembering definitions when you should be working through philosophical puzzles.

I have also minimized the use of variables in this book. A variable is a 0.11 device that people use to precisely speak in highly general terms. Sometimes philosophers use them unnecessarily, and that can result in unfortunate sentences such as, "All persons P have inherent dignity." In that sentence, the addition of a variable "P" for persons is pointless. But sometimes introducing variables can help make an idea easier to understand. In those cases, the introduction of variables is like the introduction of technical jargon, and its introduction is justified in a similar way. Here's an example to illustrate this. Consider the following sentence: "Every positive real number is the sum of two other real numbers such that both of them are smaller than it but one of them is bigger than the other one." That's a pretty clunky sentence, and it's nowhere near as clunky as sentences like this could get. If we rewrite this with variables and use the standard technical jargon from arithmetic ("+" for "sum" and ">" for "greater than"), we get a clearer sentence: "For every positive real number n, there are two positive real numbers l and m such that $l+m=n$, $n>l$, $n>m$, and $m>l$." I will do my best to not subject you to sentences with variables in what follows. But when I do use variables, it is because I want to speak generally yet clearly at the same time, and the easiest way to do this is with them.

0.2 Philosophy, Including Metaphysics, is for Everyone

0.12   There are terrific philosophers making important contributions from all walks of life. No matter what your background is, *you can do philosophy*, and you can do it well provided you are willing to work at it.[1] *Philosophy is easy for no one*. But everyone can think philosophically if they are willing to work hard at it—and it is deeply rewarding for those who do.

0.13   This is why I recommended a strategy for reading and working through the book. This book will challenge you, but I encourage you not to give up.

0.14   I think philosophy matters. I wouldn't have written this book if I didn't. We'll even discuss in Section 7.5 whether and in what way metaphysics matters. Because I believe that it matters, I want everyone to have a shot at pursuing philosophy to the best of their ability.

0.15   Really, I hope this book is for everyone.

0.16   I'm excited to get started on the metaphysics! But it might be helpful to situate metaphysics alongside some of the other important subfields of philosophy before we do. This way you'll get a clearer idea of what's in store for you if you continue reading this book.

0.3 An Overview of Metaphysics and Other Areas of Philosophy

0.17   You probably want more information about what you are in for. Fair enough. This book is a guided tour of contemporary metaphysics. That is why its title is *This Is Metaphysics*! Metaphysics is an important subfield of philosophy. Philosophy, like every academic discipline—anthropology, psychology, mathematics, comparative literature, physics, musicology, and so on—encompasses a wide variety of subfields, each of which focuses on a specific set of topics and issues. One way to understand what a discipline is up to is to look at its subfields, the questions pursued by the people working in those subfields, and the methods they use to pursue those questions.

---

[1] http://looksphilosophical.tumblr.com/

That's basically the route that I take here. Philosophy has many subfields—too many for me to try to list, let alone describe, here—so, to narrow things down, I will focus on *epistemology, logic, ethics, metaphysics,* various *philosophies of X,* and the *history of philosophy.*

I'll tell you a bit about the first three subfields of philosophy first. And I'll mention how knowing a little about them is important when thinking about metaphysics. Then we'll get to metaphysics. Finally, I'll discuss some philosophies of X and the history of philosophy. 0.18

Epistemology is the subfield of philosophy that studies what makes knowledge different from mere true belief, what it is for something to be evidence for a belief, what kinds of evidence we have, and where those kinds of evidence come from. Suppose Fred believes that 2 + 2 = 5. Does he know that 2 + 2 = 5? Of course not, because in order to know something, the thing in question must be true. Suppose Ross believes that the love of his life is thinking about him right now because this is what his horoscope says. Suppose Ross's belief is true—still he doesn't know this because he doesn't have good evidence for this belief. What kind of evidence would Ross need in order to know that the love of his life is thinking about him? Suppose Elizabeth knows that 2 + 2 = 4 and that the sky is blue. Is the kind of evidence she has for believing that 2 + 2 = 4 the same as the kind of evidence she has for believing that the sky is blue? Elizabeth knows that the sky is blue because she can see it with her own two eyes. Are the truths of mathematics known by perception in this way? 0.19

It's hard to avoid thinking about epistemology when doing any other branch of philosophy. Whenever a philosopher makes a claim, it is natural to wonder what the evidence for that claim is. Once you have worked through this book on metaphysics, you will naturally start to wonder about the epistemology of metaphysics. In fact, some questions in the epistemology of metaphysics will be briefly discussed in Section 7.2. 0.20

Logic is the subfield of philosophy that studies what makes an argument a good argument. When philosophers use the term "argument," they don't mean something like the fight you have with your mom or dad when you can't borrow the car. An *argument* is a sequence of claims, the last of which is supposed to follow from the previous ones. The last claim in an argument is the *conclusion* of that argument, and the claims that are supposed to provide support for that conclusion are the *premises* of that argument. Here is an example of an argument: "All pieces of cheese are delicious. This yellow cube is a piece of cheese. So, this yellow cube is delicious." We'll call this argument *the cheese argument,* since we'll want to refer back to it in a minute. 0.21

0.22   There are two ways for an argument to fail. First, the premises of the argument could be false. Second, the premises of the argument could fail to support the conclusion of the argument, regardless of whether the premises are true.

0.23   To see the difference, consider the following arguments. Here's the first argument:

> "The moon is made of Parmesan cheese. If the moon is made of Parmesan cheese, then the moon is delicious. So, the moon is delicious."

Call this argument *the cheesy moon argument*. The cheesy moon argument is clearly a silly argument because the first premise of the argument is false. But there is nothing wrong with the *logic* of the argument: *if* the premises *were* true, the conclusion *would* also be true. Contrast the cheesy moon argument with this argument, which we'll call *the dog argument*:

> "Kris McDaniel is a human being. Ranger McDaniel is a dog. So, Parmesan cheese is delicious."

The premises of the dog argument are true—and so is the conclusion. But it is still a lousy argument, because the premises have nothing to do with the conclusion and they certainly do not in any way provide support for the conclusion. The *logic* of this argument is messed up.

0.24   Logicians call an argument *valid* (this is a technical term!) when it is not possible for the argument to have all true premises and a false conclusion. The cheese argument and the cheesy moon argument are valid arguments in this technical sense. Logicians call an argument *factually correct* when all of its premises are true. The dog argument is not valid, but it is factually correct. Logicians call an argument *sound* when it is *both* valid and factually correct. Sound arguments are great!

0.25   Logic is super important to all areas of philosophy, including metaphysics. Philosophical discussions typically proceed by evaluating arguments for interesting claims, and to do this you need to figure out whether the conclusion really follows from the premises.

0.26   Ok, let's move on to the next subfield of philosophy. Ethics is the subfield of philosophy that is concerned with (among other things) the questions of what makes an action right or wrong, what makes a life a life worth living, and what character traits are admirable or despicable. Who hasn't wondered about this stuff? One of the things we'll discuss at the very end of the book (Section 7.5) is whether thinking about metaphysics can make our lives go better for us. In short, we'll do a bit of the ethics of metaphysics.

Now for metaphysics. Metaphysics is the philosophical study of reality. In 0.27 a way, metaphysics is the least applied and most theoretical of the subfields discussed so far. Both ethics and epistemology concern themselves with what we should do and what we should believe, and the study of logic is super important for reasoning correctly. But metaphysics is a purely theoretical investigation of reality, and it is not directly practical in the way that ethics, epistemology, and logic are.

Metaphysics addresses questions that cannot be fully answered by empir- 0.28 ical scientific investigation alone. This does not mean that empirical scientific investigation is never relevant to any metaphysical question. On the contrary, it frequently is. But empirical scientific investigation alone can't fully answer metaphysical questions. Among the questions that metaphysics addresses are:

Do we have free will?
What is the nature of human persons—are we purely physical beings or do
    we have a non-physical part or aspect?
How is time different from space?
Is everything a particular or are there universals?
What is the nature of possibility and necessity?

Many of these questions will be discussed at length in the chapters to follow. For some of these questions, the connections to empirical science will be more obvious—such as the question of how time is different from space. For other questions, the connections will be less obvious. The metaphysician should not dogmatically assert that empirical science can shed no light on metaphysical questions. But it is also an equally open question whether empirical science always can. I recommend a "wait and see" attitude towards this question as you read through the book.

Time for some more subfields, so that you can get a clear sense of what 0.29 philosophy is about and how metaphysics fits in with the rest of philosophy. Every aspect of our lives can generate philosophical questions, and this is why there exist the subfields of philosophy I am calling *philosophies of X*, such as the philosophy of religion, philosophy of science, philosophy of language, philosophy of sports, feminist philosophy, philosophy of art, and so on. Each of these subfields is unified by its focus on a particular X—but each of these subfields also overlaps in various interesting ways with epistemology, logic, ethics, and metaphysics. Consider, for example, one of the central questions in the philosophy of religion: Is there a God? This central question is also an important question in metaphysics, though it won't be addressed in this book. Now consider the question of whether the testimony from various holy texts provides evidence for the existence of God. This is an important question in the philosophy of religion, but it also clearly connects with an important question in epistemology, namely, whether testimony provides good evidence for beliefs. Finally, consider the question of whether we have a moral obligation to worship God, provided that such a being exists. This is an important question in the philosophy of religion, but it is also a question that ethicists might ponder. Similar observations can be made about each of the various philosophies of X. The subfields of philosophy are not cleanly separated. Rather, in philosophy, every question leads to further questions.

0.30   Finally, there is the history of philosophy, which is devoted to the study of the history of various philosophers, their arguments, their views, and so on. There is an interesting philosophical question about the relation of the history of philosophy to the rest of philosophy: not many academic disciplines incorporate the study of the history of their discipline into their core curriculum. How relevant is the history of mathematics or the history of biology to the research of contemporary mathematicians or biologists? On the face of it, it is not very relevant at all, which is probably why there are few such classes taught in mathematics or biology departments, and, even when they are taught, they are rarely classes that one must take in order to complete one's degree in that major. Yet in most departments in North America, not only is the history of philosophy taught but typically several classes in the history of philosophy are required in order to complete a philosophy major. Does this difference suggest that the history of philosophy is important to contemporary research in philosophy?

0.31   This is a hard question, I think. But regardless of what the correct answer to this question is, this will be a book focused on contemporary metaphysics, which means we will engage in very little historical reflection in what follows. Occasionally though, I will mention important figures in the history of philosophy when their views or arguments are relevant to the contemporary material I am discussing.

0.32   Hopefully this brief overview of the various subfields of philosophy and their relations to metaphysics will be useful for what follows. As I mentioned earlier, I'm going to do my best to make the journey as smooth as possible, but since philosophy is inherently tricky, you should expect to hit the occasional roadblock. You should also be prepared to never finish the journey: metaphysics rarely delivers definitive answers to the questions it asks. I do not expect to teach you the answer to any given metaphysical question, although I believe that there usually is a correct answer. Rather, what I hope to do is to teach you how to think carefully about metaphysical questions, and how to reason through arguments for metaphysical conclusions. Once you know what metaphysics is and how metaphysical inquiry is conducted, you are all set to do metaphysics on your own.

And this is important since metaphysical questions can be found any- 0.33 where. Here is an example that illustrates how quickly you can find oneself facing a metaphysical question, at least once you have been trained to see them. Suppose you are trying to decide on whether to invest in a soda pop company or in a computer company. Part of what you do when making this sort of decision is you ask yourself what *would* happen were you to select some course of action out of the options available to you. You think to yourself thoughts like, "If I were to do this, then that would happen, but if I were to do this other thing, then that other thing would happen." In short, you contemplate what philosophers call *counterfactuals*, which are claims about what would happen if something else were to happen. And you are going to successfully deliberate about what to do only if you have some reason to think that these counterfactuals can be true. But now for the metaphysical question: What makes a counterfactual true? (We'll have more to say about this question in Section 4.4.)

In general, metaphysical questions are lurking behind pretty much every 0.34 corner. Having some insight into how to think about them might be a skill worth picking up. One of my goals is to help you develop that skill.

Although the title of the book is *This Is Metaphysics*, I don't cover every 0.35 topic that is discussed by metaphysicians. As I said a moment ago, metaphysical questions lurk behind every corner, and so it is unlikely that any book would cover every topic. Still, I want to be clear that there are important topics that metaphysicians do talk about that are not discussed in this book. My main reason for not discussing them is just that the goal of this book is not to cover every topic in metaphysics—if this were the goal, maybe the book would be titled *This Is All of the Metaphysics*—but rather to introduce you to the activity of doing metaphysics. An omission of these topics is not an admission of their unimportance. If, by working through this book, you develop the skills needed for thinking about metaphysics, you will be well prepared to think hard about these other topics as well.

0.4 Remarks for Instructors

0.36   As the section title indicates, I'll briefly say some things to instructors who are considering whether and how to use this book in their classes. Given how I've pitched the book, I believe that it can be used in introductory philosophy classes, either as the sole text or as a text that you use along with others. It would also be useful as a text in an upper-division metaphysics class, especially if it is coupled with contemporary articles that go into more depth or present contrasting points of view.

0.37   The latter is particularly important. I have written this book to be an engaging introduction to a variety of metaphysical issues rather than as a treatise advocating the positions that I think are definitely correct. This book succeeds as a textbook to the extent that it provokes students into thinking about metaphysics in a productive way. In my own teaching, I have found that it is easiest for me to use a text that is interesting and provocative but often mistaken (from my point of view) in the positions it defends. I have tried to give you a book that your students can enjoy wrestling with, and that maybe you can enjoy correcting as well. For this reason, I have opted for a conversational writing style rather than presenting the material with excruciating rigor.

0.38   I have also chosen to throw a large number of arguments and ideas at the reader rather than selecting a smaller subset and engaging more rigorously with those. In my experience with teaching undergraduate classes, no topic resonates with—or captures the interest of—every student in the class. But, unless I am extremely unlucky, every student finds at least one topic fascinating. More topics covered equals more opportunities to grab a student's attention. You as the instructor can then elect which of the topics covered you want to discuss in more depth, perhaps based on your students' reactions to the readings.

0.39   Instructors will also notice that this book is not as modular as some other introductory philosophy books. I have chosen a less modular approach largely because I believe that, in general, metaphysical claims connect in intricate and important ways with other metaphysical claims, and that it benefits a reader to see this. Metaphysical questions are very hard to answer conclusively, but this isn't because there are no answers to them. Rather, one reason they are hard to answer is that while attempting to answer one metaphysical question, you almost always end up having to answer many others in the process. Probably we will never run out of metaphysical questions to answer.

At the end of each chapter is a section titled Doing Metaphysics that con- 0.40
tains further questions that the student might be wish to ponder or the
instructor might wish to discuss in class. This section also contains recommendations for further reading.

0.5 Acknowledgments

I thank Elizabeth Barnes, Ross Cameron, Cody Gilmore, Carrie Jenkins, 0.41
Brad Skow, Jennifer Saul, and Jason Turner for looking at chapters in this
book and giving me very useful comments. Jeremey Dickinson, Steve Hales,
Hud Hudson, and Joshua Spencer read through entire drafts and gave me
very useful feedback on each chapter. I also had great comments from three
anonymous referees. Byron Simmons provided me excellent philosophical
comments and also edited the penultimate draft of the book; he did a splen-
did job. Finally, Steve Hales was a very patient editor even though I was a
very annoying author to work with.

1

CLASSIFICATION

1.1 Introduction

1.1 This chapter focuses on the common-place activity of distinguishing and classifying objects of various kinds. You might wonder: Why start a book on metaphysics with a discussion of classification?

1.2 There are a couple of reasons. First, lurking behind this common-place activity are a lot of metaphysical puzzles and questions! One of the cool things you'll discover as you study metaphysics is that the world is a lot more complicated and much stranger than you initially might have thought. A good way to illustrate this is to start with something down-to-earth and rooted in our ordinary ways of thinking and talking. Once you see that even something that is seemingly straightforward has a tangle of puzzles hiding behind it, you'll start to suspect that philosophical perplexities can arise about pretty much anything.

1.3 Second, the metaphysics of classification will provide a nice springboard for the discussions to follow on the metaphysics of properties (in Chapter 2) and the metaphysics of parts and wholes (in Chapter 3). These parts of metaphysics are somewhat more abstract than the more down-to-earth things we'll begin with here, but they are intimately related to the metaphysics of classification, as we will see later on.

1.4 Let me give you a breakdown of this chapter. In Section 1.2, I will introduce and explain a distinction between two different ways of classifying objects: an objective and a subjective way. In Section 1.3,

This Is Metaphysics: An Introduction, First Edition. Kris McDaniel.
© 2020 John Wiley & Sons, Inc. Published 2020 by John Wiley & Sons, Inc.

I will discuss some cases in which it seems that we have mistakenly taken a merely subjective classification to be an objective one. But even if we sometimes do make this sort of mistake, it does seem like we still often succeed in objectively classifying objects. Section 1.4 will present an argument for the conclusion that some things do objectively belong to each other. In Section 1.5, we will explore the question of what it takes for things to objectively belong together. This will naturally lead us to a discussion of the connection between the metaphysics of classification and the metaphysics of properties in Section 1.6. (And Chapter 2 will be focused more generally on the metaphysics of properties.) Finally, in Section 1.7, we'll close with some further questions about classification to consider.

1.2 Two Kinds of Classification

Let's start with something that seems easy. Think about this list of things: a cat, a dog, a kangaroo, a fish, and a loaf of bread. Suppose you were asked, "Which one of these things *does not belong* with the others?" I don't think you'd have a problem answering. You'd unhesitatingly single out the loaf of bread. This wouldn't even be a hard question for a small child. My five-year old unhesitatingly singled out the loaf of bread too.   1.5

Suppose we take out the loaf of bread from the list and ask again, "Which one of these things *does not belong* with the others?" You might struggle a bit more this time, but you'd probably exclude the fish, although that isn't the only defensible answer. For example, you might exclude the fish because each of the remaining three is a mammal. However, you might instead exclude the kangaroo on the grounds that each of the remaining three is commonly taken as a pet. (Even in Australia, it is not very common for someone to have a pet kangaroo.)   1.6

But suppose I gave you the following list of things: a neutron star, the number 2, the dream you had last night, and a blade of grass. Now the question "Which one of these *does not belong* with the others?" is much harder to answer. Why is this? I suggest that it is because any way of excluding one of these items from the list leaves us with a list of three things that don't really belong together any more than the original four. And you recognize, at least implicitly, this fact.   1.7

But why do some groups of things belong together while other groups of things do not? A complete answer to this question requires some metaphysics: 1.8

specifically, we need a theory that explains what belonging together amounts to in general. This theory will be a metaphysical theory of classification. (We'll discuss this further in the Section 1.5.)

1.9   A classification of a group of things is just a way of breaking up that group of things into groups. Let's say that a classification of things is a *good* way of classifying things when it breaks things into groups, and anything in one of those groups belongs with all the other things in that group but doesn't belong with the things that are in a different group. Venn diagrams provide a good way of illustrating this idea.[1] Suppose we have a group of things *w*, *x*, *y*, and *z*.

Suppose that *w* and *x* belong together and that *y* and *z* belong together, but also that no collection of exactly three of them belong together. Then a good classification would divide up our initial group of four things into two groups of two things. We could represent this classification with a picture:

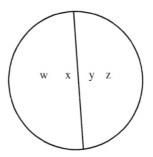

In this classification *w* and *x* have been put together and separated from *y* and *z*, and *y* and *z* have also been put together.

---

[1] http://www.mathsisfun.com/sets/venn-diagrams.html

So far, we have kept things pretty simple. One complication is that 1.10 belonging together probably comes in grades or degrees. That is, some things will belong together to a greater extent than other things. Think about this list of things: me, my wife, my two daughters, and my dog Ranger. Ranger is the odd man (odd dog?) out in this list. But now consider a larger list: me, my wife, my daughters, my dog Ranger, and the number 2. Despite being even, the number 2 is the odd number out. What this shows is that although Ranger doesn't belong in the first group as much as my daughters do, he definitely belongs in the second group much more than the number 2. So, he must belong with me, my wife, and my daughters to some extent.

What this means is that instead of focusing simply on the question of 1.11 whether a specific classification is a good way of classifying, we should also consider the more general question of when a given classification is a *better* classification than another. We won't have a complete theory of classification if we don't consider this more general question.

The second complication is that there are different reasons why we judge 1.12 that things belong together, and these different reasons will sometimes lead to different and apparently conflicting ways of classifying objects. But these different ways of classifying objects don't really conflict. We already saw an illustration of this phenomenon. Let's return to one of the lists of things that we thought about at the beginning, specifically the one that consisted of a cat, a dog, a kangaroo, and a fish. There seemed to be two equally respectable ways of breaking this list into groups. We might separate the fish from the remaining three on the grounds that the remaining three are mammals; but we may also separate the kangaroo from the remaining three on the grounds that only the remaining ones are commonly taken as pets. Is there any point in trying to decide which of these two classifications is *better*? Isn't how we classify things largely dependent on what we are interested in, what we care about, what we desire, and so forth?

Sort of. There's an important difference between the two kinds of clas- 1.13 sifications just mentioned. One of them classifies animals by looking to see whether they are related to *us* in some interesting *social* way: the classification that excludes kangaroos is based on the observations that *we* don't interact with kangaroos in (some of) the ways in which we interact with dogs, cats, and fish. But it wasn't inevitable that we don't typically have kangaroos as pets. Imagine a possible situation in which we have kangaroos as pets instead of cats: if that possible situation had actually happened, then we probably would have felt that it was cats rather than kangaroos that do not belong on the list.

1.14   But now think about the other kind of classification, the one that excludes fish because they are not mammals. This classification isn't based on our desires or interests, and it doesn't classify things on the basis of how these creatures relate to *us*. Mammals could have existed even if no human beings had ever evolved on the planet. And mammals still would have belonged with each other in a way that cats, dogs, fish, and kangaroos do not. Moreover, we can't easily imagine possible scenarios in which, for example, dogs fail to be mammals. We can imagine possible situations in which there are things that have the same outward physical appearance as dogs and that have similar behaviors to dogs, which aren't themselves mammals. But that's not the same thing as imagining a situation in which dogs aren't mammals.

1.15   One lesson to draw from these observations is that, roughly, there can be (at least) two kinds of systems of classification. We might classify objects because we are interested in how they relate to *us*. We can think of these as *subjective classification systems* because they are driven by our interests, desires, values, and so on. But a system of classification might also classify things on a more objective basis, that is, on grounds that are independent of whether that system of classification reflects anything about how reality relates to us or what we care about. Some things *objectively belong together*. An objective classification system is one that classifies things together in a way that matches how they objectively belong together.

1.3 Classification Confusions

1.16   Sometimes we make mistakes about what things objectively belong together, and these mistakes are discovered only after painstaking scientific investigation. Here are some relatively straightforward examples to consider. An ordinary culinary classification might lump carrots, beets, and tomatoes into one group, while lumping oranges, apples, and grapes into another group. But from a more scientific perspective, tomatoes objectively belong more with oranges, apples, and grapes than they do carrots and beets. And as awareness of this fact has spread, how people use language to classify things has changed.[2] Two hundred years ago the sentence "Tomatoes are fruits" might have seemed

---

[2] Whether tomatoes are fruits might seem completely trivial, but interestingly this is a question that has been addressed by no less than the Supreme Court of the UnitedStates!http://www.npr.org/blogs/money/2013/12/26/256586055/when-the-supreme-court-decided-tomatoes-were-vegetables

like a ridiculous thing to say to your average speaker of English, but that's not the case today. Now many of us are happy to utter, "Tomatoes are fruits," and believe that we say something true when we do. There is an interesting question of whether the word "fruit" has changed its meaning over time as a result of a greater awareness of the fact that tomatoes objectively belong more with grapes than they do with carrots. If the word has changed its meaning, then what was said two hundred years ago by "Tomatoes are not fruit" might well have been true too! But it would still have been false that tomatoes objectively belong with carrots more than they do with grapes.

A similar observation can be made about the word "fish." Are whales   1.17 fish? They used to be classified with other things that were called "fish," but now we know that whales do not objectively belong with fish to the extent they were once thought to, and as a consequence, there is pressure not to call whales "fish."[3] One of the things that such scientific discoveries can teach us is that our beliefs about which things objectively belong together are subject to serious revision. An even more recent case is the reclassification of Pluto as not being a planet.[4]

Social scientists—psychologists, sociologists, anthropologists, and so   1.18 on.—would be good people to consult if we wanted to know why people lump things together for subjective reasons. Maybe biology, zoology, animal psychology, and other sciences like them, might also play a role in helping us figure this out. And it will sometimes be a tough job. Occasionally the explanation for why a group of people ended up classifying some objects as belonging together can be so subtle that the people doing the classifying aren't even aware of these reasons. And when this happens, sometimes people falsely believe that the things that they have subjectively lumped together really objectively belong together. As we will see in a moment, at times this can also affect how people classify each other.

Consider, for example, the practice of classifying persons on the basis of   1.19 race. Many scientists believe that racial classifications are not backed up by the biological facts.[5] Consider, for example, how a parent classified as belonging to one race can have a child classified as belonging to another

---

[3] If you are curious about why whales are not fish: http://scienceline.ucsb.edu/getkey.php?key=2536

[4] Here's what NASA has to say about Pluto: http://www.nasa.gov/audience/forstudents/k-4/stories/what-is-pluto-k4.html#.U6nCQ_ldWSo

[5] The concept of race is in need of retirement, according to Professor Jablonski. http://edge.org/responses/what-scientific-idea-is-ready-for-retirement

race. The parent and child will likely have more biologically in common with each other than they would with other members of "the same race." But as any student of the history of racism is aware, people discriminated on the basis of race because they thought that "racial classifications" grouped people into collections that objectively belonged together.[6]

1.20   If this is correct, then racial classifications are very subjective in the sense described earlier: racial classifications are based on contingent features of societies rather than on genuinely important objective features of the world. This seems to be a view that most people who accept the idea that race is socially constructed accept, though many augment this basic position with other philosophical theses.

1.21   Some philosophers have argued for an even stronger conclusion: there are no races. This is the position defended by the philosophers Kwame Anthony Appiah and Naomi Zack, among others.[7] We'll call this position *race eliminativism*. Here are the basic ideas behind race eliminativism: not all attempts at classifying entities are guaranteed to succeed. Sometimes we introduce terms to stand for groups that we initially take to objectively belong together—but because they don't objectively belong together, we actually fail to classify things with those terms. Here's an uncontroversial example of a failed attempt to classify people. A while ago, certain women were thought to have magical powers and were persecuted as a consequence. These persecuted women were called "witches." According to their persecutors, not all women are witches—just those who have important characteristics in common, specifically magical abilities. The people who labeled these women "witches" thought that the women they persecuted objectively belonged together. But since there aren't magical powers, the persecutors' attempt to

---

[6] The *Stanford Encyclopedia of Philosophy* is a wonderful resource. It's filled with excellent introductions. Here is the one for "race," which I highly recommend: http://plato.stanford.edu/entries/race/

[7] Appiah is currently a professor of philosophy and law at New York University. His website is: http://www.appiah.net Most of his published papers are available there, including: http://appiah.net/wp-content/uploads/2010/10/The-Uncompleted-Argument-Du-Bois-and-the-Illusion-of-Race.-Critical-Inquiry-12.1.-1985.pdf This paper discusses Appiah's views on the metaphysics of race.

Zack is currently a professor of philosophy at the University of Oregon. Zack's views on the metaphysics of race can be found in her book *Philosophy of Science and Race* (London: Routledge, 2002). Her faculty profile is here: http://philosophy.uoregon.edu/profile/nzack/

classify these women together was a colossal failure. The lesson we learn from their failure is that while there might be women who were thought to be witches, there really are no witches. Similarly, according to race eliminativism, when words that allegedly refer to races were first introduced, the people who introduced these words thought that there were really important and deep biological differences between human beings, and on the alleged basis of these differences, they attempted to objectively classify people. But these differences have proven to be either non-existent or merely superficial. So, the attempt to objectively classify individuals on the basis of race is a failure just like the attempt to objectively classify individuals as witches. And so, according to race eliminativism, just as we learned that there are no witches, we should also conclude that there are no races.

One of the key theses of race eliminativism is that classification by race is 1.22 *intended* to be an objective classification. And since this intent failed, the attempt to classify via race fails too. And so, there are no races. But if race eliminativism is true and there are no races, why do people talk as if there are? It is important to keep in mind the distinction I noted earlier, between two sorts of classification: one that is based on whether things objectively belong together and the other that is based on more subjective reasons. Probably the full explanation for the prevalence of classifying people on the basis of "race" will be understood only once we have better grappled with both the historical and contemporary reality of various forms of racial stratification and oppression. The fact that we do classify for subjective reasons might generate the appearance that there are races even though, according to race eliminativism, there really aren't any.

This is not to say that there are no biological bases at all for apparent 1.23 racial differences. There is a biological explanation for why, for example, two people have different skin colors. But the existence of these sorts of explanations doesn't mean that classification on the basis of races is particularly objective. Here's an analogy to consider. Suppose that instead of thinking of people in terms of "races" we thought of people in terms of "heights." People under 5' tall were called "the lows"; people 5' to 5'2" were called the "low mids"; people 5'2" to 5'6" were called "the mids"; and so on, and so on. Presume, in this other possible culture, that what height you belonged to mattered as much as race sometimes seems to matter in our culture. (Suppose, for example, that there was systematic discrimination against the lows.) Clearly, these classifications of people in terms of height are much more subjective than objective, even though in each case there is going to be a biological explanation for why a person is of a given height.

1.24   Race eliminativism isn't the only position in the philosophy of race. It's a rich and varied field, like all areas of philosophy! Recently, the view that races are biologically real has been defended in a series of interesting papers by Quayshawn Spencer, who argues that, at least in the United States, racial classifications correspond to five global population groups corresponding to genetic clusters.[8] On Spencer's view, dividing the human population into these five groups results in genetic clusters that minimize genetic differences among individuals within a group but maximize genetic differences among individuals from different groups. Spencer clearly notes, however, that these genetic differences do not imply any moral or intellectual differences between the groups. (There are some suggested readings at the end of this chapter for those of who you wish to pursue topics in the philosophy of race more.)

1.25   Let me briefly sum up what has been discussed so far. We've explored two kinds of classification systems: those that classify on the basis of our subjective interests, feelings, and whatnot, and those that attempt to classify things on the basis of whether the things in question objectively go together. We've seen that we can make mistakes about whether some things objectively go together, and that some of these mistakes can even be very harmful. We discussed classification by race as an illustration of one way this might happen.

1.26   But the fact that we can and often do make mistakes about what things objectively go together shouldn't by itself automatically make us skeptical that nothing really objectively belongs with anything else. In order to get us to be skeptical across the board about the possibility of objectively classifying entities, we'd need a much more powerful argument than one that begins with the premise that we often screw it up (and that we are really bad at it when it comes to classifying people). On the other hand, it would be nice to have a positive argument for the conclusion that some things really do objectively belong together. We will discuss one such argument in the following section.

1.4 Do Things Objectively Belong Together?

1.27   One of the most obvious ways in which we classify things is by using language. We make use of general terms, such as "dog," "cat," and "table" to group things together under common headings. Once we've done this, we

---

[8] Quayshawn Spencer is currently a philosopher at the University of Pennsylvania. His webpage, which contains many of his published papers, can be found here: https://sites.google.com/site/qnjspencer/publications

can use these terms in sentences that communicate very general facts, such as that dogs typically are furry and friendly. In addition to terms like "dog" and "cat" that seem to stand for kinds of things, we can also classify things by way of predicates like "red" and "circular."

But there are some interesting apparent differences: dogs do seem to 1.28 form a kind of thing in a way that, say, red things do not. Suppose I tell you that I have a red thing in a box: it would be reasonable to ask what kind of thing it is, and if you did ask this question, and I replied by saying that it is a red thing, or a colored thing, you'd probably think that my answer was pretty weird. Suppose I tell you that I have a dog in a box: it would be a little odd to ask what kind of *thing* is in my box, though it wouldn't be at all odd to ask what kind of *dog* is in my box. (You should probably also ask *why* I put a poor dog in a box, but since this is a book about metaphysics rather than ethics, we won't pursue that question further.) We use words like "dog," "cat," "car," "desk," "proton," and "human being" to stand for kinds of things, and we use words like "red," "tall," "solid," "fast," and "furry" to stand for features of things. There might be an important metaphysical difference between kinds of things and features of things. But there is also an important similarity that is relevant to our discussion of classification: we use both of these types of expressions to mark differences in things: these things are the things that are red, rather than those things that are some other color, such as green; these are things that are dogs rather than those things that are some other kind of animal.

Reflecting on the various ways we use language to classify objects can 1.29 open us up to new philosophical problems. Here is an interesting thought experiment suggested by Eli Hirsch.[9] Suppose we were to encounter a community of human beings who speak a language that is in many respects like English but with some significant differences. First of all, these people don't have words for colors like "red," "purple," "green," and so forth in their language, and they don't even have any words that are synonymous with those words. They also don't have words for shapes, such as "circular," "triangular," and so forth. Although these kinds of words are missing from their language, this is not because the people in this community differ from us in

---

[9] Eli Hirsch is currently a professor of philosophy at Brandeis University: http:// www.brandeis.edu/facultyguide/person.html?emplid=3b8c58f368269c9b2a81bea2 caf5cd32e3d4e84a An important book by Hirsch on the subject of classification (among other metaphysical topics) is *Dividing Reality* (New York: Oxford University Press, 1993).

what they can perceive with their eyes. (I suppose that if human beings had never evolved with the ability to see things, we wouldn't have had words for colors either.) Their language does contain some words that English doesn't contain. For example, it contains the word "gricular," which stands for a feature that things have when they are *either* green *or* circular, and it contains the word "grincular," which stands for a feature that things have when they are *either* green *or not* circular, and it contains the word "ngricular," which stands for a feature that things have when they are *either not* green *or* are circular. Let's call this language "the gruesome language."

1.30   The gruesome language is peculiar. I'll say a few more things about the gruesome language that will probably amplify that impression. There are some words in English that can be explicitly defined. A stock example is the word "bachelor," which can be explicitly defined as "someone who is an unmarried, eligible to be married, adult human male." Competent users of words like "bachelor," which is a word that is capable of being explicitly defined, should be able to at least gesture at its definition. If a person whose first language is not English asks you what "bachelor" means, it would be appropriate to provide her with the abovementioned definition. But not every word in English is capable of being explicitly defined, even by fully competent speakers of English. When you give an explicit definition of a word, obviously and unavoidably you do this by using other words. Some of these words might themselves be capable of being explicitly defined, but at some point the chain of definitions has to come to an end. There must be some words in English that aren't capable of being explicitly defined, even by competent users of English. I suspect that words like "red" and "green" are good examples of words that we can't explicitly define. Suppose a person whose first language is not English were to ask you what "green" meant. You could do the following things to help her out. You could show her samples of things that are green, such as American dollar bills, or the color of grass or leaves in late spring, or if you are especially fortunate, some lovely emeralds. In other words, you would help this person learn what "green" meant by *pointing at things that happen to be green*. That's a very different activity from giving an explicit definition of the word "green." I suppose that you could also say that green is the color that things have when they reflect light with a wavelength of around 510 nanometers, but you shouldn't think that by doing this you are giving a *definition* of "green." Definitions of words are the sorts of things that lexicographers discover, but that green things reflect light of a wavelength in the neighborhood of 510 nanometers is a discovery of physics. Perfectly competent speakers of English hundreds of years ago knew what "green" meant but most of them knew next to nothing about the physics of light. (That's true of a lot of competent speakers of English today too.) Competent speakers of English can't give an explicit definition of "green."

The speakers of the gruesome language are in a similar position with respect to the words "gricular," "ngricular," and "grincular." If you asked them what they meant by "gricular," they would have to resort to gesturing at things that are gricular and hope that we get the general idea. A few of the more scientifically literate speakers of the gruesome language might tell us that gricular things are those things that either reflect light of a wavelength of around 510 nanometers or are shaped so that the points on its boundary are all some fixed distance from a center point and from a continuous figure. But they wouldn't be giving you a *definition* of "gricular." What they would be doing instead is similar to what we do when we say what wavelength of light green reflects. Gricular is not a word in their language that can be explicitly defined in terms of other words in their language, not even by speakers fully competent in the gruesome language. 1.31

Speakers of the gruesome language classify things in a way that seems odd to us. Just consider all of the things that are grincular. Is this a list of things that objectively belong together? If nothing objectively belongs together with anything else, then their way of classifying objects is not objectively better or worse in this way, although there might be practical reasons to prefer continuing to classify objects in the way that we do instead of changing wholesale to their systems of classification. 1.32

I am going to begin to develop an argument for the conclusion that some things objectively belong together. This argument turns on the idea that certain words are *projectable* while others aren't, and then goes on to claim that a classification system is a bad one if the words it uses to classify objects aren't projectable. 1.33

The key technical term to be explained here is "projectible." The very rough idea is that a projectable term is one that you can justifiably use to describe things that you don't directly perceive. Let's work our way up to a definition of this key technical term. We frequently make generalizations on the basis of a limited number of observations, and if it is irrational for us to do this, the kinds of generalizations we want to make in the course of doing science are irrational as well. Here are some examples. It's snowing outside and you don't want to be cold so you put on a heavy coat rather than just go outside in a t-shirt. Why do you do this? Because you know that thicker clothing is generally warmer than thinner clothing. This is a generalization that you believe, but it is one that you believe on the basis of 1.34

sampling a relatively small collection of clothing. There are probably millions of heavy coats in the world, and probably millions of t-shirts as well. You haven't tried on each heavy coat. And you haven't tried on each t-shirt. Does this shake your confidence that, in general, heavy coats are warmer than t-shirts? I doubt that it does—although you haven't sampled *every* coat and t-shirt, you have tested *enough* to be justified in believing the general claim that heavy coats are warmer than t-shirts.

1.35   Here's a second example. You notice that whenever you drop something heavy on your bare foot, like a laptop computer, it hurts quite a lot. You also notice that whenever you drop lighter things on your bare foot, such as a shoe or a pencil, it hurts a lot less. On the basis of these observations, you conclude that heavier things falling on bare feet tend to hurt more than lighter things falling on bare feet. (You should probably also conclude that you need to wear shoes more often.) You definitely believe this conclusion: were you forced to choose between dropping a feather on your foot or a piano, you know which one you'd choose. But you haven't observed every possible object that could be dropped on your foot in order to assess how painful that experience would be. You are prepared to form a very general belief on the basis of a very limited number of observations, and you take yourself to be perfectly rational in doing this.

1.36   The general pattern of reasoning we seem to be using in these situations is the following. Whenever we encounter a *sufficiently large sample* of things that each have a certain feature F, and each member of this sample also has the feature G, we generalize and believe that *all* things that have F also have G. Philosophers call this kind of reasoning "inductive generalization," and the method of deriving conclusions in this way, "induction." It's hard to see how we can get by in the world if we aren't justified in believing the conclusions of inductive generalizations. How do I know that this bread will nourish me rather than cause me to explode? Because every time I have sampled bread in the past, it has nourished me rather than caused explosions. My sample size is limited but I nonetheless conclude that I'll be ok next time I have a sandwich.

1.37   So far, so good. But now we are ready to consider the following puzzle, due originally to a philosopher by the name of Nelson Goodman, called "the New Riddle of Induction."[10] Once we see how the puzzle works, we'll be able to define "projectable."

---

[10] This puzzle appeared in chapter 3 of Nelson Goodman's book *Fact, Fiction, & Forecast* (Cambridge, MA: Harvard University Press, 1995).

Here we go. Let's think about emeralds. Emeralds have lots of features. 1.38
Some emeralds are pretty. Some emeralds are covered in dirt, and some
emeralds will probably never be seen by anyone, at least not during our
lifetimes. Some emeralds have been visually inspected by us, or at least will
be, during our lifetime. Let's say that something is *grue* if and only if it is
either both inspected by us during our lifetime and is green, *or* it is blue but
not inspected by us during our lifetimes. (As you can probably guess, "grue"
is another word in the gruesome language.) Because the idea of grue is a
little complicated, it's good to read that definition a couple of times, and
then work through some examples. All the emeralds in a jewelry store were
visibly inspected by someone during your life and they are green—and so
they are also grue.

Here's the new riddle of induction. We haven't seen absolutely all of the 1.39
emeralds in the world. Yet we have seen a large sample of them. And all of
the ones that we have seen have been green. So now we are ready to make
an inductive generalization: since we have seen a sufficiently large sample
of emeralds, and all of these emeralds are green, we infer that all emeralds
are green. However, notice this. All of the emeralds we have seen are also
grue. So, we've observed the exact same number of grue emeralds as we
have green emeralds. So, we should also be willing to make a second inductive generalization: given that all of the emeralds that we have seen are grue,
and we have seen a heck of a lot of emeralds, we should be willing to infer
that all emeralds are grue too. So, as the result of inspecting the same sample of emeralds, we conclude both that all emeralds are green and that all
emeralds are grue.

The problem is that the claim that all emeralds are green is incompatible 1.40
with the claim that all emeralds are grue, since there are emeralds that we
have never seen and that won't be observed during our lifetime. Consider
an unobserved emerald, which I will call "Eddy." If all emeralds are green
and all emeralds are grue, Eddy is both green and grue. But no one has or
will observe Eddy in our lifetime. So, Eddy can't be green and observed in
our lifetime. Since Eddy is grue, and not green and observed in our lifetime,
it follows that Eddy must be blue and not observed in our lifetime. So, Eddy
is blue. But just a moment ago we said Eddy is green. Nothing can be both
blue and green at the same time. So, the same sample set and the same
method of forming more general beliefs from that sample set led to inconsistent results. Not good. That's the puzzle of the new riddle of induction.

What seems plausible then is that we shouldn't indiscriminately make 1.41
inductive inferences. It is ok to infer from our sample size that all emeralds

are green. It is not ok to infer from that same sample that all emeralds are grue, even though every emerald in that sample is both green and grue. Don't believe that whenever we encounter a *sufficiently large sample* of things that each have a certain feature F, and everything that has F also has another feature G, we should generalize and so believe that *all* things that have F also have G. Instead, consider something more complex and careful. Only some of those Fs and Gs are ones that license inductive inferences. We are finally ready to define "projectible": an expression is *projectable* if and only if it stands for a feature that we can justifiably make inductive inferences about. "Green" is plausibly a projectable expression, but if it is, then "grue" can't also be projectable.

1.42   But what makes an expression a projectible expression? One answer to this question is that an expression is projectible to the extent that the expression corresponds to objects that objectively belong together. If this is the correct answer, we also have an argument that some objects objectively belong together. The argument is this. We are sometimes justified in making inductive inferences. But we are sometimes justified in making inductive inferences only if some of the words we use to make those inferences are projectible. And those words are projectible only if they classify objects that objectively belong together. So, some objects objectively belong together.

1.5 Two Questions about Classification

1.43 I hope that we now have a decent enough grip on the distinction between what I have called "subjectively belonging together" and "objectively belong together" that we can proceed to ask some interesting questions about this idea of things objectively belonging together. Let's now turn to two of the most important general questions.

1.44   I want to distinguish the question of *what it takes for some things to objectively belong together* from the question of *which things objectively belong together*. Both questions are important questions, and knowing the answer to one could help us learn the answer to the other. But the answers to these questions are by no means guaranteed to be the same.

1.45   The first question, the one that asks "What does it take for some things to objectively belong together?," is an example of a type of question that philosophers are prone to ask. The type of question of which this first question is an instance is "What does it take for a thing to be X?" where X is some feature that a thing could have. Here are some other examples of this type of question: "What does it take for a belief to count as knowledge?"; "What does it take for an action to be one that we morally ought to do?"; and "What does it take for an action to be done freely?" Let's briefly think about one of these questions so that we can get a feel for this type of question in general. We'll focus on the first one, the question of what it takes for a belief to count as knowledge.

There are some beliefs that don't count as knowledge. For example, some people have false beliefs, and no false belief can be knowledge. The other day, I was trying to find my wallet. I had a very strong belief that I had left it on top of the fridge the previous evening. My wife insisted that I hadn't, and I replied that I knew that I had. It turns out that I had left my wallet in my office. Given where my wallet in fact was, I didn't know that I had left my wallet on top of the fridge. I only thought that I knew. Reflecting on this story makes it clear that a belief counts as knowledge only if that belief is true. But it's also clear that merely having a true belief is not sufficient for that belief to count as knowledge. Suppose someone, who we will call "Fred," reads the story I just told and as a consequence comes to believe that my wallet had been in my office. Fred's belief is true, but does it count as knowledge? Well, you might think that Fred actually doesn't have that great of a reason for believing that I left my wallet in my office. It is a well-known fact that philosophy professors make up stories all the time just to provide vivid illustrations of some point that they want to make. Fred doesn't have enough evidence to rule out the possibility that I am just making up a story. So, even though Fred's belief is true, Fred's belief doesn't count as knowledge. It just doesn't have what it takes to count as knowledge. Ok, so what does it take for a belief to count as knowledge? In other words, what are the necessary and sufficient conditions that something has to meet in order for it to be an instance of knowledge? This might be the most important question of epistemology, and if this were an epistemology book, we'd focus on it further.

The question "What does it take for a belief to count as knowledge?" is a different question from "Which beliefs count as knowledge?" The first question asks for insight into what knowledge is, while the second question asks for a list of beliefs that are known. In principle, someone could answer the second question simply by exhaustively listing all of the beliefs that count as knowledge, which include Jason's knowledge that the sky is blue, Marcy's knowledge that $2 + 5 = 7$, Raul's knowledge that World War II took place prior to the first Gulf war, Shamik's knowledge that emeralds are green, and so on. But this sort of list doesn't by itself answer the question "What

1.46

1.47

does it take for a belief to count as knowledge?" If we had an answer to *that* question, we'd know *why* all the items on the list of beliefs that count as knowledge belong on this list.

1.48   The same idea applies to the two questions "What does it take for some things to objectively belong to each other?" and "Which groups of things objectively belong together?" An answer to the first question provides necessary and sufficient conditions that a group of things have to meet in order to objectively belong to each other, while an answer to the second question could simply take the form of a list: *these things objectively belong together, and so do those other things*, and so on.

1.49   Even though we've distinguished the two questions, as I said earlier, finding the answer to one of these questions might help us find an answer to the other. If we had an accurate list of which groups of things objectively belonged together, we could use that list to test alleged answers to the first question. Suppose, for example, that a proposed answer to the first question said that having X is what it takes for some group of things to objectively belong together, but one of the groups on our accurate list did not have X. We'd be able to deduce that this proposed answer to the first question is mistaken. On the other hand, if we had an answer to the first question, we'd hopefully have some guidance on how to go about making our list of things that do objectively belong together.

1.50   So, we should distinguish our two questions, but keep in mind that the strategies for answering them might not be completely independent of each other. In the following section, we are going to focus on the first question of what it takes for some things to objectively belong to each other.

1.6 Classification and Properties

1.51   Here is a natural train of thought. Things objectively belong together when they are similar in important ways. Things are similar in some way if and only if there is some way that those things all are. We call ways that things are *properties*. So, what it is for things to belong together is for them to share certain important properties.

1.52   But although this train of thought is natural, someone might reasonably worry that we won't travel very far on it. After all, this train of thought leads us to the question "What makes a property an important property?" If our only answer to that question is that important properties are those that things have when they objectively belong together, we are riding the train on a circular track, and we are no better off than we were when we started. (Circular explanations seem to get you nowhere, intellectually speaking.)

The question "What makes a property an important property?" matters 1.53 if we assume both that there are some important properties *and* that there are some unimportant properties as well. But maybe the latter assumption is one that we shouldn't make; maybe we should believe that the only properties that exist are the important properties. If the only properties that exist are the important properties, then we can say that things objectively belong together if and only if they have a property in common. This train of thought is less obviously on a circular track. We still need to face the question of what properties there are though.

In order to address the question of what properties there are, it might be 1.54 useful to have a quick discussion about how we attribute properties to things in ordinary language.

Consider the sentence "Kris is short." The subject of this sentence is the 1.55 name "Kris." The remainder of the sentence is the predicate "is short." Very roughly, in general, a predicate is that part of a sentence which contains a verb and is used to state something about what is named by the subject of that sentence. Other examples: in the sentence, "Ranger is a dog," "Ranger" is the subject and "is a dog" is the predicate; in the sentence "Ben eats French fries," "Ben" is the subject and "eats French fries" is the predicate; in the sentence "José was an awesome teacher," "José" is the subject and "was an awesome teacher" is the predicate. I hope this rough definition of the word "predicate" and the examples just mentioned have succeeded in giving you the idea of what a predicate is.

Predicates are used to say something about what is named by the subject 1.56 of the sentence. Does this mean that, for every predicate, there is a corresponding property? Should we say that, since we can state something true of Ranger when we say "Ranger is a dog," there is a property of being a dog? Ranger is a dog. Is there therefore a property of being a dog that Ranger has? This thought might seem plausible at first—what is the *something* that is true of Ranger if it is not a property had by Ranger? But if there is a property corresponding to every predicate, then there must be unimportant properties as well as important properties. For the following sentence is true: "Ranger is a dog or a fish or an automobile," and so corresponding to the predicate "is a dog or a fish or an automobile" is a property, namely, the property of being a dog or a fish or an automobile. If there is a property of being a dog or a fish or an automobile, it is a property had by Ranger, the fish in my daughter's fish tank, and the leaf-filled convertible rusting on the street down the block. But these things do not objectively belong together simply because they have this property. The property of being a dog or a fish or an automobile is not an important property.

1.57   So, we have a choice to make. One option is to believe that for every predicate, there is a corresponding property and some, but not all, of these properties are *important*, and then give a theory of what it is for a property to be an important property. Another option is to deny that every predicate corresponds to a property: on this option, although it is, for example, true of both Ranger and Mars that they are either dogs or planets, nonetheless there is no property of being a dog or a planet. On this second option we don't obviously need a theory of when some property is an important property, since we can just say that all properties are important properties. (That said, if being an important property is something that comes in grades or degrees—if all properties are important but some important properties are *more* important than other important properties—then we still need a theory of grades or degrees of importance.) We do need a theory to tell us which predicates have properties corresponding to them. I suspect that on either option, the theories that we will give will look very similar to each other when they are fully developed, but I encourage you to see whether this suspicion ends up being correct. (We will further discuss the idea of an important property in Sections 2.4 and 2.9.)

1.58   Here's another idea worth considering: maybe we can't define or explain what it is for some things to objectively belong together in terms of anything simpler. Instead of trying to define this concept, we could try to use it to define other concepts—such as, for example, the concept of an important property. It's not clear to me how to do this, but that doesn't mean this isn't a project worth pursuing, especially since we already know that some expressions in our language can't be explicitly defined.

1.59   Either way, the metaphysics of classification and the metaphysics of properties are deeply connected. And so, if we want to know more about the former, it will help to know more about the latter. Chapter 2 will focus on the metaphysics of properties, although we will on occasion revisit some of the issues discussed in this chapter.

1.7 Doing Metaphysics

1.60   We've barely scratched the surface of the metaphysics of classification. Here are some further questions to consider:

We distinguished between subjective and objective ways of classifying objects. Are there other ways of classifying objects that aren't neatly categorized as either subjective or objective?

Are there *degrees* of objective belonging? That is, does it make sense to talk about quantities of objective belonging, for example, these objects belong to each other to degree *n*? If not, is there a best way to understand *grades* of objective belonging?

Are there other classifications of people that seem at first to be objective but really are subjective? If so, what are they, and why do they seem (to at least some people) to be objective?

How would you solve the new riddle of induction? Are there good solutions that don't claim that some things objectively belong together?

If not every predicate stands for a property, when does a predicate stand for a property?

Further Reading

In addition to the readings I mentioned earlier in this chapter, here are some suggestions for further reading, along with very brief descriptions of them:

Anjan Chakravartty (2011) "Scientific Realism and Ontological Relativity," *The Monist*, vol. 94, no. 2, pp. 157–180.[11]

This is an important paper on the metaphysics of classification from a perspective from the philosophy of science rather than metaphysics.

Sally Haslanger (2012) *Resisting Reality: Social Construction and Social Critique*, Oxford: Oxford University Press.[12]

This collection of essays contains important discussions of the metaphysics of social groups, including discussions of the metaphysics of race and gender.

Ned Hall's discussion of David Lewis's views on the natural and non-natural property distinction in the *Stanford Encyclopedia of Philosophy*.[13]

An important philosopher discusses one way of cashing out the distinction between important and non-important properties discussed earlier in this chapter. (And in Chapter 2 as well.)

---

[11] http://monist.oxfordjournals.org/content/monist/94/2/157.full.pdf

[12] https://global.oup.com/academic/product/resisting-reality-9780199892624?cc=us&lang=en&#

[13] http://plato.stanford.edu/entries/lewis-metaphysics/natural-distinction.html

2

PROPERTIES

2.1 Introduction to the Metaphysics of Properties

2.1 Chapter 1 focused on some problems in the metaphysics of classification. As the chapter ended, we saw that there are interesting questions about properties that are closely related to those issues concerning classification that we focused on. In this chapter, concerns about classification will move into the background, while questions about properties will take center stage.

2.2 There are a number of fun topics that we will look at in this chapter. We are going to examine arguments for the existence of properties. We are also going to examine the following questions about what properties are like. Are properties *universals*, capable of literally being shared by different things? Or are they *particulars* just as the different things that have them seem to be?

2.3 And how do objects relate to the properties that they have? Is an object nothing more than the sum of its properties? You have many properties: you have a certain height, shape, chemical constitution, and so on. Are you nothing more than the bundle of those various properties? This is what the friend of the *bundle theory of particulars* believes; we'll just call this "the bundle theory" in what follows. According to the bundle theory, there is nothing more to an object than the properties that the object has. If the bundle theory is false, what else is there in an object?

2.4 Suppose that an object is distinct from its collection of properties. There might still be something that is built up out of an object and its properties.

This Is Metaphysics: An Introduction, First Edition. Kris McDaniel.
© 2020 John Wiley & Sons, Inc. Published 2020 by John Wiley & Sons, Inc.

According to some philosophers, there are things called "facts" (sometimes also called "states of affairs") that are composed of objects and their properties. According to them, whenever an object has a property, there is a fact that consists of that object having that property. And whenever two things are related to each other in some way, there is a fact that is made out of those two things plus the relation that relates them. Should we believe in facts in addition to objects and properties?

Shape, mass, weight, color, beauty, and fragility are plausible examples of 2.5 properties. But there are interesting differences between these kinds of properties that are worth drawing out. An object's shape seems to be, in some sense, something that the object could in principle have independently of how that object relates to anything else: whether an object is, for example, a triangle, has to do with *how that object is in itself* rather than how that object is situated with respect to other things. Maybe that is also true about an object's mass. But now think about the difference between mass and weight. The mass of an object doesn't necessarily change when it is moved from, for example, the earth to the moon. But an object's weight definitely does. A philosophy professor who weighs 150 pounds on the earth weighs substantially less on the moon, although her mass is exactly the same.[1] An object's weight is partially determined by how that object relates to other things that exert gravitational force on it.

Intrinsic properties are those properties that objects can in principle have 2.6 independently of how those objects relate to other things. *Extrinsic* properties are properties that objects have because of how they are related to other things. This is a rough, first-draft way of defining "intrinsic" and "extrinsic," but there does seem to be an important difference between intrinsic and extrinsic properties. We can get an intuitive handle on this difference by thinking about plausible examples: mass and shape seem to be intrinsic properties while weight is definitely an extrinsic property. It would be nice to replace our first-draft definition with something more precise. So, another question we will look at in this chapter is how best to define the difference between intrinsic and extrinsic properties.

One reason to look for a better way of distinguishing between intrinsic 2.7 and extrinsic properties is that there are hard questions about whether certain properties are intrinsic or extrinsic, and a more precise way of

---

[1] Do you want to know how to calculate your weight on the moon? https://van.physics.illinois.edu/qa/listing.php?id=16364

drawing the distinction might help us answer them. I mentioned that shape, mass, weight, color, beauty, and fragility are plausible examples of properties. Are colors, like blue, red, and green, intrinsic properties? If they are extrinsic properties, what sort of things must a red thing be related to in order to be red? We will look at some cool arguments for the view that colors are extrinsic properties that things have because of how they are related to creatures like us. If this view is correct, had creatures like us never existed, then nothing would have ever been red or any other color for that matter. (The things that are actually red, such as rubies or lava, might still have existed, but they wouldn't have been red.) People often say that beauty is in the eye of the beholder, so perhaps beauty is an extrinsic property. If this view about color is correct, then, in a way, red, green, and all the other colors are also in the eye of the beholder. We'll look at this view of colors as well as some others.

2.8   One of the interesting theories of color that we will examine is that colors are *dispositional* properties. A dispositional property is a tendency or liability to bring about some effect in the appropriate circumstances. An example of a dispositional property is being flammable. Flammable things are more apt to burn up than non-flammable things: a piece of paper is highly flammable, one soaked in gasoline even more so, but a metal desk is not very flammable. Fragility is another example of a dispositional property: things that are fragile are more disposed to break than things that are not. However, something can have a disposition to bring about some effect without it being likely that it will bring about that effect. For example, a piece of paper drenched in gasoline is highly flammable. But if that gasoline-soaked piece of paper is placed in an airtight safe and dropped into the ocean, it is extremely unlikely that it will ever burn. And there's a reason why we take really good care when mailing packages containing fragile things to surround the fragile things with those weird packaging peanuts—those packing peanuts make it unlikely that the fragile thing will break. These two examples both involve things with dispositions in inappropriate circumstances. In order to understand the theory that color is a dispositional property, we will need to know two things: What are the effects that colors tend to bring about, and what are the appropriate circumstances in which those tendencies are activated?

2.9   We explained intrinsic and extrinsic properties by talking about whether things having them had to be related to other things. That is, by whether things stood in certain relations to other things. But what is a relation?

Plausible examples of them are easy to produce: being five feet from, being between, being taller than, being similar to. The majority of the arguments about properties that we will discuss can be broadened to be about relations too.

We've got a lot on our plate to work through and digest, but before we   2.10 start eating, a little more place setting is a good idea. Specifically, let's discuss how to conceive the debate over the existence of properties. This discussion will take place in Section 2.2. How to conceive the debate has consequences for how we try to answer these questions about the nature of properties. In Sections 2.3 and 2.4, we will look at arguments for the existence of properties that are based on considerations about how we use language. Sections 2.5–2.7 will explore arguments for the existence of properties that are based on concerns about the metaphysics of causation, of events, and of material objects respectively. In Section 2.8, we'll turn to the question of whether properties are particulars or universals. Section 2.9 will discuss the distinction between intrinsic and extrinsic properties. And, in Section 2.10, we'll talk about perceptible qualities, such as colors and sounds. Finally, in Section 2.11, we'll end with some further questions about the metaphysics of properties.

2.2   Are Properties Theoretical Posits?

The important question to be contemplated here is whether we should   2.11 think of properties as *theoretical posits* or rather as entities that we were already acquainted with before we did any philosophy. As we will see in later chapters, this sort of question arises frequently in metaphysical discussions.

Very broadly, a theoretical posit is something that we believe in on the   2.12 basis of indirect evidence rather than direct observation. We posit its existence in order to explain certain things that we can directly observe. Consider electrons. Why do we believe in them? Not because we observe them in our day to day lives; we believe in electrons because they, along with the other unobservable things physicists talk about, explain so much about why the things that we do observe behave in the ways that they do. If a better theory came along that explained the same things that positing electrons currently explains, and that theory didn't say that there were electrons, we'd probably stop believing in electrons.

2.13   On the other hand, there are things that we directly observe, and that's why we believe in them. We believe in dogs because we see dogs and interact with dogs in various ways. One of them is staring at me right now and demands to be taken for a walk. Dogs are directly observed, rather than merely posited. Now we believe many things *about* dogs because of some theory; a biologist could tell you a lot of facts about dogs that you couldn't learn through direct observation. But believing something *about* dogs on the basis of a theory is different than believing *in* dogs on the basis of a theory. Biologists teach us new facts about dogs, but biologists don't teach us that dogs exist. People knew that dogs existed even before there were biologists.

2.14   There is not always a clear-cut distinction between what we know through observation and what we know through theory. Thanks to remarkable technological innovations, we can now, in some sense, observe what was previously unobservable. Have you ever seen a virus? Or do you believe in viruses only because people have told you that they sometimes explain why you are sick? But scientists can observe viruses in electron microscopes. We do need a theory to tell us that this is what they are observing, but perhaps that is also true in cases of ordinary observation as well.

2.15   Now let me be clear: although I have just distinguished between things that we believe in for theoretical reasons and things that we believe in by direct observation, I don't want to give you the impression that I am a skeptic about theoretical posits. I believe in electrons, and I think that it is rational to believe in them. Given our current scientific evidence, it might even be irrational not to believe in electrons. That said, our evidence for believing in things that we can directly observe is stronger than our evidence for believing in things solely on the basis of theory, which is probably why there is the cliché that "seeing is believing." An example: our evidence for the existence of trees is stronger than our evidence for the existence of electrons. And if you directly observe what seems to be an entity of a certain sort, you shouldn't disbelieve in that entity without very strong evidence to the contrary. It is hard for the evidence you get from a good theory to beat the evidence you get from direct observation, which is probably why we say that "seeing is believing" but not that "theorizing is believing." (It is an interesting epistemological question whether philosophy can provide sufficient evidence to beat observation.)

2.16   We've distinguished between things that we believe in because they are the posits of a good theory and things that we believe in because we directly observe them. Are properties entities that we should believe in because of what they can purportedly explain, or are properties things that we can directly observe? This way of asking the question is not ideal, since it presupposes that there are properties, and perhaps when we first start thinking about the metaphysics of properties, it is better to be neutral about whether they even exist. Perhaps a better of way of asking the question is this: Do we seem to observe properties and believe in them because we apparently observe them, or should we believe in them only because they explain things that we can directly observe? And if they explain things, then what exactly do they explain?

The question of whether we directly observe properties is surprisingly 2.17 tricky to answer. You might think that, if you are directly observing something, then it is obvious that you are directly observing it. And yet it is relatively easy to get yourself to start doubting whether you directly observe properties. One of the earliest and most famous theoreticians of properties was Plato. Antisthenes, an early critic of Plato's theory, is reported to have said, "Oh Plato, I see a horse, but I do not see horseness."[2] And you can get the feel for what concerned him: we see dogs, but do we see the property of being a dog? (I got bitten by a dog once, which is another way of observing dogs. But, as far as I know, I've never been bitten by a property.) On the other hand, with respect to some properties, it seems very natural to say that we observe them; colors and shapes are probably the best examples. But again, it is obvious that we see red things. That is, we see things that are red, such as stop signs, and blood from dog bites. But do we observe redness itself? (Questions about colors might be especially tricky, and we will revisit some of them later in the chapter.)

Let's think now about the idea that properties are things we ought to 2.18 believe in only because they can provide explanations. What are the sorts of things that we might want properties to explain? We've already encountered, in Chapter 1, something that we might want properties to explain, namely, the phenomenon that some things objectively belong with each other while other things don't. What else might properties plausibly be taken to explain? In Sections 2.3 and 2.4, we'll discuss whether properties help explain how we use language. In Sections 2.5–2.7, we'll explore whether

---

[2] See Frederick Copleston's classic *History of Philosophy*, volume I, page 119 (New York, NY: Image/Doubleday, 1993). A partial e-book can be found here: http://books.google.com/books?id=aqd4ZbnDXJIC&printsec=frontcover&dq=%22A+H istory+of+Philosophy:+Greece+and+Rome%22&hl=en&sa=X&ei=h5WtU92MAt Si8gGerIGgAw&ved=0CCgQ6AEwAg#v=onepage&q&f=false

properties help us explain the metaphysics of causation, of events and other entities, and of objects.

2.19   Let's investigate how positing properties helps us understand ordinary speech.

2.3 Issues in Language: Reference to Properties in Ordinary Speech

2.20   First, there are a number of facts about how we use language that make sense if there are properties, but are more mysterious if there are not. Let's start by thinking about the distinction between *types* and *tokens*, which, when you see it once, you see it everywhere. Consider the difference between the following two scenarios:

Scenario 1: You are visiting my house. You see me in my luxurious 2003 VW Beetle, which is a true status symbol among professors of philosophy. You ask me where my wife's car is, and I reply "we have the same car; it's this one."

Scenario 2: I am visiting a fellow philosophy professor's house, and I see that she also has a luxurious 2003 VW Beetle. I say to her "we have the same car!" So far, so good. But then immediately afterwards I drive away in her car. I reason that since we have the same car, her car must be my car, and so I take it for a spin! Something has gone wrong.

2.21   Why is it that when my wife and I have the same car, it's ok for me to drive away in it, but when my colleague and I have the same car, it isn't? This isn't a serious question: the phrase "same car" is ambiguous. When I first used the expression "same car," I used it to mean "same specific car," that is, the same *token* or *instance*. When I used "same car" the second time, I meant "same type of car." My wife and I have the same specific car; we jointly own the same *token*. My friend and I have two cars of the same *type*. Even still, there are many functioning tokens of the type 2003 VW Bug.

2.22   This kind of ambiguity between tokens and types is extremely common. Here are a couple more examples:

Example 1: How many letters are in the word "ignite"? Both six and five are good answers—there are six tokens but five types.

Example 2: If you are practicing a piece on a musical instrument, you will probably play the same sequence of notes over and over again—that is, you will keep producing new tokens of the same type.

Although this ambiguity is extremely common, we usually know whether 2.23 types or tokens are meant. If I tell you that I eat the same thing for lunch every day, you might think I am a little weird, but you won't be completely revolted. But sometimes it is not clear what is intended. Consider the express checkout line at the supermarket, which usually displays a sign that says something like "ten items or less." Is that ten token items or types of items? Do I violate the policy if I put 20 Snickers bars on the conveyer belt?

Regardless of how often we get tripped up in this way, it is undeniable that 2.24 there is a distinction between types and tokens, and it appears pretty much everywhere. Why would so many of the things we say be ambiguous in this way if there weren't types, that is, properties for us to talk about? It would be pretty silly to talk about types all the time if there weren't any types to talk about.

And often we do explicitly refer to types: for example, I clarified how "same 2.25 car" was ambiguous by explicitly referring to types. And in general, we talk about properties all the time, and it is hard to see how we can avoid doing so. For example, consider the claim that there are many anatomical properties shared by whales and wolves. This claim is true, but how could it be true unless there are properties? By analogy, consider the claim that there are many people over the age of 70. Again, true, and true only if certain things, specifically, people over the age of 70, exist. In general, it initially seems that claims of the type "there are many ___" are true only "if there are some ____."

Types are a kind of properties. And it seems that ordinary speech makes 2.26 use of a distinction between types and tokens all the time. It is hard to explain why this would be unless there are types, that is, unless there are properties.

Metaphysicians say that a sentence is *ontologically committed* to some things 2.27 if and only if the only way for that sentence to be true is for those things to exist.[3] A lot of the sentences that we utter seem to be ontologically committed to properties. Consider: "Spiders have many interesting anatomical properties," "We have the same type of computer," and "His height is impressive."

---

[3] The idea of ontological commitment was explicitly formulated by W.V.O. Quine. See https://plato.stanford.edu/entries/quine/ for a discussion of him and his work. Recently, philosophers have been debating alternative definitions of "ontological commitment," and this link is a good place to read an overview of the issues: https://plato.stanford.edu/entries/ontological-commitment/

2.28   Admittedly we do need to be careful when trying to figure out whether a sentence is ontologically committed to some things. Let me give you some examples to illustrate why we need to be cautious.

Example 3: Consider the difference between "The President of the United States has two children" and "The average mother has 2.3 children."

The first sentence is true only if there is a person, namely the President of the United States, and there are two other people who are the President's kids. The second sentence, however, is true even though there is no individual who is the average mother—and, of course, no one can have 2.3 kids.

Example 4: Karen and Ted are watching a football game in the stadium. Karen turns to Ted, and says, "Our team is really kicking tail tonight. They have great team spirit." Ted looks puzzled, puts his hand up to his eyes and squints, looks left and then right, up and then down, and then finally says, "I don't see it." Now Karen is puzzled, so she asks Ted, "What is it that you don't see?" Ted replies, "The team spirit. I see the team, and I see the coach, but I don't see the team spirit. Where is it?"

Clearly, Ted is confused. Part of the reason why Ted is confused is that he took Karen's sentence to be ontologically committed to something, a team spirit, since it looks a lot like a bunch of other sentences that are ontologically committed to something. But when people say things like, "They have great team spirit," they don't mean that there is some weird spiritual thing like a team soul which is awesome in some unspecified way. When Karen says that a team has great spirit, she intends to communicate something about how the team is playing: that they are doing a good job of cooperating with each other, that they are functioning well as a unit, that they are playing with enthusiasm, and so on. There's a big difference between "The team has great team spirit" and "The team has great jerseys." The first sentence is true even though there is no such thing as the team's spirit, but the second sentence is true only if there really is something that is the team's jersey.

2.29   This is why we have to be cautious. "The team has great spirit" doesn't imply that there is a spirit that the team has. "The average woman has 2.3 children" doesn't imply that there is an entity that is the average woman. The hard question for us is whether a sentence like "Whales and wolves have many anatomical properties in common" implies that there are anatomical properties.

If talk about properties just is a manner of speaking like talk involving "team spirits" and "average women," what is it a manner of speaking *for*? When someone uses an expression like "the average woman," we know how to translate or paraphrase what they are saying in terms that don't involve that expression. For example, "the average woman has 2.3 children" means something like "the ratio of women to children is 1 to 2.3." But what sort of paraphrase can we offer for "There are many anatomical properties shared by whales and wolves?" Give it a try!

Coming up with paraphrases is tricky because the practice of talking about properties is deeply linked with other ways in which we use language, unlike, say, the way we use phrases like "the average mother" and "team spirit." We not only *quantify* over properties—that is, assert sentences like "There are scientific properties we haven't discovered," "Many properties of fish are uninteresting," and "There are exactly ten properties that could be responsible for this effect"—but we also name them and even attribute other properties to them. Here's a good example of this: After a bit of observation, some scientists notice that sometimes pairs of particles will react differently than other pairs even when the masses of those particles are the same. Sometimes two particles are attracted to each other, while other particles are repulsed. The scientists infer that there is a property that some of the particles have but that the other particles lack. (They *quantify* over this property.) They then introduce a *name* for the property; they decide to call it "charge." Later on, they theorize about how charge and mass interact with each other. (They *attribute* various relations to charge and mass.)

This is very different from the way we use phrases like "average mother" or "team spirit." We do not quantify over team spirits or average mothers, or introduce names for them. But this process of quantifying over properties, naming them, and then attributing further properties to them is analogous to how we treat other things we already believe in. Consider the following scenario. The police have been cataloging a series of murders, and have come to believe they are the work of one man, a person with a right foot substantially larger than his left foot. They decide to call this murderer, who they don't yet know the identity of, "Big Foot." Now that they have a name to use, they say things like "Big Foot is terrorizing this city" and "I hope that Big Foot does not strike again." They might attribute new properties to Big Foot on the basis of further evidence. Both "Big Foot" and "charge" are names we introduced to designate some object of study. The linguistic evidence suggests that we believe in properties as much as we believe in things like people, desks, chairs, protons, and so on.

Margin notes: 2.30, 2.31, 2.32

2.33   If all this talk about properties is a mere manner of speaking, it sure is a complicated manner of speaking! Isn't the simpler hypothesis just that it's not a mere manner of speaking and that what we say really is ontologically committed to properties?

2.4 More Issues in Language: Properties as the Referents of Predicates

2.34   Consider a sentence like "Kris is hungry." The sentence has parts, a subject and a predicate. (We talked about predicates in Section 1.6). The subject is the name "Kris." This name refers to an individual, namely, me. That's pretty much uncontroversial. But what about the predicate "is hungry"? Does "is hungry" refer to anything? A natural thought is that it does, and, specifically, that it refers to the property of being hungry.

2.35   We have the beginnings of a *semantic theory*, that is, a theory about what the expressions of a given language mean or refer to. In this theory, names refer to things—often, very ordinary things like you, your dog, or your car. And predicates refer to properties (and relations). In this theory, every meaningful predicate corresponds to a property. Properties must be abundant since there are many meaningful predicates.

2.36   Why should we accept this intuitive semantic theory? What can it explain? One thing that this semantic theory explains is the difference between genuinely meaningful predicates and things that look like meaningful predicates but aren't. For example, consider the following two strings of sounds: "Kris is hungry" and "Kris is ghrung." The second string is not a sentence because "is ghrung" is just a made-up collection of letters, rather than a real predicate. So, what does a collection of letters need in order to be a real predicate? The theory that real predicates are those predicates that really are true of some things is not right: "is both round and square" is a real predicate—it must be, because it is a meaningful expression—and yet nothing is, or even could be, both round and square. A better theory is the theory that real predicates are ones that successfully refer to properties. Since "is round and square" is a real predicate, there is a property of being round and square. (But obviously nothing does or could ever have this property. So, according to this intuitive semantic theory, there are properties that nothing actually has or even could have.)

2.37   In addition to explaining the difference between real predicates and fake ones, the intuitive semantic theory also explains when simple subject-predicate sentences, such as "Kris is hungry," are true. On the intuitive semantic picture, a subject-predicate sentence is true if and only if the object named by the name—in this case, Kris is the object named by "Kris"—has the property that the predicate refers to—in this case, the property of being hungry. We can expand the theory to cover more complicated sentences, like "Kris loves Nina." A sentence like that is true whenever the first thing named in the sentence bears the relation corresponding to the verb in the sentence to the second thing named in the sentence. And hopefully this simple but intuitive picture can be developed into a more sophisticated account of how sentences are either true or false: they are true or false because the things referred to by the parts of the sentences are related to each other in certain ways.

One potential worry about this linguistic explanation of why we should   2.38
believe in properties is that, if we aren't careful, we can get caught in a contradiction. To see this, first observe that some properties exemplify themselves. Consider the property of being a property. Red has the property of being a property, and the property of being square has the property of being a property. Moreover, the property of being a property has the property of being a property. Take a minute to make sure you understand that sentence before moving on! (Making sure you understand is always a good idea when reading, but it is especially important when reading philosophy!) That is, being red is a property, being square is a property, and being a property is a property.

Second, observe that some properties don't exemplify themselves. For   2.39
example, the property of being a square isn't itself a square and the property of being a human being isn't itself a human being. Ok, now consider the property of being a property that doesn't exemplify itself. Since that is such a mouthful, let's call this property "Graham." Does Graham exemplify itself? Suppose Graham does exemplify itself. Then Graham has the property of being a property that doesn't exemplify itself. So, if Graham does exemplify itself, then Graham *doesn't* exemplify itself! Let's consider the other side of the equation. Suppose Graham doesn't exemplify itself. Since Graham doesn't exemplify itself, Graham has the property of not exemplifying itself. So, Graham exemplifies itself if and only if Graham doesn't exemplify itself. Contradiction! RUN!![4]

This argument is both cute and deep. Here's why it is relevant to our   2.40
current discussion: The predicate "is a property that doesn't exemplify

---

[4] Run to the *Stanford Encyclopedia of Philosophy*, a wonderful resource for philosophers everywhere. Here is their article on paradoxes of self-reference: http://plato.stanford.edu/entries/self-reference/

itself" sure looks like a real predicate. If it wasn't a real predicate, we couldn't use it in true sentences. But we can use this predicate in true sentences, such as "Being a human being doesn't exemplify itself." Our semantic theory says that real predicates refer to properties. So, our semantic theory seems to license the conclusion that the property of being a property that doesn't exemplify itself is a real property. But the assumption that there is a property like this quickly leads to a contradiction, as we just saw a moment ago.

2.41   What should we do? The semantic theory seems plausible but it also appears to lead to something really implausible. One option is to try to develop a more sophisticated semantic theory that avoids the contradiction. The next question is whether that more sophisticated semantic theory would also imply that properties exist.

2.42   For now, we'll consider alternative, non-linguistic reasons to believe in properties. Sections 2.5–2.7 consider metaphysical reasons to believe in properties.

2.5 Issues in Metaphysics: Causation

2.43   The bowling ball rolls down the lane, strikes three pins, and then disappointingly disappears down the other side. Why did only three pins get knocked down? Two reasonably good explanations immediately come to mind. The first explanation appeals to how the bowling ball was when it left my hands: the angle it was thrown, the kinetic energy it had when it collided with the pins, and so on. A second explanation appeals to my poor spatial reasoning, clumsiness, and lack of hand–eye coordination. These are two reasonably good explanations of why this event happened.

2.44   Notice something about both explanations though. Both kinds of explanation explain why the event happened by appealing to *properties* of the objects involved in making that event happen. The first explanation appealed to properties of the bowling ball: its initial angle when thrown, its kinetic energy, and so on. The second explanation appealed to my properties, such as my clumsiness.

2.45   This example is pretty down to earth, but it can be used to make a very general and important metaphysical point: Whenever we explain why some event occurred, we appeal to properties of the objects involved in making that event occur. In short, events occur because and only because there are objects that have certain properties that are relevant to making those events occur. If there aren't any properties for things to have, then it is hard to see why anything ever happens.

So, one reason to believe in properties involves causation. Events happen 2.46 because certain things have certain properties. Another related reason to believe in properties, which we will look at next, involves the general question of where events belong in our *ontology*, specifically, whether we should take events to form a basic *ontological category*.

2.6 Issues in Metaphysics: The Ontology of Events

In this section, we will discuss the branch of metaphysics called *ontology*. 2.47 Whenever you see a word with "ology" as its suffix, you know that the word in question refers to the study of something or other. Some examples: psychology is the study of the psyche, that is, roughly our minds; anthropology is the study of the cultures of humanity; ornithology is the study of birds. So, what is ontology the study of? It's the study of *being*, or what there is.

An *ontological theory*, or an *ontology* for short, is a theory of what there 2.48 is. An ontology differs from other theories of what there is because it aims to provide a *comprehensive* and *exclusive* list of *fundamental categories* of what there is. Let's go through each of these important technical phrases in turn. First, an ontology will provide a list of kinds of things. A list of kinds of things is *comprehensive* if and only if every entity is a member of at least one of the kinds on the list, or is built up out of entities that are each a member of at least one of the kinds on the list. Second, a list of kinds of things is *exclusive* if and only if no entity belongs to more than one kind of thing on the list. So far, so good. The trickier idea to get is the idea that the list in question should be a list of purported fundamental categories. Let's work our way up to this idea by considering some examples.

First, consider the following comprehensive and exclusive list of kinds of 2.49 entities, which I'll call the "T-O ontology." The T-O ontology is a list that contains just two kinds of things. The first kind of thing on the list is *toaster ovens*. The second kind of thing on the list is *entities that aren't toaster ovens*. This list is comprehensive, since any given thing is either a toaster oven, in which case it belongs to the first kind on the list, or it isn't a toaster oven, in which case it belongs to the second kind on the list. And this list is also exclusive, since nothing can both be and not be a toaster oven. But the kinds *toaster ovens* and *entities that aren't toaster ovens* aren't fundamental kinds of things. Fundamental kinds of things are, at the minimum, kinds of things that objectively belong together. Consider all the entities that aren't toaster ovens. Do these things objectively belong together in the sense discussed in Chapter 1? No.

2.50   The first lesson to draw from the failure of the T-O ontology as an ontological theory is that a kind of thing is a fundamental category only if the entities in that category objectively belong together.

2.51   But this isn't the only constraint that a kind must meet in order to qualify as an ontological category. Ontological categories should also be *highly general* kinds of things. Let's have a second example to play with. Consider what I will call the "Commonsensical Ontological Theory." The Commonsensical Ontological Theory is composed of the following lists of kinds of things: *material objects, properties, times, events, numbers, facts, and possibilities.* I call this theory the Commonsensical Ontological Theory not necessarily because it is commonsense that this theory is true (does commonsense have opinions on fundamental metaphysical questions?) but rather because this is the theory suggested by observations of what various commonsensical claims seem to be ontologically committed to. Tables, trees, toaster ovens, you, me, and Ranger are all material objects, and the bulk of what we say does ontologically commit us to things of this sort. We've discussed properties already. With respect to the other alleged categories, we can consider the following kinds of claims:

1.   Times: This is what you said to me the last time we had this discussion. I have a stopwatch to measure how much time it takes me to run a mile. I still remember the first time we met.
2.   Events: The earthquake happened in California. The worst thing that that ever happened to me in college was that my girlfriend dumped me by email. Check the events listing in the paper to see what's happening this weekend!
3.   Numbers: There are many prime numbers between 3 and 3,000,000. The number of moons of Jupiter is really big, maybe bigger than 50. The number 2 is the only even prime number; all other prime numbers are odd numbers.
4.   Facts: The fact that Hille is taller than Carrie cannot be disputed. There are many facts about the case that are yet to be discovered. Just the facts, ma'am.
5.   Possibilities: There are five different possible ways in which Shinya can win this chess match. If that possibility had obtained, we all would have died. When your life starts, there are all these possibilities open to you, but as you get older, many of these possibilities disappear.

The sentences in (1) make explicit reference to times; the sentences in (2)   2.52
make explicit reference to events; the sentences in (3) make explicit reference to numbers; the sentences in (4) make explicit reference to facts; the
sentences in (5) make explicit reference to possibilities. All of these
sentences could either be true or sensibly uttered in various contexts. How
could any of these sentences be true or sensibly uttered unless there are,
respectively, times, events, numbers, facts, and possibilities?

Is the Commonsensical Ontological Theory comprehensive? Note that we   2.53
also speak of *places* as well as times. Do places belong to any of the kinds
already listed? Or can they be built out of items on the list? Another category
worth considering is the category of *propositions*, where propositions are the
kinds of things that are expressed by complete sentences, or are the objects
of beliefs. (More will be said about propositions in Section 4.5.) Some people
might also want to add a category of *immaterial concrete objects*, such as God
or immaterial souls. If the Commonsensical Ontological Theory isn't comprehensive, then it will need to be augmented with additional categories.

At least at first glance, it does seem that the Commonsensical Ontological   2.54
Theory is exclusive. No material object, for example, is a time, or an event,
a number, or a way something could be. (In Chapter 4, we'll revisit the question of whether the category of material objects really is distinct from the
category of possibilities.) And the categories of the commonsensical ontological scheme do seem to be both highly general categories and consist of
things that objectively belong together. So that's a plus too.

However, maybe the Commonsensical Ontological Theory is not the best   2.55
theory. One of the things that metaphysicians try to do is construct ontological theories that differ in important ways from the Commonsensical
Ontological Theory and then assess the evidence in favor of these alternative
ontological theories. Some metaphysicians defend alternative ontological
theories that have fewer categories in them than in the Commonsensical
Ontological Theory. Some of these metaphysicians appeal to Ockham's Razor,
which says that, when trying to explain some phenomenon, we should prefer
simpler theories to more complex ones. Ockham's Razor motivates seeking
fewer categories: a theory that says that there are five fundamental kinds of
things is a more complex theory, everything being equal, than one that says
that there are four fundamental kinds of things. An ontological theory that
posits fewer ontological categories but that can explain why all the sentences
in (1)–(5) (and others relevantly like them) are true has an advantage over the
Commonsensical Ontological Theory, at least with respect to Ockham's
Razor. (We will further discuss Ockham's Razor in Section 7.2.)

2.56   So how to gain that advantage? The rough idea, which we will develop more in later chapters, is that we reduce the number of categories in our ontological theory by analyzing some of the kinds listed by the Commonsensical Ontological Theory in terms of other kinds. The idea is basically this: If we can explain what it is to be a K by appealing to other kinds we are already committed to, there is no reason to take K as a *fundamental* kind, that is, as an ontological category.

2.57   Let's see this rough idea in action. In the previous section, we discussed the role that the properties of things play in the production of events. It's hard to deny that there are events. But do events form a fundamental category? Here is a reason to think they don't. First, events always occur at some time or other: all happenings happen at a time. (They might occur at a moment, or over a stretch of time, but they always occur in time.) Baseball games, weddings, flashes of lightning, and earthquakes all take place at certain, specific times. Second, events always involve objects: there are no events in which objects don't participate. A baseball game happens only if there are baseball players, baseball bats, baseballs, and so on. No wedding can occur without people to be wed. Even flashes of lightning and earthquakes require the presence of various objects to happen. Third, events always involve the properties and/or relations of the objects that participate in them. This third claim about events played a role in the proceeding subsection of this chapter. This tells us the following: we have an event *only if* there are some objects having some properties at a given time. I think the converse is also true: *if* there are some objects having some properties at a given time, then there is an event consisting of those objects having those properties at that time. The event might be a boring event. But it's happening just the same. (There are events that consist simply of a person staring at a wall for an hour. They are pretty boring. But they happen from time to time.)

2.58   What these three facts about events suggest is that an event is nothing more than an object (or objects), a time, and a property (or relation) that the object (or objects) has (or have) at that time.[5] In slogan form, an event is an object's having a property at a time. If this is the case, then events don't form a fundamental ontological category: they are built out of properties,

---

[5] This is the view of events defended by Jaegwon Kim, who is an emeritus Professor of Philosophy at Brown University. One place Kim defends this view is in Kim, J. "Events as Property Exemplifications," in *Action Theory*, edited by M. Brand and D. Walton (Dordrecht: Reidel, 1976) pp. 159–177. Kim's faculty profile page is here: http://www.brown.edu/Departments/Philosophy/people-facultymember.php?key=12

times, and objects. We have a more parsimonious ontological theory if we scratch off events from the list of fundamental kinds.[6]

But notice that we can simplify our ontological theory in this way only if 2.59 the materials that we are using to, so to speak, "build up" events actually exist. In other words, we can simplify our ontological theory in this way only if there are properties. This is because properties are appealed to in the construction of events. You cannot reduce events to something that doesn't exist. So, if the reduction of events to objects, properties, and times is correct, then properties must exist.

2.7 Issues in Metaphysics: The Ontology of Material Objects

In the previous section, we looked at whether we can reduce events to 2.60 something more basic, because if we can, then events won't be a fundamental ontological kind. In this section, we explore a similar idea: Do material objects form a fundamental ontological category or are material objects built up out of their properties?

The view that material objects are built up out of the properties is some- 2.61 times called *the bundle view*. Ockham's Razor, mentioned in the previous section, provides one reason to take the bundle view seriously.[7] But there are additional arguments for the bundle view that are worth considering. We'll look at one such argument in a bit.

First, let's examine some rivals of the bundle view. Suppose the bundle 2.62 view is false, because there's more to an object than a bundle of properties. In addition to the object's shape, size, color, mass, charge, and so on—that is, in addition to that object's properties—there is something else, traditionally called the "substance" of the object. Once a substance is brought into the picture, we have a metaphysical question to address: What is the relation between this substance and the material object? One theory says that this substance is a component of the object that, along with the object's properties, constitute or make up the object. According to this theory,

---

[6] Kim's theory is not the only theory of events worth considering. As always, the *Stanford Encyclopedia of Philosophy* is a terrific resource. Here is their article on events: http://plato.stanford.edu/entries/events/

[7] Laurie Paul, a metaphysician at Yale University, defends a version of the bundle theory on this basis. http://www.lapaul.org/See especially Paul, L. (2002) "Logical Parts," Noûs 36, 578–96.

which we can call *the constituency view*, an object, such as a table, has two very different sorts of constituents. The table's shape, size, color, and so on, and the table's substance are all components of the table. A second theory says that an object's substance simply is the object itself. The substance of a given table just is the table. On this theory, which we can call *the relationalist view*, an object like a table doesn't have properties as components; instead, the only components of a substance like a table are other substances, such as the legs of the table. But relationalists believe that objects nonetheless stand in a relation to their properties: objects *have* their properties, they *exemplify* their properties. But the properties are not really parts of the objects in question.

2.63   To sum up, on the bundle view, the properties of the table are the only parts of the table; on the constituency view, the table has a further part, namely, a substance which exemplifies the properties of the table; and finally, on the relationalist view, the table simply is the substance, and it exemplifies various properties, none of which is a part of the table.

2.64   How do we know that substances exist? Fans of the bundle theory worry that there isn't a great answer to this question. To understand why, recall our discussion of methodology from Section 2.2. The big question discussed there was whether we should believe in properties because we see them or because theories that posit that they exist are good explanations for various phenomena. There is a similar question about substances. Are the primary things that we observe substances or are they bundles of properties? In other words, are substances or properties perceived objects or posited objects?

2.65   The bundle theorist argues that properties are what we perceive and that substances are just posited entities. And by the lights of the bundle theorist, it is not clear what it is that substances explain. If the existence of substances does not explain anything, then we don't have a good reason to believe in substances over and above their properties. Is the bundle theorist right? Let's see. What do you see? Colors, shapes, sizes—and all of these are properties. What do you feel? Smoothness, hardness, softness, scratchiness—and all of these are properties. Ok, we've considered some of what we observe in ordinary contexts. What about scientific observations? What we detect, measure, and quantify in instances of scientific observations are properties. We do not seem to observe substances.

2.66   Why then believe in a substance that is not observed? If substances explain something that properties don't, we'd have a reason to believe in them. But what might substances explain?

A friend of substances might respond as follows: Substances explain how   2.67
there can be distinct things that nonetheless share all of the same properties.
If an object is nothing more than the bundle of properties that it has, then it
seems like there can't be two objects that are made up of exactly the same
bundle of properties—in such a case there would just be one bundle, rather
than two. Perhaps no two snowflakes are exactly alike. Maybe every person is
special in their own special way. But aren't every two electrons *exactly* alike?
Once we get to the fundamental building blocks of matter, there's a case to be
made that there are many distinct things that nonetheless enjoy the same
bundle of properties. If the bundle theory were true, then it seems that there
would have to be exactly one electron, but that's not the case.[8] This argument
isn't conclusive—probably no argument in metaphysics is conclusive, and
maybe no argument for anything is conclusive—but it is initially compelling.
If it is right, we do have a reason to believe in substances; they are what explain
why it is possible for there to be multiple things that are exactly alike.

One issue on which this argument turns is whether properties are them-   2.68
selves universals or particulars. Let's say that a property is a *universal* if and
only if one and the same property can literally be shared by more than one
object. Consider two red stop signs, sign A and sign B. If red is a universal,
then the redness of sign A is literally numerically identical with the redness of
sign B, that is, there is exactly one redness that both signs exemplify. But if
properties are *particulars*, then two things can't share exactly one property. At
most, these two things can have properties that perfectly resemble each other.
With respect to our example, if properties aren't universals, then the redness of
sign A might perfectly resemble the redness of sign B, but it is nonetheless the
case that there are at least two different rednesses. Friends of properties who
believe that properties are just as particular as the things that have them call
their properties *tropes*.[9] It's an ugly name, but it's common in the literature.[10]

If properties are tropes, then the argument for substances sketched ear-   2.69
lier breaks down. Suppose properties are tropes and material objects are
bundles of properties. The original worry we had was that, if objects are

---

[8] Or is it? http://www.physicsforums.com/showthread.php?t=25167
[9] To learn more about tropes: http://plato.stanford.edu/entries/tropes/
[10] The name itself comes from D.C. Williams, an important proponent of trope
theory: http://plato.stanford.edu/entries/williams-dc/ A recent collection of
Williams's papers, edited by Anthony Fisher, *The Elements and Patterns of Being:
Essays in Metaphysics*, 2018. Oxford: Oxford University Press. Fisher also has a
forthcoming book on Williams's metaphysics titled *The Metaphysics of Donald C.
Williams*. Basingstoke: Palgrave Macmillan.

bundles of properties, and every electron is exactly alike, then there is exactly one electron, since each electron would be made of exactly the same bundle of properties. But if properties are tropes, then, for example, the negative charge of electron one is not numerically identical with the negative charge of electron two, even though those negative charges are themselves exactly alike. Therefore, the two electrons do not share the same properties (although each has a property that perfectly resembles a property of the other one), and so the respective bundles of properties are not identical with each other. Hence there can be more than one electron.

2.8 Tropes, Universals, and States of Affairs

2.70   We've looked at a number of reasons to believe that properties exist. We'll now switch gears and examine some questions about their nature. We discussed in the previous section whether properties are particulars or universals. We'll continue to explore this question, and then afterwards we will dive into some of the other questions.

2.71   Let's start with a claim about truth. A true proposition is true because it says something about how things are, and what it says really does describe how those things are. In short, whenever a proposition is true, there are items in the world that make it true. We can make this idea more precise by explaining what "makes true" means. For our purposes, the following definition of "makes true" will do the job: An entity x makes proposition C true if and only if it is impossible for x to exist without C's being true. That is, an entity x makes a proposition C true provided that the existence of x guarantees the truth of C. With this definition in our pocket, we can now consider what is called *the truth-maker principle*: Whenever some proposition C is true, there is something that makes it true.

2.72   Here's a short argument for the truth-maker principle. The argument takes the form of what philosophers call a *reductio ad absurdum* argument, or a *reductio* for short. One begins a reductio by initially assuming the opposite of what one actually wants to prove, and one then proceeds to demonstrate that this assumption generates an absurd conclusion. (This is why this style of argument is called a "reduction to an absurdity.") In this specific case, we'll begin by assuming that the truth-maker principle is false and see where that takes us. So, assume that the truth-maker principle is false. It then follows that there is some truth, T, that isn't *made* true by anything that actually exists. Consider the group, G, of all the things that actually exist: nothing in G is sufficient for T to be true. Given that nothing in G is sufficient for T to be true, there is a possible situation in which exactly all the same things exist in G but T is false rather than true. In which case, it looks like there is in principle no explanation of why T is true rather than false. This is what denying the truth-maker principle leads one to.[11]

The truth-maker principle is, however, a powerful principle, and whether 2.73 it is true is relevant to the question of whether properties are universals or tropes. Let's start by assuming that properties are universals. Consider now a pretty boring truth, namely, the truth that my shirt is red. My shirt is a particular object, but its redness is a universal. In fact, my shirt is red in the same way that a typical stop sign is red, and so, on the theory that properties are universals, one and the same entity—in this case, redness—is literally exemplified by my shirt and the stop sign. Alright, let's now ask what in the world makes it true that my shirt is red? That is, which entity is it whose existence guarantees that it is true that my shirt is red?

Not my shirt! My shirt could exist without being red. In fact, now that my 2.74 five-year old daughter has gotten into painting, a lot of things around my house have acquired new—and not always attractive—colors. My shirt could very easily cease to be red. So the existence of my shirt does not guar-antee the truth of the claim that my shirt is red. What else might? Not the property of redness! The property of redness is a universal, and so capable of existing independently of any given particular that has it. Remember that the redness of my shirt is the same redness as the redness of a typical stop sign. Suppose we completely burn my shirt to ashes. This would destroy my shirt. But it wouldn't destroy the redness it previously had. That redness would still exist, and would still be had by many stop signs around the world. So, neither my shirt nor the property of being red guarantees the truth of the claim that my shirt is red. The truth-maker principle accord-ingly demands that there be a further entity beyond my shirt and redness, which must be some sort of combination of my shirt and redness. Entities of this sort are called *facts* or *states of affairs*. On this metaphysical picture, what makes it true that my shirt is red is the fact that my shirt is red.

The upshot seems to be that, if properties are universals, then either we 2.75 need more than particulars and properties in our ontology or we need to reject the truth-maker principle. We need entities whose existence

---

[11] For more on the truth-maker principle: http://plato.stanford.edu/entries/truthmakers/

guarantees the truths of claims like the claim that my shirt is red. In general, in order to avoid counter-examples to the truth-maker principle, for every contingent claim of the form "x is F," there needs to exist, in addition to x and the property of being F, a fact that consists of x and being F.

2.76   What if properties are tropes rather than universals? If properties are tropes, we have some interesting questions to consider.

2.77   First, should we think that tropes are *transferable*? Consider the particular redness of my shirt; call this particular redness R1. Consider now the particular redness of a given stop sign; call this R2. R1 and R2 are perfectly alike but numerically distinct. My shirt has R1. The stop sign has R2. Could my shirt have had R2 instead of R1? Or is it impossible for a trope to transfer in this way?

2.78   Second, are tropes *metaphysically dependent* on the particulars that have them? One thing is metaphysically dependent on another if the dependent thing can't exist without the other thing existing. Could the redness of my shirt survive the destruction of my shirt? Or is it impossible for the redness of my shirt to exist without my shirt also existing?

2.79   A case can be made for the claim that, if the bundle theory of objects is true, then tropes are transferable and are not metaphysically dependent on the particulars that have them. The rough idea is that, on the bundle theory of objects, the properties (the tropes) are the metaphysically basic items, not the objects that are made up out of them. In a sense, these properties are like metaphysical atoms: just as the chemical atoms that make up your body existed before they made up your body and will continue to exist after you die and your body disintegrates, so too the tropes that constitute objects can pre-exist and survive the destruction of the bundle.

2.80   What about the bundle itself? Can a bundle of tropes survive gaining or losing a trope? If my red shirt just is a bundle of tropes, which includes its redness, its shape, its mass, its texture, and so on, can it lose its redness and continue to exist? If the answer is that it couldn't, then on this particular metaphysics there is no need to posit states of affairs over and above the tropes: the existence of the red shirt itself guarantees that the proposition that my shirt is red is true. In this case, the trope view would be more parsimonious than the theory that properties are universals. We wouldn't need to add a category of states of affairs to our ontology.

2.81   Ok, but what if properties are tropes and the bundle theory of objects is false? In this case, objects are something over and above the bundles of properties that they have. And so, it is less clear whether tropes are transferable or metaphysically dependent on the particulars that have them.

Suppose they are not transferable and are metaphysically dependent on the particulars that have them. Then, once again, we do not need to posit states of affairs or facts to avoid a counter-example to the truth-maker principle. For, on this metaphysical picture, the redness of my shirt cannot exist without belonging to my shirt. Therefore, the redness of my shirt metaphysically guarantees the truth of the claim that my shirt is red. So, on this metaphysical picture, the trope view would be more parsimonious than the theory that properties are universals.

We've looked at some of the reasons to think that properties are tropes. 2.82 Let's now consider the following consideration against taking properties to be tropes. Remember, one of the reasons to believe in properties was that the type/token distinction is ubiquitous. (We discussed this in Section 2.3.) Suppose we have two tropes of the same shade of redness. (Say that they are both tropes of scarlet.) To talk of tropes being of the same shade is to talk about types rather than tokens. But what is a type for a trope theorist? If we say that a type of trope is a universal shared by the tropes that are tokens of that type, then we have added universals into our ontology in addition to tropes. But if we don't, how do we make sense of talk of types? Tropes are particulars, not types. Tropes are tokens, through and through. If properties are tropes, are there no types? What is a type of thing for a trope theorist? If there is no good answer to this question, should we conclude that properties are universals after all?

2.9 Intrinsic and Extrinsic Properties

When I first illustrated the distinction between intrinsic and extrinsic 2.83 properties, I mentioned mass and weight, since the difference between mass, which is plausibly an intrinsic property, and weight, which is definitely an extrinsic property, is well-known. We have a rough idea of the difference between intrinsic and extrinsic properties: roughly, intrinsic properties (such as mass) are properties that a thing can just have, independently of what it is related to, while, roughly, extrinsic properties (such as weight) are properties a thing has because of its relations to other things. It would be nice to have a more precise statement of this distinction though. For one thing, the rough way of drawing the distinction isn't only rough—it also arguably says the wrong thing about certain properties.

One reason it would be nice to have a clearer understanding of the dif- 2.84 ference between intrinsic and extrinsic properties is that one of the deep questions about our capacity to acquire knowledge of the world is the question of whether we have any knowledge of the intrinsic properties of those objects that could have existed completely independently of us. There are things that exist independently of us, and some of their properties are had by them independently of how they relate to us or to other things around them. In other words, there is a real world out there, made of things that have their own intrinsic properties. To assess how much we *know* about the intrinsic properties of things, it would be helpful to have a clearer account of what it means to say that a property is an intrinsic property.

2.85   As mentioned earlier, we have the rough idea that intrinsic properties are properties that a thing can just have, independently of what it is related to, while extrinsic properties are properties a thing has because of its relations to other things. Unfortunately, this rough idea seems to have some false consequences. Consider the property of being maximally isolated: a thing is maximally isolated whenever it doesn't stand in relations to anything other than its parts. Does anything have this property? Maybe. Perhaps our universe is maximally isolated; if there is nothing more to reality than what is found in the universe, then it is maximally isolated. But now focus on the property of being maximally isolated, rather than on whether any entity has it. Is the property of being maximally isolated an intrinsic or an extrinsic property?

2.86   Consider something that has the property of being maximally isolated, and now consider a possible situation in which that thing and something additional exist. By adding that second thing into the possible situation, you subtract maximal isolation from the first thing. Because of the relation that the first thing bears to the second, the first thing is not maximally isolated. And yet, if something is maximally isolated, then it isn't maximally isolated *because of how that thing is related to anything else* (other than its parts). So, our rough way of drawing the distinction between intrinsic properties and extrinsic properties misclassifies the property of being maximally isolated as an intrinsic property.

2.87   It is surprisingly hard to come up with a successful replacement for our rough way of drawing the distinction between intrinsic and extrinsic properties. Consider the alleged counter-example of our universe. If this counter-example works, it works because there are properties that are extrinsic not because of the relations that the universe bears to other things, but rather because of the lack of relations that the universe bears to other things. Being maximally isolated is an example of an extrinsic property that something has because there are no things for it to be related to. We need a broader definition that can take this into account.

Perhaps a property is an intrinsic property if and only if it can be had by   2.88
something regardless of whether that thing is related to other things or not,
and a property is an extrinsic property if and only if it is not intrinsic. Let's
call this idea Proposal 2 (our rough idea was Proposal 1) and state it a bit
more precisely in the following way:

Proposal 2: A property F is an intrinsic property if and only if (i) it is possible that a maximally isolated thing has F and (ii) it is possible that
something that is not maximally isolated has F; a property is an extrinsic
property if and only if it is not an intrinsic property.

Notice that the property of being maximally isolated is correctly labeled as
an extrinsic property according to Proposal 2, since it fails to meet condition (ii). (Nothing that is not maximally isolated can have the property of
being maximally isolated!)

But there are still some problems. Consider the property of being the big-   2.89
gest thing that there is. This sure sounds like an extrinsic property. But
Proposal 2 classifies it as an intrinsic property! Something could be the biggest thing that there is even though it is related to other things besides its
parts, which means that it satisfies clause (ii). And it also satisfies clause (i)
albeit in a rather trivial way: suppose that something is the only thing that
exists; then it is, of course, the biggest thing that there is, and so it has the
property. So, it looks like we have a counter-example to Proposal 2 as well.
(I'm going to foreshadow Chapter 3: this counter-example works only if
composition is restricted. After you read Chapter 3, it might be fun to
return to this section and then think about why this counter-example has
this limitation.)

Let's take a look at one more initially promising proposal, which was   2.90
developed by the metaphysician David Lewis.[12] We'll call this Proposal 3.
The neat thing about Lewis's proposal is that it attempts to define the idea
of an intrinsic property in terms of an idea we already encountered in
Section 1.6, specifically, the idea of an important property. Remember that
important properties are those properties that explain why the things that
have them objectively belong together. Lewis used the term "natural

---

[12] David Lewis was the preeminent metaphysician of the 20th century. See http://
plato.stanford.edu/entries/david-lewis/ for more information. David Lewis develops this proposal in *On the Plurality of Worlds* (Basil: Blackwell, 1986), pp. 61–63.

property" instead of "important property," and in what follows, we'll use Lewis's terminology.

2.91   The proposal also appeals to the ideas that some properties are more natural than others and that a select few are more natural than any of the rest. Lewis calls the most natural properties "perfectly natural properties." (In our old terminology, we could say that these are the "most important properties.")

2.92   As I mentioned, Lewis's account of the difference between intrinsic and extrinsic properties uses the idea of a perfectly natural property. Before we dive into Lewis's proposal, let me pause for a second to explain why this is neat.

2.93   In the course of engaging in any sort of theoretical enterprise, new technical terms will get introduced. This includes philosophy, which is why we had a brief discussion of my "philosophy of technical terms" in Section 0.2 of the Introduction. As I said there, in the ideal case, when a technical term is created, it is explicitly defined using only words that were previously understood before that technical term got made. Much of the time this is possible; but is this always possible? Maybe not. Sometimes we need to introduce new technical terms because we discover that there are important differences between things, but we lack the ability to express them. This is the third reason for introducing technical terms that I alluded to in Section 0.1.

2.94   Let me illustrate this with a fictional story in which people need to introduce new vocabulary to make distinctions that their old words can't express. Suppose there is a biological species that is a lot like ours with one big exception. Up until just recently, no member of this species had the ability to see anything—that is, they all lacked visual perception. However, due to a random mutation, a few members of this species have recently acquired vision, and these few can see colors. They can now make distinctions they couldn't previously make—they can distinguish red objects from blue objects, for example. If they want to communicate with each other about these differences in color that they can now observe, they must introduce new words into their language. (It's hard to talk without words.) But it is not clear how they could explain what these new words mean to the majority of the people of their species, who, after all, still lack visual perception. (Recall how we talked about what can be explicitly defined in Section 1.4.)

2.95   The moral that I draw from this fictional story is this: sometimes when you discover a distinction between things, you also discover that you don't have a good way to use your existing vocabulary to explain what that distinction is. You must introduce words to express this distinction, but if you are in this sort of situation, you won't be able to offer *definitions* of those new words. And maybe this can happen when doing philosophy! Sometimes when thinking hard about some phenomenon, you discover an important distinction, and in the context of offering a theory about it, you introduce a new technical term—a technical term that you cannot yet define. Philosophers call this activity of introducing a new technical expression without defining it *taking an expression as primitive*. A related idea is that of an *undefined expression in a theory*, which is an expression that is used to state the theory but is not given a definition by the person stating that theory. Finally, let's say that an expression is *primitive* if and only if it cannot be explicitly defined.

One of the possibilities we discussed in Section 1.6 was that the notion of   2.96
objectively belonging together might be an expression that cannot be explicitly defined, that is, is primitive. An alternative theory we considered was that we can define "objectively belongs together" in terms of sharing natural properties but that we can't define "natural property," and so we would need to take "natural property" as primitive.

Now let's tie this discussion of taking expressions as primitive with the   2.97
proposal for defining "intrinsic property" developed by David Lewis and labeled "Proposal 3" by me. As I mentioned earlier, Lewis tries to define "intrinsic property" in terms of "natural property." Here's why this is cool. Whenever you introduce a new expression, you should be a little nervous, especially if you think that it is a primitive expression. Introducing a new primitive expression into philosophical discussion is a pretty bold move: it involves claiming that you have discovered that there is an important distinction and also that this distinction is not expressible using words that people understood before you made this discovery. One way to reduce your nervousness is to find other concepts that can be explained using this primitive expression. If you can explain a lot of things by using this primitive expression, then you have some reason to believe that your distinction is a real one instead of some sort of intellectual mirage. For example, if you can explain the distinction between intrinsic and extrinsic properties by using the distinction between natural and non-natural properties, then you have an additional reason to think that the distinction between natural and non-natural properties is an important distinction rather than an illusion.

Ok, let's see how Proposal 3's explanation of the difference between   2.98
intrinsic and extrinsic properties works. We'll start slow, since it is complicated. The main idea is this: Since intrinsic properties are those properties that can never differ between *duplicates*, if we can explain what it is for two

things to be duplicates of each other by appealing to natural properties, we can then use the notion of duplication to explain the difference between intrinsic and extrinsic properties.

It's helpful to take Proposal 3 in steps.

Step 1: Give a rough idea of duplication. Roughly, things are duplicates when they are perfect copies of each other.

2.99   Go to your computer and print out two copies of the same file. Print something nice, like a picture of a puppy. Place the two copies side by side, and look at them—see how they seem to be exactly alike? That is, see how they seem to be duplicates? This is the idea we are trying to capture.

2.100   For another example, think about mass-produced products. The manufacturer of mass-produced products wants their product line to be as consistently produced as possible, which is why they employ people to check for what they call "quality control." In the ideal case for the manufacturer, every product produced in that product line would be perfectly similar to every other product in that line. In short, they would all be duplicates of each other.

2.101   This idea of duplication is related to the idea of intrinsic properties, since two things are duplicates if they have all of their intrinsic properties in common. So, maybe if we get clearer on what it is for two things to be duplicates of each other, then we will be able to get clearer on what it is for a property to be intrinsic.

Step 2: Refine this rough idea of duplication into something precise. Here we go. Two things x and y are duplicates if and only if there is a one-to-one correspondence between the parts of x and the parts of y that has the following features: (i) for any part of x that has a perfectly natural property, F, the corresponding part of y has F as well (and vice versa) and (ii) for any parts of x that stand in a perfectly natural relation, R, to each other, there are corresponding parts of y that stand in R to each other as well.

2.102   To see this refined idea in action, pick up those two pieces of paper that you printed, each of which has the same picture of a puppy printed on it (Figure 2.1). You know that each of these printouts is made of a bunch of parts that stand in various relations to each other, and it is clear that there is a correspondence between the parts that generates a mirror of these relations. This is why in both pictures the puppy's ears are depicted as being

Figure 2.1 Two Puppy Pictures.

attached (in the exact same way) to the puppy's head and not to the puppy's feet. The pictures show that the puppy's ears are attached to the puppy's head because they are both made of fibrous material covered with ink, and this material in turn is made of smaller things (molecules, atoms), until we get to the bottom level of fundamental physics, where we find objects exemplifying perfectly natural properties and relations. If our two pictures of puppies really are exact duplicates of each other, then they are particle per particle duplicates of each other.

Here is another example. Look at Figure 2.2. Let A, B, C, and D represent four different objects, each of which is composed of exactly three parts—represented by circles—that are at various spatial distances from each other. Let's assume that spatial distance is a perfectly natural relation. The lines drawn between the circles are proportionate to the actual distances between the parts of the objects depicted. The shadings within the circles representing these parts depict different perfectly natural properties had by these parts.

Which of them are duplicates of each other? A is not a duplicate of B because a part of A (specifically, the top part of A) has a perfectly natural property that the corresponding part of B (specifically, the top part of B)

Figure 2.2 Each of A, B, C, and D is composed of exactly three parts that are at various distances from each other.

doesn't have. (This is also why B is not a duplicate of either C or D.) A is not a duplicate of D because the spatial relation between A's two bottom parts is not the same spatial relation as the one between D's two bottom parts: A's two bottom parts are further apart than D's two bottom parts. (This is also why D is not a duplicate of B or C.)

2.105   A and C are the only ones that are duplicates of each other. One interesting fact about the definition of duplication that is worth noting then is this: how the objects are oriented with respect to one another is not relevant to whether they are duplicates of each other. So, in principle, a left hand could be an exact duplicate of a right hand!

Step 3: Define "intrinsic property" in terms of duplication. Here we go. A property F is intrinsic if and only if there are no possible objects that are duplicates of each other such that one of them has property F and the other does not.

In slogan form: it is impossible for an intrinsic property to differ between duplicates.

2.106   Proposal 3 avoids the counter-examples confronting its predecessors. Let's focus on the last one and consider the property of being the biggest thing that there is. According to Proposal 3, this property is extrinsic. The reason is that the biggest thing that there actually is has a possible duplicate that is not the biggest thing that there is. (Maybe the physical universe is actually the biggest thing that there is. Consider now a possible physical universe which is just like the actual one but has a few extra stars in it. This merely possible physical universe has a part that is a duplicate of the actual physical universe, and this duplicate isn't the biggest thing that there is in this possible situation.)

2.107   Let's consider two possible concerns about Proposal 3 before moving on. First, this proposal is ontologically committed to possible objects. It won't yield the right result unless there are other possible situations in which objects are or fail to be duplicates of actual objects. We'll have more to say about the metaphysics of possible objects in Chapter 4. Second, it is a consequence of Proposal 3 that any property that as a matter of necessity all objects have (such as the property of being self-identical) will automatically count as an intrinsic property. Perhaps that's ok, but it's worth thinking about whether this consequence is plausible. Are there properties that, necessarily, everything has but which nonetheless are extrinsic properties?

2.10 Perceptual Qualities

The status of properties such as colors, tastes, smells, textures, and sounds, 2.108
which for the sake of brevity we'll call *perceptual qualities,* has troubled philosophers for a long time. For example, René Descartes, Galileo Galilei, and John Locke all worried about what to say about perceptual qualities, and they've all been dead for quite a while.[13] Let's focus on colors: red, blue, yellow, and the rest. Are colors intrinsic properties? If so, great—we know some of the intrinsic features of the world by seeing them, which goes some way towards answering the question discussed in the beginning of the previous section about how much of the objective world can be known by us. If colors are not intrinsic properties, then they are extrinsic properties. Are they extrinsic properties that things have because of how they related to other things (such as, perhaps, us)?

Here is one argument for thinking that color properties are not simply 2.109
intrinsic properties of the objects that have them. Consider a red stop sign, and consider that exact shade of red that the stop sign is, which I'll call "stop-sign red." If stop-sign red is an intrinsic property of the stop sign, then the stop sign would be stop-sign red regardless of whether anything else existed, and it would be stop-sign red regardless of whether the lights were on or off or how well lit the stop sign was. This is what being an intrinsic property entails.

If there is an intrinsic property of being stop-sign red, then there is a 2.110
set of ideal viewing conditions for seeing it accurately, and these ideal viewing conditions should in principle be ones that we can figure out. An object's color can seem very different in different lighting conditions. Which lighting conditions are the optimal conditions to have an accurate perception of stop-sign red? Late in the evening, stop-sign red will seem darker than it does in the middle of the day. One might be tempted to say then that the best time to get an accurate perception

---

[13] Galileo worries about the status of colors, tastes, and smells in *The Assayer,* a portion of which can be found here: http://www.princeton.edu/~hos/h291/assayer.htm

In many places, Descartes worries about the status of colors, tastes, and smells; see for example his sixth meditation in his *Meditations on First* Philosophy, here: http://oregonstate.edu/instruct/phl302/texts/descartes/meditations/Meditation6.html

Locke discusses the distinction between primary and secondary qualities in his *Essay Concerning Human Understanding,* which can be found here: http://oregonstate.edu/instruct/phl302/texts/locke/locke1/Book2a.html# Chapter VIII

of stop-sign red is in the middle of the day. But why be confident that the middle of the day is the best time to get an accurate impression of stop-sign red? And when exactly in the middle of the day is the best time? Lighting conditions change subtly all the time and these changes subtly affect how objects look to us. We can't figure out the ideal viewing conditions for accurately seeing stop-sign red. How would you even go about determining which apparent perceptions of stop-sign red are accurate?

2.111   Some philosophers find it helpful when thinking about whether colors are intrinsic properties to distinguish the physical properties of the surface of an object that dispose it to reflect light rays of certain wavelengths and the qualities of the subjective experiences a person has when she encounters the object in certain lighting conditions. The physical properties of the surface of an object might be intrinsic properties of that object's surface. But the qualities of the subjective experience you have when viewing the object—*the ways you feel* when you look at something colored—are not properties of the object, let alone intrinsic properties of the object. They are properties of you. These philosophers think that, once this distinction has been made, there is no interesting question about the metaphysics of colors.

2.112   Are these philosophers correct? Don't these philosophers owe us something further? Don't they still need to tell us which of these kinds of properties they are identifying with color properties? (Or is their position really that there are no such things as color properties?)

2.113   So, let's discuss some views about the nature of color.

View 1: Colors are dispositions that objects have to reflect, absorb, or emit light waves of certain wavelengths.[14]

2.114   A *disposition* is a tendency or liability to bring about an effect in appropriate circumstances. How to define "tendency" in this context is tricky, because something can have a specific disposition to produce a characteristic effect without it being likely that it will produce that effect. Consider fragility and flammability, which are dispositions: a thing that is fragile is more apt to break than one that is not and an object that is flammable is more apt to combust than one that is not. These were the properties we

---

[14] Perhaps this view about color is presupposed here. But in any event the pictures sure are nice! http://science.hq.nasa.gov/kids/imagers/ems/visible.html

briefly discussed in Section 2.1. Suppose I douse a stack of newspapers in gasoline. I thereby make something extremely flammable. I then stick this gasoline-soaked stack of newspapers in an airtight safe and deposit the safe at the bottom of the ocean. It is now extremely unlikely that the stack of newspapers will ever burst into flame—but it is still extremely flammable nonetheless. Similarly, when we mail things that are fragile, we take great care when packing these fragile things—and because we do, the fragile items are not very likely to break during transit. As these examples show, the task of defining "tendency" is really tough. I'll assume in what follows that you have enough of an understanding of a disposition or tendency for me to proceed.[15] (In other words, I am taking "disposition" as primitive, although I doubt that it really is primitive.)

Let's now consider a second view of colors: 2.115

View 2: Color properties are identified with the properties of perceivers or their subjective experiences.

Here is an argument against View 2. Suppose that stop-sign red is a property of subjective experiences. The stop sign is not a subjective experience. So the stop sign does not have the property of being stop-sign red. So the stop sign is not stop-sign red. The problem is that the stop sign, but not my subjective experience of the stop sign, is red, but according to View 2, my subjective experience, but not the stop sign, is red. So, if View 2 is correct, nothing that actually seems to be stop-sign red really is stop-sign red, and plenty of things that don't seem to be red at all are actually red.

Here is a third view about the metaphysics of colors: 2.116

View 3: Color properties are dispositional properties of objects, but rather than being the disposition to reflect light rays of certain wavelengths, they are dispositions to cause human beings with normal visual capabilities (and other animals with visual capabilities similar to such human beings) to have certain subjective experiences.

View 3 seems to imply that colors are *extrinsic* properties. An object is red not only because of what its surface is disposed to do, but also because of how most of us are and how the majority of us are disposed to react when

---

[15] For more on the metaphysics of dispositions, start here http://plato.stanford.edu/entries/dispositions/

confronted with red objects in suitable viewing conditions. If View 3 is true, stop-sign red is a property of the stop sign, but it is a property that the stop sign has only because the typical human being's visual system is set up in a specific way.

2.117   Which view is true? Here is an interesting line of thought. Suppose you are forced to stare into a very dim white lightbulb. It isn't fun to have to stare at it, but at least it doesn't hurt. Not yet, anyway. But then the bulb grows increasingly brighter and more intense. Gradually, your eyes begin to hurt. Soon the pain is very intense. You hear the philosophers behind you laughing like maniacs, but you should try not to focus on that. Consider this instead: There is a physical object, namely the light source, that is interacting with another physical object, specifically your visual system. Because of this interaction, you have two different experiences. First, you have an experience of an aspect of the white color, namely its brightness—you seem to be seeing something very bright. Second, you have an experience of pain. These are distinct sensations, since you are experiencing pain *because* your experience of brightness is so intense. One object—in this case, the light source—is disposed to bring about two different kinds of subjective experiences in creatures like you. We say that an object is *painful* when it is disposed to bring about sensations of pain in creatures like you and me. If View 3 is true, then the property of being bright white or being red or any other color is just like the property of being painful.

2.118   Nothing would be painful if there weren't creatures around capable of feeling pain. But couldn't something be red even if no creatures were around that were capable of seeing red? If every living creature in the world became suddenly blind, then no creature would see colors. But would things suddenly cease to be colored? If View 3 is true, the answer is yes. If View 1 is true, the answer is no.

2.119   Suppose View 1 is true and that the property of being red just is the property of having a surface that is disposed to reflect light rays of certain wavelengths. (Remember that, according to View 1, colors are dispositions to reflect light rays of certain wavelengths.) Is being red an intrinsic property? It might be, but only if dispositions can be intrinsic properties.

2.120   Here is a suggestive line of reasoning for the claim that all dispositions must be extrinsic properties. Remember that a dispositional property is a tendency to produce a characteristic effect in appropriate circumstances. But things have dispositions not only because of the intrinsic properties that they have, but also because of how the laws of nature work. Consider the disposition that things have when they have mass. In Newtonian physics, two massive things are attracted to each other by a gravitational force that is proportionate to the product of their masses divided by the square of the distance between them.[16] This principle precisely tells us how massive things are disposed to act towards each other. But is this principle necessarily true—that is, actually true and true in all possible situations—or merely contingently true—that is, actually true but possibly false? (We'll explore issues concerning necessity and possibility in Chapter 4.) Perhaps it's merely contingently true. (I'm setting aside the fact that Newtonian physics is not strictly speaking true at all!) Consider two objects that are at some specific distance from each other. Could exact duplicates of these objects exist yet be disposed to have a different gravitational attraction to one another? That is, could duplicates of these objects exist in a possible situation in which the law of gravitation was different than it actually is? If so, then this disposition is an extrinsic property.

More generally, if every dispositional property depends on the laws of 2.121
nature in this way, and these laws could have been different, then it looks like every dispositional property is an extrinsic property. This case has a serious hole in it if the laws of nature couldn't have been different. So, this is not an airtight case, but it is still worth thinking about.

Two fundamental questions about dispositions are relevant to assessing 2.122
the suggestive line of thinking we just discussed. First, is there a genuine distinction between dispositional properties and non-dispositional properties? Consider fragility. It is natural to think that an object has this disposition—that it is fragile—because of the other properties that it has. It has a disposition to break *because* it is composed of molecules that are arranged in such and such a way, for example. Something can't simply be fragile without having other properties that make it fragile. These other properties form the *basis* for this disposition. But perhaps the properties that form the basis for a given disposition are themselves dispositional properties. Perhaps there are no non-dispositional properties.

But if every dispositional property has some other property as its basis, 2.123
and every property is a dispositional property, then every object has infinitely many dispositional properties. Perhaps this is true, but it would still be surprising. So, let's explore an interesting question that assumes that

---

[16] To find out how gravitationally attracted to various things around you, go here http://www.physicsclassroom.com/class/circles/u6l3c.cfm

there are some non-dispositional properties that are the bases of all the dispositional properties. In the metaphysics literature, such properties are usually called *categorical* properties. (But don't confuse categorical properties in this sense with the ontological categories discussed earlier in Section 2.6.)

2.124   Are dispositions necessarily or contingently determined by their bases? A dispositional property D is *necessarily determined* by a categorical property C if and only if any possible object that has C will also have D—that is, there is no possible situation in which an object has C but lacks D. A dispositional property is *contingently determined* by its basis if and only if there are possible situations in which something has C but doesn't have D, but in the actual world anything that has C has D. If massive objects could exist in possible situations with different laws of gravity, then massive objects would have different dispositions than they in fact have.

2.125   Tough stuff indeed!

2.11 Doing Metaphysics

2.126   As we've seen, the metaphysics of properties is surprisingly complicated, and we have barely scratched the surface. (What madness lurks beneath these depths?) Here are some further questions to ponder:

Does the study of how we speak and what we say—that is, the study of our language—provide a good guide to what ontology we should accept? If it isn't a good guide, what should we trust instead?

The commonsense ontological theory is commonsensical. But is the fact that a theory is commonsensical itself a reason to believe the theory? (If all your friends believe the theory, should you?)

If the bundle theory of particulars is true, does an object have a property if and only if that property is one of its parts?

In addition to properties, there also seem to be relations. Do relations create philosophical problems or puzzles over and above those created by properties?

Suppose the bundle theory is true. Are relations ever included in a bundle that is an ordinary object?

We distinguished between intrinsic and extrinsic properties. Can a similar distinction be drawn between intrinsic and extrinsic relations? What does this distinction between relations consist in?

Suppose that a left hand is a duplicate of a right hand. What makes one of
them a *left* hand?

We only talked about a limited number of views about the nature of color.
What other views should we consider?

Further Reading

If you are looking for even more to read, over and above the suggestions made earlier, check these out:

Toby Handfield (editor) (2009) *Dispositions and Causes*, Oxford: Oxford University
Press.
A collection of important papers on the metaphysics of dispositions.

C. L. Hardin (1998) *Color for Philosophers: Unweaving the Rainbow*, London:
Hackett Publishing.
An important book on the metaphysics of colors.

Rae Langton (1998) *Kantian Humility*, Oxford: Oxford University Press.
An interesting take on an important philosopher (Kant), but also interesting as
an exploration of whether we have knowledge of the intrinsic properties of objects.

Anna-Sofia Maurin (2010) *If Tropes*, London: Springer Publishing.
An important book-length defense of tropes.

D. H. Mellor and Alex Oliver (1997) *Properties*, Oxford; Oxford University Press.
A classic anthology on the metaphysics of properties.

3

PARTS AND WHOLES

3.1 Introduction

3.1   We got into questions about the metaphysics of properties by first considering questions about classification. We will get into our next big metaphysical question in a similar way. This big metaphysical question is "When do
some things compose a whole?" An alternative way of expressing this big
metaphysical question is "When are some things parts of something else?"

3.2   This is how the question of when composition happens is related to the
metaphysics of classification. Classification, at rock bottom, involves putting things into groups: when we classify things, we say that some of them
belong to one group while others belong to a different group. So, if you want
to classify things, you have to start by thinking of which things you are
going to put into which groups.

3.3   But what guarantees that you are really thinking about a collection of
things to begin with? Suppose you observe what you take to be a weirdly
shaped animal approaching from far away. You try to classify "it." As "it"
gets closer, you see that what you thought to be a single thing is really just a
tiger and an elephant that have been cruelly duct-taped together. Is there a
single object made up of the tiger, the elephant, and the duct tape? If there
is no such object, then your attempt to classify "the thing that you saw
approaching you" fails, because you can't classify what doesn't exist! In that
case, there would be *things* approaching you, but there would be no single
thing made out of the tiger, the elephant, and the duct tape. And it was a
single thing that you had hoped to classify.

This Is Metaphysics: An Introduction, First Edition. Kris McDaniel.
© 2020 John Wiley & Sons, Inc. Published 2020 by John Wiley & Sons, Inc.

In general, it seems that a lot of the things that we try to classify are mac- 3.4
roscopic objects that have parts. Some examples are tables, chairs, human
bodies (and maybe human persons, if we are not identical with our human
bodies), dogs, plants, stars, planets, diamonds, rivers, and castles. The
objects that we can move or manipulate with our bodies are things that have
parts. Unless we are making a big, systematic mistake, there are things that
have parts, and so there are things that are parts of other things, and so
sometimes composition occurs—and so there should be an explanation, in
principle, that will tell us when composition occurs.

This chapter is highly indebted to the work of Peter van Inwagen, an 3.5
important metaphysician whose ground-breaking work on composition
captured the attention of a generation of metaphysicians. Specifically, his
book *Material Beings* is devoted to raising what he calls the "Special
Composition Question," and to defending his own answer to this question.[1]
The Special Composition Question is this: What are the necessary and
jointly sufficient conditions a bunch of things must meet in order to compose a single thing? Van Inwagen's answer is roughly that composition
occurs only when the parts in question form a living thing. We'll spend a
bunch of time on the Special Composition Question before we move on to
other interesting questions about parts and wholes.

Van Inwagen distinguishes between the Special Composition Question 3.6
and what he calls the "General Composition Question." The difference
between these two questions is basically this: The Special Composition
Question asks when composition occurs, that is, what are the conditions in
which some objects compose a whole. But it doesn't ask what composition
is. That's what the General Composition Question asks. Compare the difference between asking when a person is free and asking what freedom is.
(Freedom is the focus of Chapter 6.) Our focus, like van Inwagen's, will be
on the Special Composition Question. That doesn't mean that these two
composition questions are completely distinct. If we had an answer to the
General Composition Question, maybe that answer would help us answer
the Special Composition Question too. (Recall a very similar discussion we
had in Section 1.5.)

---

[1] Van Inwagen, P. *Material Beings* (Ithaca: Cornell University Press, 1990). Professor
van Inwagen's webpage at the University of Notre Dame is here: https://philosophy.
nd.edu/people/faculty/peter-van-inwagen/ Also of interest is Andrew Bailey's page
compiling van Inwagen's publications: http://andrewmbailey.com/pvi/

3.7   Here's the layout of what will happen in the rest of the chapter. In Section 3.2, we'll discuss a proposed answer to the Special Composition Question that says that composition occurs when objects are sufficiently stuck together. Section 3.3 will explore a proposed answer that says that whether composition occurs in some way depends on our interests or desires. In Section 3.4, we'll discuss van Inwagen's proposed answer, which is roughly that composition occurs when objects form a living thing. In Section 3.5, we will digress from our discussion to talk about the nature of vagueness. This will set the stage for Section 3.6, in which we will discuss some complications for answers that allow it to sometimes be vague when composition happens. Sections 3.7 and 3.8 will look at two radical answers to the Special Composition Question: the answer that it never occurs (in Section 3.7) and the answer that it always occurs (in Section 3.8). Up until then, the focus will have been on the Special Composition Question, but in Section 3.9, we will discuss a smorgasbord of other questions about parts and wholes. Section 3.10 will provide you with further questions for you to consider on your own.

3.2 The Sufficiently Stuck Together Theory

3.8   Maybe you think that the question of when composition occurs is easy to answer: some things make up a whole whenever those things are suffi-ciently stuck together. "Sufficiently stuck together" is a vague phrase—and, as we will discuss later (beginning in Section 3.4), there is an interesting argument for the conclusion that the correct answer to the Special Composition Question can't be vague in this way.

3.9   Let's first get clear on what metaphysicians are up to when they ask this question about composition. They are asking a question that is intended to be fully general: in *all* possible cases, when are some things parts of a whole? An answer to the metaphysician's question will tell her the necessary and sufficient conditions for composition to happen. So, if we are to understand this "Sufficiently Stuck Together Theory" (SSTT) as an answer to the Special Composition Question, we need to under-stand it in the following way:

(SSTT): In all possible cases, some objects make up a whole if and only if those objects are sufficiently stuck together.

Is SSTT true? SSTT does seem to get a lot of possible cases right, at least   3.10
depending on what is meant by "sufficiently stuck together." So, let's be a
little more precise and say that some things are sufficiently stuck together
when the following conditions are met. First, they move together as a unit,
that is, if you push or pull one of them in a certain direction, the rest of
them will also be moved in that direction; and, second, the things are in
physical contact with each other and some amount of force is needed to
make them not be in physical contact with each other. But how much force
are we talking about? Think about a typical homework assignment. When
you hand in a paper for a class, what you hand in is some small number of
pages that are held together by a single staple. Your completed homework
assignment seems to be a whole made out of parts. The parts of the assignment move together as a unit—that's the point of the staple! But it would
take very little force to separate the parts of the homework assignment. If
quite a bit of force is required for composition to occur, then, strictly speaking, there is no single thing that is your homework assignment. On the
other hand, if very little force is required, then there will be something
made out of the tiger, the elephant, and the duct tape that we talked about
in Section 3.1.

Suppose SSTT is true. What happens when two objects are stuck   3.11
together, then separate, and then are stuck together again? Van Inwagen
suggests the following experiment.[2] Find a friend and shake his or her
hand, but when you do this, try as hard as you can to not let your friend
break your grip. If you succeed, you and your friend will now move
together as a unit, you will be in physical contact, and it will take a lot of
force to separate you two—it will take a lot more force to separate you two
than it would to separate the pages of your homework assignment. Let's
suppose that this is enough force for SSTT to imply that you and your
friend compose a whole.

Don't let go of your friend yet, since we aren't done. Let's give this com-   3.12
posite object a name. Let's call it "Fred." Ok, let go—quit holding your
friend's hand. Given that you and your friend are no longer sufficiently
stuck together, SSTT implies that you and your friend no longer make up a
whole. What happened to Fred? Did Fred go out of existence when you
separated? What happens if you shake hands with your friend again and

---

[2] See *Material Beings*, p. 36.

hold on just as tightly as before? According to SSTT, something would then be made out of the two of you. Would that something be Fred again, popping back into existence after a brief period of nonexistence? Or would it be something new?

3.13   These are hard questions to answer, which is not to say that one couldn't try to answer them. But these questions might also make you wonder whether being sufficiently stuck together is all that it takes for some things to make up a whole. For if being sufficiently stuck together were enough, then something would come into existence every time you shook hands with someone with a firm grip, or held on tight while on an amusement park ride, or for that matter, buckled your seatbelt when you got in a car. The point of a seat belt is to make your body sufficiently stick to the seat so that in a crash you don't sustain further injury. But is there a whole composed out of you and the seat when you buckle up? If the answer to this question is no, then being sufficiently stuck together is not sufficient for some things to make up a whole. That is, things can be sufficiently stuck together and yet still fail to compose a whole.

3.14   And it might be that being sufficiently stuck together isn't even necessary for some things to make up a whole. For an earthly example, consider the United States of America, which at the time of my writing this book is composed of fifty states, but only forty-eight of those states are actually in contact—Hawaii and Alaska are not part of the contiguous United States. So, in the sense of "sufficiently stuck together" we have been using, the United States is not sufficiently stuck together. Sure, the parts of the United States are gravitationally attracted to one another to some degree. But so are the Statue of Liberty and your nose. If all that is needed for some objects to compose a whole is that there is some gravitational attraction between them, you and your buddy composed something even before you held your buddy's hand ever so tightly. And you still do now even after you have let go.

3.15   Probably there is some other meaning for "sufficiently stuck together" in which some other kind of "force" is responsible for "sticking" the parts of the United States together. (Yes, those are scare quotes, which I am using to indicate here that the words "force" and "sticking" don't have the same literal meaning that they had when I used these words earlier.) Perhaps the parts of the United States are stuck together by political "forces." Hence maybe what is necessary is being stuck together in some sense of "being stuck together." What this tells us is that, at best, SSTT is both vague and ambiguous, which is not a great feature for a theory to have.

And there still might be counter-examples to the necessity of being stuck 3.16 together. That is, some things might compose a whole even though they are not sufficiently stuck together. Consider the Big Dipper, which is allegedly composed of stars that are trillions of miles apart.[3] The stars that make up the Big Dipper are not sufficiently stuck together in the sense that we have been using. (Sure, there is some weak gravitational attraction between these stars, but there is also some weak gravitational attraction between your nose and the Statue of Liberty.) The stars that make up the Big Dipper are no more stuck together than many other random collections of stars. It is just that, from our perspective, the stars that compose the Big Dipper are arranged in an interesting shape.

Let's explicitly discuss some metaphysical theories about collections of 3.17 stars. Thinking about these theories will help us down the road to think about more comprehensive theories. The first theory we will look at is:

Theory 1: The stars that "make up the Big Dipper" do not compose a whole.

According to Theory 1, there are only the stars and nothing more: the stars that we in our day to day lives label as "making up the Big Dipper" don't actually compose a whole.

Suppose that there is no metaphysical difference between the stars that 3.18 "make up the Big Dipper" and other random collections of stars that we don't find visually interesting. If this is the case and Theory 1 is true, then a bunch of stars never succeed in adding up to anything bigger: there are just stars that are arranged in various ways. But sometimes when we find some ways in which stars are arranged interesting, we come up with new names such as "the Big Dipper" to label those stars. That is, we might act as if these stars make up a whole, and we might treat these stars as if they make up a whole, but they don't really make up a whole.

If SSTT is true, then Theory 1 is true. (And we will see later in this chap- 3.19 ter that there are other theories about when composition happens that also imply Theory 1.) If Theory 1 is true, then, really, the Big Dipper doesn't exist; there are just the stars that supposedly make it up. If the Big Dipper doesn't really exist, "it" can't have the properties that "it" is commonly said to have: "it" can't have any properties at all, since there isn't an "it" to begin

---

[3] http://earthsky.org/favorite-star-patterns/big-and-little-dippers-highlight-northern-sky

with! (Once again, the quotation marks are scare quotes.) So, for example, the sentence "The Big Dipper is a large object made of stars that are many, many light years away" is false if Theory 1 is true.

3.20   But Theory 1 does not imply that people who believe that the Big Dipper is a large object made of stars are hallucinating. When Carrie looks up at the night sky and sees the stars that she takes to compose the Big Dipper, she isn't hallucinating. Theory 1 presupposes that there really are stars out there arranged in certain ways. (We will look at other theories that do no presuppose the existence of stars in a bit.) However, when Ben looks up at the night sky and sees a full-colored image of Elvis Presley, he is having a full-on hallucination, and he should see a doctor right away. Carrie has made a metaphysical mistake, but Carrie still has many true beliefs: when she sees stars arranged in a Big Dipper kind of way, there really are stars arranged in that way. When Ben hallucinates Elvis Presley, he doesn't have any corresponding true beliefs about how individual stars are arranged. This distinction between false beliefs that are nonetheless tracking something real in the world and false beliefs that are completely off base will be important to keep in mind when we talk about other theories of composition.

3.3 The Mind-Dependence Theory of Composition

3.21   The Big Dipper is an interesting example to think about. The only thing that seems to be different about the stars that compose the Big Dipper and most other random collections of stars is that the stars that make up the Big Dipper are visible to us and arranged in a way that we find visually interesting. Does that make these stars special in a way that other stars that are not arranged in a visually interesting (to us) way are not?

3.22   The next theory we will consider answers "yes" to this question:

Theory 2: The stars that "make up the Big Dipper" do compose a whole, namely, the Big Dipper. But the reason that these stars compose a whole is that we have taken an interest in the stars that make it up. Stars that are not arranged in ways that are interesting to us do not compose a whole.

On Theory 2, although the fact that there are stars in the night sky arranged in a certain way is totally independent of us and our interests, the fact that these stars compose something is not. On this theory, what it takes for some stars to add up to a whole is for us to pay attention to them and to find their arrangement visually interesting. Most of the stars in the universe are not lined up in a way that we find visually interesting; in fact, most of them are not even detectable with the naked eye. On Theory 2, these other stars do *not* compose a whole. On Theory 2, the reason these other stars do not compose a whole is that we have not taken a significant interest in them.

Theory 2 suggests a more general theory of when composition happens, 3.23 which I am going to call the "Mind-Dependence Theory of Composition," or MDTC for short. We'll state this theory as follows:

(MDTC): In all possible cases, some objects make up a whole if and only if those objects are arranged in a way that is interesting to us.

Remember that what we are looking for is a theory that will give us necessary 3.24 and sufficient conditions for some things to make up a whole. MDTC does this.

In our statement of MDTC, the phrase "arranged in a way that is interest- 3.25 ing to us" appears. In the previous section, we talked about stars being arranged in a way that was visually interesting to us. We might be visually interested in some things because the pattern they make is pretty, really ugly, geometrically intriguing, painful to look at, and so on. There are even more ways for an arrangement of things to be interesting besides being visually interesting. The arrangement of notes in a melody is interesting to our ears rather than our eyes. Remember our earlier example of the United States of America: its parts are arranged in a way that is *politically* interesting to us.

Melodies, and musical compositions in general, provide a second sort of 3.26 example we can use to assess how plausible MDTC is. Consider the difference between the following two situations. In both situations, there are two musicians playing in a park. The first musician, who I will call Larry, is playing notes on a lute. The second musician, who I will call Dana, is banging on a drum. In both situations, they are doing the same sort of things with their instruments, playing the same notes in the same sequence, at the same tempo, in the same rhythm, and so on. They are playing from the same distance as each other, and are playing at the exact same time. In other words, in both situations, the arrangement of notes and beats is exactly the same. Ok, now here are the differences between the two situations:

Situation 1: Larry and Dana are not playing together; they aren't even paying attention to what the other person is doing. Each musician has attracted a crowd to listen to him or her. Larry's crowd is interested in the notes Larry is playing, and Dana's crowd is interested in the beats she is banging out. No one—none of players and none of the audience—is interested in both Larry's notes and Dana's beats.

Situation 2: Larry and Dana are playing together; they are paying attention to what the other person is doing and responding accordingly, and people in the audience are interested in both the notes and the beats together.

3.27   Remember that there is no difference in what is played by Larry and Dana in either situation. It seems that, in Situation 1, the notes and the beats don't compose anything, just as it seems that the notes and a random car honk don't compose something. But in Situation 2, it seems that the notes and the beats compose a piece of music. Suppose things are as they seem. If so, what explains why composition occurs in Situation 2, but not in Situation 1? The difference in why composition happens in one situation but not in the other can't be due to the arrangements of notes and beats themselves, since they are the same. One thing that differs in these two situations is whether anyone is interested in that arrangement. In the first situation, no one is. Some people are interested in the arrangement of notes played on the lute, and other people are interested in the arrangement of beats banged out on the drum, but no one is interested in both the notes and the beats. But in the second situation people are interested in the notes and the beats. MDTC says that this difference in interests is why composition happens in Situation 2 but not in Situation 1.

3.28   MDTC seems to say the right thing about arrangements of stars and arrangements of musical elements. Maybe it also says the right thing about the existence of countries, such as the United States of America. Take a look at a globe. Pick up a marker. Draw some random continuous shape on the globe. Maybe you managed to exactly enclose some politically important entity, such as country, a city, or a lake. More likely than not you've just drawn some weird shape around some weird group of parts of politically important entities, but you haven't drawn a shape around exactly one. A mere collection of geographical locations doesn't add up to anything politically interesting. Maybe that's why they don't compose anything. If there's nothing else about them that we find interesting, then MDTC says they don't compose anything.

3.29   We can sum up this discussion as an explicit argument: MDTC says plausible things about the cases we have discussed; if MDTC says plausible things about the cases we have discussed, then we have a reason to believe MDTC; so, we have a reason to believe in MDTC.

3.30   We started this chapter by discussing how the topic of composition is related to the topic of classification. At this point, we might wonder whether anything actually does objectively belong together if MDTC is true. For MDTC basically says that composite objects exist only when we have certain subjective interests—that is, only when we classify their parts for

subjective reasons. But note that, even if MDTC did imply that no composite objects objectively belong together, it doesn't imply that nothing objectively belongs together. For example, it is consistent with MDTC that
fundamental particles that have no parts objectively belong together.

Now let's examine arguments against MDTC. The first concern about 3.31
MDTC is that it is *anthropocentric*. A theory is anthropocentric when it
treats human beings as being especially important or superior in some
respect. MDTC talks about things that are of interest to *human beings*—we
are what are referred to by the "us" in the statement of the theory. But what
makes us so special? Why is the fact that an arrangement of objects is of
interest to *us human beings* necessary for composition to occur? To see how
radically anthropocentric MDTC is, consider the following scenario that, for
all we know right now, is actually true. Suppose that there are aliens somewhere else in this gigantic universe who stare up at their sky and see stars
that we cannot see. Some of these stars are arranged in ways that are visually
interesting to them. They think that some of those stars compose constellations and give those apparent constellations names. But none of the arrangements of those stars is of any interest to us, since we can't even see them. So,
none of the collections of stars viewed by the aliens succeeds in composing
anything if MDTC is true. This is arbitrary—why would our interests alone
be relevant to when composition occurs? (We will discuss in more detail
whether arbitrariness is a reason to reject a metaphysical theory in Section 7.2,
and we will also see in the pages to come other instances of the claim that the
arbitrariness of a theory is a reason to reason to reject that theory.)

Moreover, we aren't the only sentient species on this planet: chimpanzees 3.32
and dolphins are also really smart. Other animals are interested in certain
arrangements of objects rather than others. MDTC as stated implies that
our interests are more metaphysically important than other conscious creatures.[4] However, if this is a good objection, there are ways to broaden
MDTC so that everyone's interests count. Consider this way:

(MDTC*): In all possible cases, some objects make up a whole if and only if
those objects are arranged in a way that is interesting to a conscious being.

---

[4] MDTC seems to be an instance of *speciesism*, which roughly is the view that
human beings matter more than other species do simply because they are human
beings. The idea that speciesism is objectionable is defended by Peter Singer, a philosopher at Princeton University. https://uchv.princeton.edu/people/peter-singer
See also: http://www.britannica.com/EBchecked/topic/1304228/Speciesism

MDTC* isn't objectionably anthropocentric. It gives dolphins, chimps, and aliens a say in when composition occurs.

3.33   Note that, if we accept MDTC*, then we should be hesitant about our judgments that composition *doesn't* occur. Consider a random collection of garbage on someone's front lawn. There's an old, moldy couch. About three feet from it is an overturned trashcan lid. A few centimeters to the right of the lid is an empty beer bottle. We might think that these things do not compose a whole because they are just randomly distributed left-over garbage. And yet perhaps some creature is interested in how these three things are arranged. Maybe that bird nesting in the tree nearby finds their arrangement significant. The moral of this observation is that, although we are often confident that a bunch of things don't compose something because *we* aren't interested in how those things are arranged, if MDTC* is true, we shouldn't be this confident.

3.34   This raises an interesting question. We have two sorts of beliefs about composition: beliefs about when composition does occur, and beliefs about when composition does not occur. Do we have equally good evidence for both sorts? If not, should we trust our judgments about when composition occurs more than our judgments about when composition does not occur (and vice versa)?

3.35   Here is a second argument against MDTC*, which I'll explicitly state first, before exploring reasons for believing the premises. We are composite objects made up of various smaller parts, such as bones, organs, and so on, which in turn are composed of even smaller parts, such as protons, electrons, and so on; the same is true of other conscious beings on our planet. In short, creatures with interests are themselves composite objects. If creatures with interests are composite objects, then MDTC* has a counterexample. And If MDTC* has a counterexample, then MDTC* is false. So MDTC* is false.

3.36   The first premise of the argument just mentioned is that we (and other creatures with interests) are composite objects. If we are not composite objects, then we are not physical objects at all. (We are not partless physical objects, like an electron or something.) The alternative then is that we are a non-physical object, such as soul. The question of what kind of thing we are is a central question in the branch of philosophy called *the philosophy of mind*.[5] And we won't hope to settle that question here. So,

---

[5] If you want to know more about philosophy of mind, there is a book on exactly that topic in the same series as the book you are reading now: Mandick, P. *The Philosophy of Mind* (Oxford: Wiley-Blackwell, 2013). http://www.wiley.com/WileyCDA/WileyTitle/productCd-0470674474.html

what I will do is present one argument that you are a composite physical object for your consideration. The argument is based on the central idea that you have certain capabilities. For example, you can think about philosophical arguments and evaluate them. You can remember what oranges taste like. You can communicate in a common language with other people. You can recognize the face of your mother. There are a lot of things that you are a capable of doing.

You aren't the only thing that has capabilities. Cellphones have capabilities: they can transmit texts or emails, take pictures or movies, record sounds, and display where you are currently located and how to get to where you want to be located. A cellphone is a composite physical object, and it has these capabilities because of how its parts are arranged. If you change how these parts are arranged by, say, removing some of them or damaging others, you destroy some of the capacities of the phone. If you destroy the lens of the phone, it can't take pictures or movies any more. If you turn on a phone and then forget about it for a while, it will go into sleep mode. If its battery runs out, it won't do anything at all. It will just be an expensive coaster or paper rest, at least until you've recharged it. If you do enough damage to the phone, you will permanently eliminate any hope of restoring its capabilities, and it will just be dead weight. 3.37

When certain things happen to the physical object that is your body, *you* lose certain capabilities. Serious damage to your brain (itself an apparent composite object) can leave you without the capacity to remember what oranges taste like, or to speak a language, or to recognize the face of your mother. Periodically you go into sleep mode as a result of physiological changes that are as of yet not fully understood. If you suffer enough damage, you will permanently lose the capabilities you care about. You'll just be dead. 3.38

You are substantially more complex than a cellphone—as much as a phone can do, you can do so much more, and these more impressive capacities are the result of your parts being arranged in much more complex and impressive ways. The general claim is this: if a capacity of a thing can be destroyed or affected by changing how certain objects are arranged, then we have a strong reason to think that these objects are part of that thing. The fact that your mental capacities are so strongly tied to how your physical body is structured—specifically, to how the parts of your brain and nervous system are arranged—provides a strong reason to think that you are a physical object, differing only from other physical objects in how amazingly complex your parts are arranged. At rock bottom, you and your phone are 3.39

built out of the same stuff: protons, electrons, and whatnot. The same is true of the other creatures on our planet that have interests.

3.40   That was the first premise of the argument against MDTC*. The second premise is that if creatures with interests are composite objects, then MDTC* has a counterexample. To assess this premise, let's ask why our parts compose a whole. Let's consider a particular person, Li, and ask why her parts compose a whole. Here are the two options given MDTC*:

Option 1: Li's parts compose her because she is interested in how her parts are arranged.
Option 2: Li's parts compose her because something else is interested in how her parts are arranged.

3.41   Here's an argument against Option 1. In general, when explaining why something exists, you can't appeal in your explanation to the fact that the thing exists. Otherwise your explanation will be a circular explanation: among the reasons why x exists is the fact that x exists. Circular explanations do not explain what they are attempting to explain. When explaining why Li exists, we'll need to appeal to the fact that her parts compose a whole. If we then explain why those parts compose a whole by appealing to the fact that Li is interested in some way in those parts, then we will have assumed Li's existence as part of our explanation of why Li exists. And so, our explanation would be circular. Option 1 is not really an option.

3.42   So, let's turn to Option 2. There's someone or something else that is interested in the arrangement of Li's parts, and this why there is a composite object made out of them. Let's call this something else "Michaela." We now ask why Michaela's parts compose a whole, and we are faced with the same two options as before, and the same reason for rejecting the first option. Note that we can't assume that Li is the person who is interested in the way in which Michaela's parts are arranged. Because if we do, then the existence of Li will be assumed in the explanation of the existence of Michaela, but the existence of Michaela was supposed to be part of the explanation for the existence of Li. So it looks like we need to drag a third individual into the picture in order to have an explanation for why Michaela's parts compose a whole. Call this individual "Sergio." And now we have the same question about Sergio and why his parts compose a whole. And we can't appeal to Li's or Michaela's interests when answering that question.

3.43   At each stage of the explanation for why Li exists, we need to bring in a new individual with interests. Could such a chain of individuals, each of whose interests form part of the explanation for the existence of the previous person in the chain, go on forever, that is, be infinitely extended? I don't know. I think that's a hard question: arguments of this sort are called "vicious regress arguments," and they can be tough to evaluate.[6] But we can set this question aside, since we know that there are not infinitely many creatures with interests on our planet. And regardless of whether there are intelligent beings on other planets, it is extremely unlikely that they are aware of what is going on our planet or have any interests in the creatures on it. So, such a chain must terminate somewhere on earth with some particular individual. And this particular individual must therefore be a counterexample to MDTC*, since the explanation of why her parts compose a whole can't involve the interests of herself or the interests of anyone else. In short, if all creatures with interests are composite objects, then MDTC* has a counterexample.

And if MDTC* has a counterexample, then it is false: MDTC* is intended 3.44 to cover all possible cases of composition, and so one actual case in which it gets the wrong result would be sufficient to refute it.

3.4 Life is the Answer?

Suppose that the SSTT and the Mind-Dependence Theory were refuted by 3.45 the respective arguments against them. One might think then that neither binding things together with physical bonds nor grouping things together because of our interests are what is relevant to composition. Perhaps this is because both theories claim that there are wholes even when there is a lack of real unity between the parts. (Recall the example of the tiger duct-taped to the elephant.) But what kind of unity is real unity?

Think about the differences between a living organism and a heap of 3.46 toys. A living organism not only has parts but it has parts that have functions. And these functions are often to engage in activities that sustain the life of the living organism. For example, the function of the heart is to pump blood, the circulation of which is necessary to stay alive. A living organism is a dynamic object in a way a heap of toys is not: a living organism takes in

---

[6] One paper on the topic worth thinking about is Clark, R. "Vicious Infinite Regress Arguments," *Philosophical Perspectives* 2, Epistemology (1988), 369–380. https://www.jstor.org/stable/2214081?seq=1#page_scan_tab_contents

things from its environment to sustain itself and to grow, it repairs itself when it is damaged, and it can reproduce with the assistance of other living organisms. Living organisms are dynamic, self-sustaining unities; their lives are dynamic, self-sustaining processes. Maybe this idea will help us develop another putative answer to the Special Composition Question:

DSU: In all possible cases, some objects make up a whole if and only if the activities of those objects constitutes a dynamic, self-sustaining process.

3.47   Are there non-living things that are also dynamic, self-sustaining unities? I'm unsure. Suppose the following is true: Necessarily, the activities of some objects constitute a dynamic, self-sustaining process if and only if the activities of those objects constitute a life. If we take this claim and conjoin it with DSU, we can derive the following theory:

Life: In all possible cases, some objects make up a whole if and only if the activities of those objects constitutes a life.

And this is more or less van Inwagen's own answer to the Special Composition Question. (Though van Inwagen does not argue for Life in this way, but rather argues for it by arguing that its competitors, some of which are discussed in this chapter, face serious difficulties.)

3.48   Let's see what Life says about some of the cases we've discussed. First up, the duct-taped elephant and tiger. According to Life, these objects do not make up a whole, for two reasons. First, the activities of the elephant, tiger, and duct tape do not constitute a life. There is no living thing made out of these three objects. Second, if Life is true, the duct tape strictly speaking doesn't exist either! Life implies that the only composite objects are living things. Life is consistent with the existence of physical objects that aren't alive, but such objects must lack parts. If Life is true, the only physical objects are either things like fundamental physical particles or living organisms like cats, plants, and people. This means that Life also implies that there is no composite object that is the Big Dipper, and that no composite object is created when you shake hands with your friend, even if you hold on really tight. But Life also implies that no composite object is a table, house, guitar, car, dead tree, dead animal, or water molecule; none of these alleged things is an object without parts or a living thing.

3.49   At this point, one might reasonably ask what it is to be alive. I wish I had a good answer to this question. Currently, there is a debate among biologists—whose job it is to study living things—and among other scientists as well over what the answer to this question is.[7] There are hard cases such as viruses. It might be that the answer to what it is to be alive is vague, and so, if Life is true, there are possible situations in which it is vague whether composition occurs. Life is not the only theory that implies this; the SSTT does so as well. So, let's turn next to a discussion of vagueness, and whether vagueness poses an especially sticky threat to these theories.

3.5 Vagueness

Let me be clearer about what I mean by "vagueness." First, what I don't 3.50 mean: I don't mean by "vague" what some people mean by "general." Consider the sentence, "There is some number between 2 and 2,000,000." That sentence is true, and it is also highly general, that is, non-specific. But it is also a perfectly precise sentence: it's not vague in the sense I have in mind.

It's hard to say something positive about the nature of vagueness without 3.51 stepping into controversial waters. For our purposes, the following remarks should be enough to get us going. We'll start with two paradigmatic examples of vague words, "bald" and "rich."

Mike is a person with a full head of hair. (He has great hair.) He currently 3.52 has 150,000 strands of hair on his head. He's definitely not bald. We take a tweezer and carefully pull out one of the hairs on his head. Ouch! Still, he's definitely not bald, although now he has 149,999 strands of hair on his head. Slowly and methodically, we pull out one strand of hair from his head, and then another, and then another, and so on. After each hair is removed, one of us marks down on a piece of paper whether Mike is bald or not. He definitely was not bald when we started. He definitely is bald sometime before we end. Can the removal of a single hair make the difference between being bald and not being bald? If it can, at what number of hairs did Mike become bald?

I offer up access to my bank account for the good of philosophy. I am 3.53 currently not rich. One penny at a time will be added to my account.

---

[7] Here is an interesting interview with a NASA scientist about how they are understanding what it is to be alive: https://www.space.com/22210-life-definition-gerald-joyce-interview.html

Eventually, I will become rich. When did I switch from not rich to rich? Can the addition of a single penny convert someone from being not rich to being rich? If it can, which penny made the difference?

3.54   The words "bald" and "rich" are similar in many ways. First, there is a spectrum such that at one end of the spectrum, there are the things that are definitely bald or rich and at the other end of the spectrum, there are the things that are definitely not bald or not rich. And in the middle of this spectrum are a bunch of things that we don't know what to say about. But the reason that we don't know what to say about these cases isn't that we are ignorant about where they are on the respective scale. Think about our two examples. With respect to Mike, at every stage of our philosophy experiment, we know exactly how many hairs he has, how those hairs are arranged, and so on. But, at some point, we enter a kind of grey area where we aren't sure whether he has become bald. Similarly with my bank account. At each stage of the experiment, we know exactly how much money I have, but at certain stages, that information isn't enough to definitely classify me as being rich or as not being rich. Moreover, it is exceptionally hard to see what kind of further information we could acquire that would shed light on when Mike became bald and I became rich.

3.55   Both "bald" and "rich" are associated with one-dimensional scales that have measurable units. Not all vague words are like this. Consider color expressions, for example. Colors are multi-dimensional phenomena. Look at a fancy color wheel.[8] There are some parts of the color wheel that are definitely not red. There are some parts of the color wheel that are definitely red. And then there are parts of the color wheel that are neither definitely red nor definitely not red. What extra information about the colors on the wheel are we missing that would help us decide whether a given color on the wheel really is red? The whole wheel is in front of us, and we can see where any particular precise shade is relative to any other. But even though I see the whole color wheel, I can't decide whether that particular shade is red.

3.56   Let's say that an expression is *vague* if and only if there is a spectrum of possible cases such that (i) in some of the cases, the expression definitely applies; (ii) in some of the cases, the expression definitely does not apply;

---

[8] Like the ones here: https://www.google.com/search?q=continuous+color+wheel &es_sm=93&tbm=isch&tbo=u&source=univ&sa=X&ei=HO69U_GyEM-myASIq YCwBg&ved=0CBwQsAQ&biw=1366&bih=667

and (iii) in the remainder of the cases, the expression neither definitely applies nor definitely doesn't apply. We've made some progress on getting clearer on the notion of vagueness of interest to metaphysicians, but now we enter into contested terrain: what more can be said about the cases mentioned in clause (iii)?[9] And what is meant by "definitely"? In what follows, I'm going to mention and explain three theories about what vagueness is: the theory that vagueness is a kind of irredeemable ignorance, the theory that vagueness is the result of not fully specifying what we mean, and the theory that there is vagueness in the world. On this third theory, some vagueness is metaphysical.

Let's start with the theory that says that vagueness is just ignorance: 3.57

The epistemic theory of vagueness: Vague expressions do have sharp cut-offs. Vagueness is simply our unfixable ignorance of where in a given spectrum the sharp cut-off happens to be. Something is definitely F if and only if it is F and it is a clear case of being F.

According to the epistemic theory of vagueness, there is a single hair such that if you remove that hair, Mike will go from being not bald to being bald. But we can't know which hair it is. According to the epistemic theory of vagueness, a penny can make the difference between being rich and not being rich, though we can never know which penny makes that difference. Moving a millimeter to the left on the color wheel can take you from red to not red, although the two colors will look almost exactly the same to us.[10] However, some people are clear cases of being bald (e.g., Patrick Stewart), some people are clear cases of being rich (e.g., Bill Gates), and some objects are clear cases of being red (e.g., a stop sign). These are cases of being definitely bald, definitely rich, and definitely red, respectively.

One argument for the epistemic theory of vagueness is that it is logically   3.58 conservative. Specifically, if the epistemic theory of vagueness is true, the existence of vagueness does not imply that well-formed declarative sentences which contain vague expressions are neither true nor false.

---

[9] Here is *Stanford Encyclopedia of Philosophy*'s awesome article on vagueness. http://plato.stanford.edu/entries/vagueness/

[10] The two biggest champions of the epistemic theory of vagueness are Roy Sorensen and Timothy Williamson. Professor Sorensen's webpage is here: http://artsci.wustl.edu/~rsorense/. Professor Williamson's webpage is here: http://www.philosophy.ox.ac.uk/members/philosophy_panel/tim_williamson

Opponents of the epistemic theory of vagueness often grant that this is a good feature of the theory, but then argue that there is no good explanation of how our vague words come to have these sharp cut-offs.

3.59   The second theory of vagueness is the *semantic theory of vagueness*. According to the semantic theory of vagueness, vagueness is the result of our failing to fully specify the meanings of our words. We failed to decide on whether to use the word "bald" in such a way that it is true that someone with exactly 1000 hairs on his head is bald. This is something we could have in principle decided, although it would be a nightmare to do this. I guess we could have an election that all speakers of English could vote in. The number that gets the most votes is the number at which someone with that many hairs becomes bald. If there is more than one number that gets the most votes, we have a run-off election. This procedure would be a nightmare to implement. And if we were to implement it, the upshot would be that we would have made precise exactly one word—and this doesn't seem like much of an accomplishment. Trying to make precise a word like "bald" is not a good use of our time. For pretty much any word in English, we haven't bothered to explicitly settle the conditions for which that word applies or fails to apply to things. For any vague word or expression, such as "bald," there are a number of possible cases that we have implicitly agreed are cases in which the word applies and there are a number of possible cases that we have implicitly agreed are cases in which the word doesn't apply. The rest of the cases are those that we never made a decision about—but since there's no one else around to make these decisions for us when we don't, in those cases, the word neither applies nor fails to apply. So, in a situation in which Mike has exactly 1000 hairs on his head, it is neither true nor false that he is bald. Instead, the claim lacks a truth-value. It has a truth-value gap. We can now state the semantic theory of vagueness as follows:

> *The semantic theory of vagueness*: Vagueness is the result of our failing to make decisions about how our words are to be used. Something is definitely F if and only if our implicit decisions about how words are to be used classify that thing as an F.

3.60   The third theory about the nature of vagueness is that (at least some) vagueness is not a feature of our thoughts or our language. The world itself can be vague, independently of how it is thought of or how it is represented. Not all vagueness is ignorance or the result of failures to make decisions about the meanings of our words. According to an influential account of metaphysical vagueness by Elizabeth Barnes, metaphysical vagueness is vagueness that would remain even if all representational vagueness were eliminated.[11] Ultimately, the world itself is intrinsically vague.

That the world might be vague is a puzzling idea. (When I think about it, 3.61 I feel a kind of intellectual vertigo.) This might be because, at least initially, vagueness seems to be a feature of representations rather than a feature of the things represented, and so when we eliminate all representational vagueness, we thereby eliminate all vagueness.

Let's explore this further. We'll start by distinguishing the features of rep- 3.62 resentations from the features of the things they represent. We'll do this by looking at two examples in which there is a clear difference between these features.

First example: Photographs are photographs *of* things. Photographs are a kind of representation—they can serve as stand-ins for the objects they depict. This is why I can point to a photograph and truthfully say "that's my oldest daughter." I can refer to my daughter by pointing to a represen-tation of her. In a sense, I point at my daughter by pointing *through* the photograph. But the photographs can have all sorts of properties that the objects they are photographs of lack. The photograph is smaller than my daughter. The photo of my daughter might be blurry while my daughter isn't really the sort of thing that can be blurry. Consider a lousy photog-rapher who has turned off the autofocus on his camera. Most of his photos are incredibly blurry swirls of colors. But the things that they are pictures of are not incredibly blurry swirls of colors, since they are pic-tures of his cats, and his cats are not incredibly blurry swirls of colors. The blurriness is a property of the photographs, not of the things photographed.

Second example: I witness an episode of real-life heroism: A hero saves two people from a burning building. Reporters are interviewing witnesses because they want to learn who this hero was. I give the following description to the reporter. "She was a woman. She had hair on her head. She was either taller than me or the same height as me. She had a coat on." My description of the hero is accurate but not super helpful, because it is highly unspecific. My description doesn't specify most of the

---

[11] Elizabeth Barnes is a professor of philosophy at the University of Virginia; her webpage is: https://elizabethbarnesphilosophy.weebly.com/

properties that the hero has. The hero that my description describes has a much fuller range of properties than my description of her mentions. The description is a representation, and it has a property, namely being highly unspecific, that the hero (the thing represented) lacks.

3.63   Blurriness, lack of specificity, and vagueness are different features. But, at least initially, they seem to belong to a common family: they are all ways in which representations can be defective or partial. When a representation has one of these features, there is a way in which that representation could have been better: a blurry picture could have been crisper, a non-specific description could have been more specific, and a vague description could have been more precise. Blurriness, lack of specificity, and vagueness don't automatically result in *misrepresentation* per se. A blurry picture of my daughter still represents my daughter, an unspecific description of the hero still describes her, and a vague predicate like "bald" might still be true of your grandfather. What is common in these three cases is that, in each case, there is a dimension along which a more informative (and so in some sense better) representation of their respective objects can be found.

3.64   Blurriness and lack of specificity are properties of representations, not of the objects they represent. And vagueness seems to be relevantly like blurriness and lack of specificity: it seems to be a property of representations and not of what is represented. This is why the idea of metaphysical vagueness is so puzzling. However, as we will see in the next section, there is an argument that some theories of composition imply that there are possible cases of metaphysical vagueness. If this argument is sound, and metaphysical vagueness is impossible, then these theories of composition are false. On the other hand, a proponent of these theories of composition might instead claim that we should accept metaphysical vagueness.

3.6 Vagueness and Composition

3.65   Let's tie the discussion of vagueness to the discussion of the Special Composition Question, which was explicitly formulated at the end of Section 3.1. An answer to this question will tell us what all the possible cases in which some objects compose a whole have in common; it will give us necessary and jointly sufficient conditions for composition to occur. Consider a possible answer to the Special Composition Question. Either you can state this answer only if you use some vague expression, or you can state it perfectly precisely, that is, without using any vague expression. An answer to the Special Composition Question that can be stated perfectly precisely won't seem very likely to be true. This is because almost all of the expressions we have in natural language are to some extent vague, and so will not appear in a perfectly precise answer. Here's an example of a perfectly precise answer to the Special Composition Question: In all possible cases, some objects make up a whole if and only if those objects are all within one light year of each other. (A light year is the distance a ray of light travels through the vacuum of space in a year.) On the assumption that the expression "light year" is precise—which it might not be if the expression "year" is vague—then we have a precise but implausible answer to the Special Composition Question.

The three answers to the Special Composition Question that we have 3.66 looked at each use vague vocabulary. "Sufficiently stuck together" wears its vagueness on its sleeve, but the notion of "interest" used in MDTC was also vague, and "life" seems to be vague as well.

Ok, so what's the big deal if the answer to the Special Composition 3.67 Question is vague? Many true answers to questions can be stated only using vague words.[12] (Here's an example: "What does Patrick Stewart's hair look like?" "He's basically bald.") Maybe the true answer to the Special Composition Question can be stated only by using vague words. But the Special Composition Question is importantly different, because it is a question about the conditions under which things exist.

To see this important difference, we will now examine an argument 3.68 for the conclusion that a vague answer to the Special Composition Question implies that there is metaphysical vagueness. Let me upfront say that this argument works only if the epistemic theory of vagueness is false. So, if you believe a vague answer to the Special Composition Question but reject metaphysical vagueness, probably your best option is to accept the epistemic theory of vagueness. With that noted, we will set the epistemic theory of vagueness to one side, and focus on the remaining two theories of vagueness. And since we are trying to see whether a vague answer to the Special Composition Question implies that there is metaphysical vagueness, we will start by assuming that some vague answer is true.

---

[12] See this famous article, in which the author claimed that almost all words in English are vague: Russell, B. (1923) "Vagueness," *Australasian Journal of Philosophy* 1 (2): 84–92. https://philpapers.org/rec/RUSV-2

3.69   Here is the first premise of the argument:

Premise 1: If the semantic theory of vagueness is true, then *the special expressions* are not vague.

3.70   There are some expressions that on the face of it do not seem vague. Which ones? Mathematical words like "one," "plus," "less than," and so on, seem to be perfectly precise. (Is "plus" vague? In what way could "plus" be vague?) Logical expressions like "and," "every," "there is," "is identical with," and "not" also seem to be precise. That's mathematics and logic. Additionally, the words "entity" or "thing" when used in metaphysical discussions are not vague: the metaphysician just means by "entity" or "thing" anything that exists, regardless of what kind of thing it is. So, on this usage, everything that there is an entity or a thing: you are a thing, a number is a thing, a property is a thing, and so on. (If the logical words just mentioned are precise, then the expressions "entity" and "thing" must also be precise, since these words are defined in terms of the logical words.) Finally, it seems that "is in space" and "is in time" are not vague. I'm going to use the expression "physical object" as an abbreviation for "an object that is in space and time." These expressions—logical and mathematical vocabulary, "entity," "thing," "is in time," "is in space," "physical object"—are the expressions that I am calling "the special expressions."

3.71   The special expressions don't seem to be vague expressions. But we are really interested in what the semantic theory of vagueness implies about them. Suppose that the semantic theory of vagueness is true, and so vagueness is the result our not making decisions about what precisely to mean by our words. We can fail to make a decision only if there are possible decisions to make. With respect to a word like "bald," it's easy to see what the possible decisions are. Each number n of hairs for which it is neither definitely true nor definitely false that a person with n hairs is bald corresponds to a possible choice we could have made: we could have said that n is the cut-off. As noted earlier, it's not worth our time to make these decisions. That doesn't mean that we couldn't in principle make them. We could subtly change the meaning of words like "bald," "rich," or "red" so that they are more precise. But think about words such as "every," "some," and "not." If they are vague, what choices could make them precise? Things are either in space or they aren't; so, how could we make "is in space" more precise? There is no decision to make. Since there is no decision to make about them, there is no decision that we have failed to make concerning them, and so the semantic theory of vagueness implies that these expressions are not vague. That's just what our first premise said.

Let's consider the next premise, which is: 3.72

Premise 2: If the special expressions are not vague, then every sentence that contains only special expressions is either definitely true or definitely false.

Given that the special expressions are not vague, any sentence that contains   3.73
only such expressions will be perfectly precise, and so the world either is as that sentence says that it is—in which case, the sentence is true—or the world is not as that sentence says that it is—in which case, the sentence is false. This means that sentences that express how many physical objects there are in a given situation are either definitely true or definitely false. (A sentence like "There are exactly six physical objects" contains only special vocabulary.)

Here is the third premise: 3.74

Premise 3: If a vague answer to the Special Composition Question is true, then some sentence that contains only special expressions is neither definitely true nor definitely false.

Remember that what the Special Composition Question asks is very gen-   3.75
eral: in all possible situations, when does an object compose a whole? We assumed that a vague answer to this question, which we'll call "Vague Answer," is true. Vague Answer (whatever it is) says that some objects compose a whole if and only if some condition C is satisfied by those objects, and since Vague Answer is a vague theory, what it takes to satisfy condition C is also vague. Given the semantic theory of vagueness, there are possible situations in which it is true that C is satisfied, possible situations in which it is false that C is satisfied, and possible situations in which it is neither true nor false that C is satisfied.

In order to see why Premise 3 is plausible, it will be helpful to consider   3.76
some principles about *necessarily equivalent statements*, that is, statements whose truth-values always move in sync with one another. The standard definition is that two statements P and Q are *necessarily equivalent* if and only if (i) any possible situation in which P is true is also a situation in which Q is true, and vice versa, and (ii) any possible situation in which P is false is also a situation in which Q is false, and vice versa. But we are now considering views on which some sentences are neither true nor false.

For example, if it is vague whether Kim is rich, then it is neither true nor false that Kim is rich. So, we should expand our definition of necessary equivalence by adding this 3rd condition: if P and Q are necessarily equivalent, then any possible situation in which P is neither true nor false is also a situation in which Q is neither true nor false, and vice versa.

3.77   Since this discussion has been and will continue to be a little abstract, it will be helpful to consider a specific example of a vague answer to the Special Composition Question. But what we'll say about this particular theory will apply to any other vague answer to the Special Composition Question. We'll consider our old friend, the SSTT. SSTT says that the necessary and sufficient condition in which some objects compose a whole is that the objects in question are sufficiently stuck together. In some possible situations, some objects will definitely be sufficiently stuck together, and hence, given SSTT, they will compose a further object. The total number of physical objects in this sort of situation will be the original objects we considered plus the whole they compose. In other possible situations, the objects in question will definitely not be sufficiently stuck together—and hence, given SSTT, they will not compose a further object. Finally, in some possible situations, it will be neither true nor false that the objects are sufficiently stuck together. What should we say about these kinds of situations?

3.78   Given our claim about necessary equivalence, if it is neither true nor false that the objects in question are sufficiently stuck together, then it is also neither true nor false that the objects in question compose a further thing. Take the example we looked at in Section 3.2. Suppose we start off with just you and your friend. Ignoring the parts of you and your friend, there are exactly two objects in this situation. You begin to shake your friend's hand. The two of you are currently not sufficiently stuck together. As you shake his hand, you squeeze tighter and tighter. When you reach the maximum pressure you can exert, you and your friend are sufficiently stuck together. Somewhere between the minimum and maximum pressure is a grey zone in which it is vague whether you and your friend are sufficiently stuck together. Focus on that grey zone. How many things exist then? Definitely at least two: you and your friend. Definitely not more than three, because you and your friend are the only potential parts here. But since it is vague whether you and your friend exist, it is vague whether there are two objects (you and your friend) or three objects (you, your friend, and the whole you two make up).

3.79   In general, suppose that there are exactly n physical objects such that it is neither true nor false whether they are sufficiently stuck together. Then it is definitely true that there are *at least* n physical objects in this situation. But it is not true that there are more than n physical objects. It is not false either that there are more than n physical objects. And it is not true that there are exactly n physical objects. And it is not false that there are exactly n physical objects.

If the SSTT theory is true, then some sentence that contains only special 3.80 expressions is neither definitely true nor definitely false. But the SSTT is just a useful example to illustrate a broader point: If a vague answer is true, then some sentence that contains only special expressions is neither definitely true nor definitely false. And that was just our Premise 3.

Here is the argument presented in summary form: 3.81

We began by assuming that the epistemic theory of vagueness is false and
  that some vague answer to the Special Composition Question is true.
Premise 1: If the semantic theory of vagueness is true, then logical and
  mathematical vocabulary are not vague, and neither are "is in space," "is
  in time," "entity," and "thing." (Call these "the special expressions.")
Premise 2: If the special expressions are not vague, then every sentence
  that contains only special expressions is either definitely true or definitely false.
Premise 3: If a vague answer to the Special Composition Question is true,
  then some sentence that contains only special expressions is neither definitely true nor definitely false.

It follows from our assumptions and these three premises that the seman- 3.82 tic theory of vagueness is not true. There are situations in which a sentence like "There are exactly three physical objects" is neither true nor false, even though none of the words in that sentence is semantically vague. Instead, the world itself is vague as to how many physical objects are in it.

In the next two sections, we will look at two answers to the Special 3.83 Composition Question that are not vague—but they do appear to be surprisingly divergent from ordinary judgments about when composition occurs.

3.7 A Radical Answer to the Special Composition Question: Compositional Nihilism

In this section, we will consider some radical answers to the Special 3.84 Composition Question. The first we will consider is *compositional nihilism*. As its name suggests, compositional nihilism is the view that composition *never* occurs: in no possible situation do some objects make up a whole. On the compositional nihilist's view, there are physical objects, but they are very tiny ones that have no parts. Let's call these physical objects *simples*.[13] According to the compositional nihilist, the only physical things are these simples. Some of them might be arranged in more interesting or complex ways than others, but they never compose something further. A complete list of all the physical simples is a complete list of all the physical objects period.

3.85   Compositional nihilism is not a vague answer to the Special Composition Question. But it also seems to disagree with commonsense judgments about composition. If compositional nihilism is true, no composite object is a human being, a plant, a car, a table, or a tower, because no composite object exists period. Is there a way to play down how radical nihilism seems to be?

3.86   In Section 3.2, I asked you to consider the Big Dipper. Remember that the stars that we think compose the Big Dipper are trillions of miles apart. These stars are lined up in an interesting shape, but that is not true of most of the stars in the universe. Compositional nihilism implies Theory 1, the view that the stars do not compose a whole. (It also implies that no simples compose a star too.)

3.87   If they don't compose a whole, why do we have a name for the whole they compose? Consider the sentence, "The Big Dipper is huge." Aren't sentences like this true only if *the* thing named in the sentence has the property designated by the predicate? (Recall the simple semantic theory we discussed in Section 2.4.) The compositional nihilist would respond that, while it's true that we have a single name, "the Big Dipper," the fact that we have a single name does not indicate anything more than that we find it convenient to refer to many things using one tag. Does a name need to refer to exactly one thing rather than many things at once in order to be a name? If it doesn't, the compositional nihilist can respond that "the Big Dipper is huge" is true because the things referred to by the name "the Big Dipper" are *collectively* huge.

3.88   Look at Figure 3.1 and consider the following sentence: "The students carried the piano up the stairs." This sentence is ambiguous in an interesting

---

[13] For an overview of questions about the metaphysics of simples, see Hudson, H. (2007) "Simples and Gunk," *Philosophy Compass*, 2, 2: 291–302. http://onlinelibrary. wiley.com/doi/10.1111/j.1747-9991.2007.00068.x/abstract

Figure 3.1 Two Ways to Lift a Piano.

way. The sentence could mean that each individual student carried the piano up the stairs all by himself or herself. Each student would have to be extremely strong for this to be the case! On this way of understanding the sentence, the predicate "carried the piano up the stairs" is *distributive*, that is, it is true of each of the students. A predicate F is a distributive predicate if and only if F applies to some things only if F applies to *each* of those things. An example of a predicate that is usually taken to be distributive is "is tall"; they are tall only if each of them is tall. But this way of understanding the sentence, "The students carried the piano up the stairs," is pretty weird. A more natural way to disambiguate the sentence is to understand it as saying that each student, working together, *collectively* lifted the piano and brought it up the stairs. The students would still have to be pretty strong, but they wouldn't have to be Incredible Hulk strong. Sometimes a predicate applies to some things without it applying to any of these things individually. In these cases, the predicate applies *collectively*. Here's another example: "The protestors surrounded the building." The natural way to understand this sentence is that "surrounded the building" applies collectively. The protestors would have to be very, very large or the building very, very small for "surrounded the building" to apply as a distributive predicate.[14]

There is a distinction between distributive and collective predicates, and a single name can refer to a plurality of things rather than a single thing. So 3.89

---

[14] Thomas McKay has done important work on the logic of distributive and non-distributive terms. See McKay, T. *Plural Predication* (Oxford: Oxford University Press, 2006). His profile page at Syracuse is here: http://thecollege.syr.edu/profiles/pages/mckay-thomas.html

maybe a lot of our beliefs aren't actually ontologically committed to composite objects. (Recall that a sentence or belief is ontologically committed to some x if and only if that sentence or belief can't be true unless x exists.) What is a beach? A beach is just a bunch of particles of sand and other debris spread over a certain expanse. There doesn't need to be a single composite object made out of these things in order for it to be true that I went to the beach. What is a constellation of stars? It's just a bunch of stars arranged in a way that is visually appealing to us. There doesn't have to be a single thing there for us to find *those things* visually appealing. The nihilist can say that, in general, what we take to be a composite object is really nothing more than some things that are arranged in an interesting way. The compositional nihilist can claim that any sentence containing a name that apparently refers to a single thing can be understood instead as containing a name that refers to many things, and that any sentence that seems to predicate a property of exactly one thing should rather be understood as containing a collective predicate. In this way, the compositional nihilist can try to show that everything that we say and think in ordinary situations is actually *compatible* with compositional nihilism.

3.90   So maybe the compositional nihilist can argue that what we say and think is compatible with compositional nihilism. But what about what we see? In addition to talking about and thinking about composite objects, don't we also observe composite objects? When I look at all my kid's toys scattered across the living room, it seems that I am looking at a bunch of composite objects. In addition to seeing them with my eyes, don't I also feel them via touch? When I step on one of them, isn't what I step on a whole with parts?

3.91   The compositional nihilist might respond that I do observe toys, and unfortunately, I sometimes also step on them. But the compositional nihilist might then also say that toys are not composite objects. A toy is not one thing, but rather "it" is many things arranged in a certain way. It is true that I stepped on a toy because I stepped on a bunch of simples that are arranged in a certain way. If this response to these examples by the compositional nihilist is correct, then in general, no observation we can make would ever provide evidence that compositional nihilism is incorrect, for compositional nihilism would be compatible with our seeing toys, chairs, trees, rocks, beaches, constellations, and so on. (No toy, chair, tree, rock, beach, or constellation would be a composite object.) Composite objects would be things that we posit rather than perceive. (Recall the discussion of methodology in Section 2.2.)

The compositional nihilist might push further and ask what reason we   3.92
have for positing composite objects. In general, absent a reason to posit an
entity, we shouldn't willy-nilly posit that entity. So, there seems to be an
interesting shift in the burden of proof: rather than searching for arguments
for compositional nihilism, we should rather be searching for reasons to
think that it is false.

Not positing an entity is different from actively denying that the entity in   3.93
question exists. Just as there is a difference between not saying that something exists and saying that it does not exist, there is a difference between
not believing that something exists and believing that it does not exist.
Compositional nihilism doesn't merely say that we have no good reason to
believe in anything more than physical simples: it says that the only physical
objects are those that have no parts. Why should we believe compositional
nihilism as opposed to just refraining from believing that there are composite objects?

Contrary to the cliché, sometimes an absence of evidence is evidence of   3.94
an absence. When I open the door to my refrigerator, I don't acquire evidence that there is a housecat in it. My lack of evidence that a housecat is
there is itself evidence that there isn't one—because I would see it if there
were one there. And we don't merely lack evidence for the existence of Santa
Claus: we positively know that there is no Santa Claus. Part of the reason
that I know that there is no Santa Claus is that there is nothing for him to
do. Even if there is, contrary to fact, a Santa Claus, he's not the one putting
toys under the trees or eating the cookies left out on the plate. Parents are
putting those toys under the trees and eating the cookies. No one has ever
observed Santa Claus, and the existence of Santa Claus is not needed to
explain anything that happens. In general, when we conclude that an alleged
entity explains nothing at all, then we have a good reason to believe that the
alleged entity does not exist, and this is because, in general, we expect the
existence of things to make a difference in some way or other.

Similarly, if composite objects are not things we observe, then we should   3.95
posit them only if they explain phenomena that we do observe.

We also have some positive evidence against the existence of Santa Claus.   3.96
If there is a Santa Claus, he definitely does not give toys to all the good boys
and girls. He just gives them to the boys and girls of parents who can afford
to give their kids toys. If a kid is from a family that is too poor, then Santa
will just pass that kid by, regardless of how good the kid has been that year.
But set aside the fact that Santa is basically a jerk, and note something else:
being a good boy or girl is pretty vague. How good do you have to be in

order to be a good boy? There are some boys that are definitely good, some boys that are definitely not good, and then there are kids for whom it is neither true nor false that they are good. What does Santa do in these third cases? Either a kid gets a present, or he doesn't. The analogy with vague answers to the Special Composition Question is hopefully clear. A vague answer to the Special Composition Question implies that there are situations in which it is neither true nor false that composition has occurred. But either a thing exists, or it doesn't. There's one way in which this analogy might break down: Santa can give a kid that is neither good nor not good something that is neither a present nor not a present. (Maybe he leaves a note under the tree that says, "Happy Holidays." Is that a present? Not clearly yes, but maybe also not clearly no.) But a thing can't sort of, kind of exist—if metaphysical vagueness is impossible. (So, if metaphysical vagueness is impossible, we have some reason to disbelieve in composite objects.)

3.97   Things are looking pretty good for compositional nihilism. There is one hitch though. What should we say about ourselves? Earlier, in Section 3.3, we discussed an argument for the claim that and you and I are composite objects. But if compositional nihilism is true, there are no composite objects. Put both those conclusions together, and you get the further surprising conclusion that you and I do not exist.

3.98   I'm going to focus on myself because I know my own name. According to the strategy for defending compositional nihilism that I discussed earlier, a name can refer to many things. So, on this theory my name—"Kris McDaniel"—refers to a plurality of simples arranged in the shape of a person. A sentence like "Kris McDaniel is short" is true if and only if the plurality of simples referred to by my name collectively has the property of being short. On this view, even "I" does not refer to exactly one thing when I use it—I am not one thing, I am many things. This doesn't really fit my self-conception: it seems to me that I am a single thing. I invite you to consider whether you find what the compositional nihilist might say about yourself to be plausible.

3.99   A second problem for this strategy for defending compositional nihilism is that it seems incompatible with the fact that I have existed for a very long time and during that time I have changed parts on many occasions. Consider all the simples that currently "make me up." How many of these simples were parts of me when I was a toddler? Probably very few. For one thing, I am substantially bigger now, which seems to mean that a lot more simples make me up now than made me up then. So, the simples that make me up now can't simply be just the simples that made me up then. Yet I was once a toddler. How can the compositional nihilist make sense of these facts? Consider the sentence "That toddler is me." Suppose I utter this while I point at a picture of myself as a toddler. On the strategy we have been considering, "that toddler" refers to one bunch of simples, and "me" refers to a different bunch of simples. Since the two bunches of simples are different, how can we make sense of the fact that the apparent wholes that they make up (at these different times) are one and the same? In general, it's hard to see how things can continue to exist even though they've changed parts over time if compositional nihilism is true. (We will return to the question of how to make sense of change of parts over time, and change over time in general, in Section 5.6.)

3.8 Another Radical Answer: Compositional Universalism

The diametric opposite of compositional nihilism is compositional univer- 3.100
salism. Compositional universalism is the view that composition always occurs. Whenever you have some things, there is a thing made out of them. According to compositional universalism, there is something made out of the stars in the Big Dipper. You and all your friends compose a whole. You and this old and forgotten hardboiled egg in the back of my fridge compose a whole. The moon, the sun, all the planets, and your mother compose a whole.

If compositional universalism is true, it is never vague whether some 3.101
things compose a whole, because it is always clear that they do. So, the argument from vagueness supports compositional universalism just as much as it supports compositional nihilism. But compositional universalism might have a leg up over compositional nihilism, since the compositional universalist can say that you and I exist and are composite objects but the compositional nihilist cannot. So, if you find the argument from vagueness to be a compelling argument, compositional universalism is a view that you should consider very carefully.

If compositional universalism is true, we are always correct when we 3.102
think that some objects compose a whole, provided that we correctly believe that those objects exist in the first place. But we are always mistaken when we deny that some specific things fail to compose a whole. All the collections of stars in the universe that we are interested in compose a whole, but so do all the collections of stars in the universe that we are not interested in.

In general, there are way more composite objects than we ordinarily seem to think if compositional universalism is true. Many of these composite objects might strike us as odd, such as the composite object that is made out of a trout and a turkey. Call such objects "odd wholes." Is the fact that compositional universalism implies the existence of odd wholes a reason to reject compositional universalism?

3.103   In Section 3.7, we discussed how the compositional nihilist might try to convince us that our ordinary beliefs about cars and trees can be true even if compositional nihilism is correct. The basic strategy of the compositional nihilist was to deny that our words mean what we might have thought that they meant. The compositional universalist might try a similar strategy to reconcile compositional universalism with ordinary beliefs about the non-existence of wholes like the one made out of your nose and the planet Mercury. We'll examine this strategy next.

3.104   In order to see how the compositional universalist might attempt this, first consider the following conversation, which involves two friends Ishani and Hille, who are at a party at Ishani's place. Hille is thirsty and has just asked Ishani where she can get something to drink. Ishani responds to Hille, "All the beer is in the fridge." What Ishani says seems to be true; she in no way lies to or deceives Hille, and she provides her with factual information about where the beer is located. But Hille can be kind of uptight about how words are used and so she says to Ishani, "Ishani, not all the beer is in the fridge. Some beer is in Milwaukee. Some beer is in those cute little microbreweries in Seattle. Some beer is in Germany. Not all of the beer is in the fridge." Now what Hille said might be rude, but what she said was also true. Now we have what looks like a puzzling situation, since it looks like Hille contradicted what Ishani said, but it also looks like Ishani and Hille both said something true.

3.105   The puzzle evaporates once we realize that when we typically use words like "everything" we don't usually mean to be talking about *absolutely everything*. Instead, we typically intend to talk only about a lot fewer things than absolutely everything. There's a technical term that linguists and philosophers of language use for this phenomenon: they call it "quantifier domain restriction." A *quantifier* is a word or phrase like "some," "all," "most," "many," "few," "exactly three." A quantifier signifies the quantity or number of things in question. Whenever we use a quantifier, there is a collection of things that we intend to be talking about: this collection is called the *domain* of the quantifier. But we might not always intend to be talking about the same domain. So, if we say something like, "all Fs are Gs," we might be intending to talk about absolutely everything, but we might not—and if we aren't intending to talk about absolutely everything, then the domain of "all" in this situation will be less than everything that there is. That is, the domain is *restricted* to less than everything that there is.

When Ishani says to Hille, "All the beer is in the fridge," what Ishani says   3.106
is true because she is not using the word "all" to mean absolutely everything that there is, but she is instead using it with a restriction in mind. Probably the domain for "all" when Ishani first uses that word is the domain consisting of all the things in the immediate vicinity of the party. And it is true that all the beer in the immediate vicinity of the party is in the fridge. When Hille uses "all," however, she is talking about a much bigger domain. Maybe she is talking about absolutely everything. And it is not true that *absolutely all* the beer is in the fridge. That's how Hille and Ishani both manage to say something true, even though it looked like Hille was contradicting Ishani. Words like "all" can be pretty flexible. Suppose later at the party Ben says "There is no more beer. Get some more beer from the nearby grocery store. They have beer." What Ben said was totally reasonable. But if "There is no more beer" meant "There is absolutely no more beer anywhere in the world"—that is, if the domain of "there is" had been absolutely everything—then Ben's speech would have been unreasonable, because if there's absolutely no more beer in the world, the local grocery store doesn't have beer either. Ben's crazy, but he's not that crazy.

The compositional universalist notes that typically when we talk, we do   3.107
not intend to talk about absolutely everything. Most of the time, we intend to speak only about a restricted domain, and typically the things in that domain are those objects that are relevant to the conversation at hand. Suppose we are in a context in which we can truthfully say "All the beer is in the fridge." In such a context, wholes made out of bottles of beers and distant stars are not relevant. Since they aren't relevant, they are not in the domain of quantification. And so, in that context, we could truthfully say, "There are no wholes made out of bottles of beer and distant stars." (We probably wouldn't say it though, because it is a weird sentence to say at a party.) So now the questions are whether there are any ordinary situations in which the domain of quantification contains everything, and whether there are any ordinary situations in which the domain of quantification contains odd wholes. If there are no ordinary contexts in which the domain of quantification contains odd wholes, then in every ordinary context we can truthfully say "There are no odd wholes," even if compositional

universalism is true! And if in every ordinary context, we can truthfully say "There are no odd wholes," then compositional universalism is consistent with what we ordinarily say, even though compositional universalism implies that odd wholes exist.

3.108   Let's consider another argument against compositional universalism. It will be easier to state this argument by using a specific example. So, consider my dog Ranger, who is made up of a lot of parts. Consider all the parts that make up Ranger except for those that make up one small toenail on his back-left foot. If compositional universalism is true, then there is an object composed of those parts, which we will call "Range." Range would be a very large part of Ranger, since it would be almost as big as he is; Ranger is just a toenail away from being the same size as Range. However, Ranger is not identical with Range any more that you are identical with your hand.

3.109   Suppose Ranger has a minor accident that causes that toenail to be cleanly separated from the rest of his body. This is the kind of accident that a dog can easily survive and so Ranger still exists after the accident. Range also survives the accident, since nothing really happened to Range: unlike Ranger, Range never had the toenail as a part to begin with. So, after the accident, both Ranger and Range still exist. But after the accident, they are made of exactly the same parts, and occupy the same place at the same time. If it is impossible that two things be made of exactly the same parts at the same time, then compositional universalism is false.

3.110   We will return to the question of whether two things can be made of the same parts in the next section, where it will be discussed along with other questions about parts and wholes.

3.9 Other Questions about Parts and Wholes

3.111   Before closing this chapter, I'd like to discuss some other interesting philosophical questions about parts and wholes.

3.112   Parthood is a relation. A relation R is *transitive* if and only if it has the following feature: necessarily, if x bears R to y and y bears R to z, then x bears R to z. *Taller than* is a transitive relation: If Jane is taller than Ignatius, and Ignatius is taller than Korman, then Jane is taller than Korman. An example of a relation that is not transitive is friendship: If Sam is friends with Jerome, and Jerome is friends with Erica, it doesn't follow that Sam is friends with Erica. Is parthood transitive?

There are some cases that suggest that parthood is transitive. My finger is 3.113 a part of my hand. My hand is a part of my body. And my finger is a part of my body. This screw is part of this table top. This table top is part of this table. And this screw is part of this table. But consider the following case. My finger is a part of me. I am a part of the department of philosophy at The University of Notre Dame. So, my finger is a part of the department of philosophy at The University of Notre Dame? That doesn't sound as good. How should we respond?

Here are three possible responses to consider. The first response is to give 3.114 up the transitivity of parthood. If we go down this route, we should explain why transitivity seems to hold in a wide variety of cases even though it doesn't hold across the board. The second response is to simply bite the bullet and accept that my finger is a part of the department of philosophy at The University of Notre Dame. The third response is that we should distinguish between two different ways of being a part. My finger is a part of me in one way, and I am a part of the department of philosophy in a different way. So, we don't have a counterexample to the transitivity of *the* relation of parthood because there is more than one relation of parthood to consider.

Is there more than one relation of parthood? Consider the following sen- 3.115 tences. The first inning is a part of the baseball game. My 33rd birthday is a part of my life. A day is made up of 24 hours. My finger is a part of my body. Each of these sentences seems true, and each attributes a relation of part to whole that involves entities of different ontological categories, respectively, events, lives, durations, and physical objects. Is the relation of part to whole the same relation in each case though? Is the first inning of a baseball game a part of the baseball game in the same way as my finger is a part of my body?

Answering these questions is important when thinking about the Special 3.116 Composition Question. If there is exactly one relation of parthood, then we need to keep this in mind when trying to answer the Special Composition Question. We didn't really do that in the earlier sections of the book. In effect, we concentrated on the question of when some physical objects compose some other physical objects, and we didn't explore the more general question of when some objects in general compose something. On the other hand, if there is more than one relation of parthood, then for each such relation there is a corresponding relation of composition—and accordingly, for each kind of composition there is the question of when things compose in that way something else. So rather than thinking about *the* Special Composition Question, we need to think through a series of Special Composition *Questions*.

3.117   Remember in Section 3.2 when we discussed the SSTT, which said that some things composed a whole if and only if they were sufficiently stuck together? I raised a worry for that theory that had to do with the United States. I noted that the parts of the United States were not stuck together, since Hawaii and Alaska are not attached to the rest of the United States. In that context, I asked you to consider whether the United States is a counter-example to the claim that being sufficiently stuck together is *necessary* for some things to compose a whole. In light of the current discussion though, you might now worry that this discussion moved too quickly. Political entities like the United States do not obviously belong to the same ontological category as physical objects like you, me, tables, chairs, and dogs. Maybe the kind of parthood relation that relates Hawaii to the United States doesn't require any sort of physical contact. But that leaves open the possibility that the different kind of parthood relation that relates my finger to my body does require physical contact. In short, the question about whether to believe in a multitude of different parthood relations or instead believe in exactly one parthood relation that can relate a multitude of different kinds of things is intimately connected with how we go about assessing the Special Composition Question.

3.118   I want you to consider one final question, before we conclude this chapter: Can two things be made out of exactly the same parts at the same time?

3.119   One possible reason that the answer might be "no" is that a whole really is nothing more than its parts: that is, the whole just is the parts considered as one thing rather than as many things. Here is a stock example designed to illustrate this idea. Suppose a farmer has a field divided into three plots. She sells the first plot to Ferris, the second plot to Samantha, and the third plot to Tomas. The farmer then sells the whole farm to a fourth person, Ripley. This seems like a messed-up thing to for the farmer to do—it looks like the farmer is scamming someone. But the farmer presents the following argument that everything is above board. She says, "I'm allowed to sell the things that I own. And I am allowed to sell different things to different people. The farm is not identical with the first plot, which is just a part of the farm, just as I am not identical with my hand, which is just a part of me. Similarly, the farm is not identical with the second plot, and it is not identical with the third plot. So, I own four things: the farm and the three plots that make it up. Since I own four things, I can sell these four things to four different people."

3.120   One way to resist the farmer's speech is to deny her premise that the farm and its plots are different things. Sure, *each* individual plot is different from the whole farm. But *collectively* the plots just are the farm. (We discussed collective predication in Section 3.5.) When the farmer sells the plots of the farm to three different people, she also sells the whole farm. None of Ferris, Samantha, and Tomas owns the farm, at least not considered on their own, but *collectively* they own the farm. So, once she sells the three plots of the farm, she has nothing left to sell to Ripley. Ripley has been ripped off.

In the metaphysics literature, *composition as identity* is the name of the view that the parts of a whole just are the whole.[15] Composition as identity is supported by this response to the farmer's scam. Composition as identity does provide an answer to whether two things can be made out of exactly the same parts at the same time: if composition as identity is true, this is not possible. Here's why. If there were two things, x and y, made out of the same parts, the Ps, at the same time, then the Ps just would be x and the Ps just would be y, assuming composition as identity of course. So, x would be identical to some things that y is also identical with. Therefore, x would be identical with y. So, there wouldn't be two things made out of the same parts after all; there would just be one thing. `3.121`

Is composition as identity just compositional nihilism under a different name? Remember that the compositional nihilist might be willing to say that some singular expressions like "the farm" refer to a plurality of things, such as the plots. (A "singular expression" is an expression that is grammatically singular. Consider the difference between "the farm" and "the farms." "The farms" is a plural expression rather than a singular one.) The compositional nihilist doesn't think that there are wholes that are in some way things over and above their parts any more than the friend of composition as identity thinks this. `3.122`

But regardless of whether composition as identity and compositional nihilism are the same view, they seem to face a similar objection. I'm currently composed of a bunch of smaller objects. Call these objects *the P1s*. In a few minutes, I'll change—I'll exhale, swallow some food, take a sip of tea, and so on—and as a consequence, I won't be made up of the same parts anymore. Call the different objects that will make me up then *the P2s*. The P1s are not the same things as the P2s. Maybe by the time the P2s come to compose me, some of the P1s won't even exist anymore. Or maybe at that time, the P1s will all still exist and compose something, but that something `3.123`

---

[15] Donald Baxter is a prominent defender of composition as identity. http://homepages.uconn.edu/~dlb02011/Home_page.html

won't be me. But I will continue to exist, regardless of what happens to the P1s. So how can I just be the P1s? The P1s and I have different futures lying ahead of us. So, I must be something different from them, something over and above the mere parts I have at a given time.

3.124   We've explored one reason to think that two wholes can't be made of the same parts at the same time, and we've critically evaluated that reason. Let's examine now a positive argument for the claim that two wholes can be made out of the same parts at the same time.

3.125   Consider the following scenario. Suppose I take a lump of my kids' play-doughand create a beautiful work of art out of it. Perhaps I make a statue of David Lewis. I call this statue "Little David." I contact the local museum curator, who is of course always looking for new and exciting works of art. After viewing my masterpiece, she decides to display it in the central location of South Bend's Metropolitan Museum of Metaphysical Masterpieces (MMMM). Millions of tourists soon flock to South Bend to see it, thus revitalizing the local economy. I am viewed as a hero in South Bend and given a key to the city by the Mayor. In short, my creation is a work of art and is treated as such. Unfortunately, there are malcontents in South Bend—evil men and women who hate us for our art and for our freedoms. Late at night, they enter the MMMM, grab Little David, drop it on the floor of the museum, and then step on it, squishing it flat.

3.126   Little David was destroyed by being squashed. This is because Little David was a statue, and statues are destroyed when they are squashed. All that remains is a flattened splat of playdough. Little David is no longer with us. But a flattened lump of playdough is with us. In fact, upon reflection, this lump of playdough was with us before Little David was destroyed. Call the lump of playdough "Lumpy." Lumpy existed before Little David existed. A lump of playdough can change its shape in all sorts of ways without going out of existence. So, Lumpy can survive being stretched or flattened. In fact, Lumpy can even survive being shaped like a statue of David Lewis. It seems then that Lumpy does not go out of existence when Little David comes into existence. This means that during the period in which Little David is on display in the MMMM, Lumpy is right there along with Little David. More precisely, during this period, Lumpy occupies exactly the same space as Little David: wherever Little David is found, there Lumpy will be found. So, there are two things that are in the same space at the same time! Moreover, any part that Lumpy has, Little David must also have and vice versa. At the very minimum, any simple that is a part of Lumpy must also be a part of Little David, and vice versa.

One important philosopher who embraces these conclusions is Lynne   3.127
Rudder Baker.[16] She calls the relation between the statue and the clay the
relation of *constitution*. On her view, it is possible for two things to be in the
same place at the same time. Not only is it possible, it happens all the time,
as the previous paragraphs demonstrate. On her view, "Little David" and
"Lumpy" are not two different names for the same thing but rather are two
different names for two different things that coincide for most of the times
that they exist.

Baker believes that the case of Little David and Lumpy is just an example   3.128
of a wide-spread phenomenon. Consider, for example, the relationship
between the lump of tissue that we call your body and yourself. When that
lump of tissue dies, do you go out of existence? Or do you continue to exist
as a dead person? Something does continue to exist, namely that lump of
tissue. Your body goes from being a living body to a dead body. Your body
doesn't have to be a living being in order to continue to exist. But, if you
have to be a living being in order to continue to exist, it seems to follow that
you aren't your body. Instead, you are a physical object that happens to
occupy the same space as your body (which is also a physical object) for a
fairly decent amount of time.

On Baker's view, not only is it possible for two things to be made out of   3.129
the same parts at the same time, its actual—and incredibly common! (Recall
the case of Ranger and Range that we discussed in the previous section.)
We'll have more to say about Baker's view in Sections 4.8 and 4.9.

3.10 Doing Metaphysics

Appropriately enough, we've only covered some parts of the metaphysics of   3.130
parts and wholes. Here are some further questions to consider:

What role does science have in telling us when composition occurs?
Can science give us an answer that conflicts with commonsense?

---

[16] Professor Baker's home page is here http://people.umass.edu/lrb/publications.
html She defends the constitution view in a number of important books, including
Baker, L. R. *Persons and Bodies: a Constitution View* (Cambridge: Cambridge
University Press, 2000).

Suppose we can't discover the correct answer to the Special Composition Question. Should our failure to find this answer make us skeptical about whether composition has occurred in particular cases?

How confident should I be that a table has parts if I can't figure out in general when composition happens?

Suppose that there is more than one parthood relation. Would it still make sense to claim that composition is identity?

We've discussed an argument that two things can be at the same place at the same time. But the statue and the clay are different kinds of things—one is a piece of art and the other is a lump of clay. Can two things of the same type be at the same place at the same time? For example, could two statues be constituted by the same piece of clay?

Further Reading

Kit Fine (2010) "Towards a Theory of Part," the *Journal of Philosophy*, vol. 107, no. 11, pp. 559–589.

 An important paper describing Fine's approach to the metaphysics of parts and wholes.

Kathrin Koslicki (2008) *The Structure of Objects*, Oxford: Oxford University Press.

 The author defends a view about the metaphysics of composition in which objects compose wholes only when they participate in an important structure.

David Lewis (1991) *Parts of Classes*, Oxford: Wiley-Blackwell Publishing.

 This book contains a defense of unrestricted composition as well as a kind of composition as identity.

Kenneth L. Pearce (2017) "Mereological Idealism," in *Idealism: New Essays in Metaphysics*, edited by Tyron Goldschmidt and Kenneth L. Pearce, Oxford: Oxford University Press.

 This article defends a version of the view that whether composition occurs is in some way mind-dependent.

4

POSSIBILITY AND NECESSITY

4.1 Introduction

This chapter will focus on the metaphysics of possibility and necessity. In
this chapter, I plan to do a number of things. First, in Section 4.2, I will
distinguish several kinds of possibility and necessity. Second, in Section 4.3,
I will introduce the idea of a *possible world*, which will lead us to a discussion of whether we should believe in possible worlds in Section 4.4. Once
we have examined the arguments for believing in possible worlds, we will
then turn to questions about the nature of possible worlds in Sections 4.5
through 4.8. In this respect, the sections on possible worlds will be a lot like
Chapter 2, which focused on properties. Remember that in Chapter 2 we
looked at two different kinds of questions about properties: Are there any
properties? And if there are, what are properties like? Here we will be asking similar questions: Are there possible worlds? And if there are possible
worlds, what are possible worlds like?

  After discussing the metaphysics of possible worlds, I will switch gears in
Sections 4.9 and 4.10, and talk about possibility and necessity as they apply
to individual objects like you and me. So, for example, there are many different ways my life could have gone differently. Instead of going to graduate
school for philosophy, I could have kept my job of moving boxes of reams
of printer paper from one of end of the warehouse onto the truck parked at
the other end of the warehouse. (This is what I did between college and
graduate school.) If I had pursued this alternative career, I would never
have written this book, but I'd probably be in better shape. In general, there

4.1

4.2

This Is Metaphysics: An Introduction, First Edition. Kris McDaniel.
© 2020 John Wiley & Sons, Inc. Published 2020 by John Wiley & Sons, Inc.

are many ways my life could have been different. I actually have certain properties, but I could have existed without having them—these are my *accidental* properties. A property of an object is an *accidental property* of that object if and only if it is possible for that object to exist without having that property.

4.3   You also have many accidental properties. You are currently reading this book. But things could have gone differently. The property of currently reading this book is an accidental property of you. Are all of your properties accidental properties?

4.4   Or are some of your properties *essential* properties? A property of an object is an essential property of that object if and only if it is *not* possible for that object to exist without having that property. You have some essential properties: you could have been taller, or shorter, or have had different hair, or different interests, but you couldn't have been a fried egg or a grain of sand. Suppose that you witness someone else suffering a misfortune. It makes total sense to think, "That sort of thing could have happened to me; I could have ended up like that." In short, you could have had those features. But suppose you see some water being slowly poured into a glass. It would be pretty wild to point to the water and say, "Yep, that could've been me; I could have been like that." You are essentially not a glass of water.

4.5   There are many properties you could not have had. You have the property of not being a fried egg essentially. These are kind of cheap and easy examples of properties that you have essentially, to bring home the point that not every property you have is an accidental property. However, there are still very interesting questions about what kinds of properties we have essentially. Are you essentially a human being? (In general, are members of biological species essentially members of those species?) Are you essentially conscious? We'll need to examine these questions in more depth. We'll also look at whether the theories of possible worlds examined earlier have any impact on these questions.

4.6   I have assumed up to this point that things could have gone differently for you—that not everything that has happened to you had to have happened. More generally, I assumed that not every truth is necessarily true. That is, there are some truths that although true could have been false. But some philosophers reject these assumptions. These philosophers think that every truth is necessarily true. On their view, there are no alternative possibilities; the actual way things are is the only way that things could have been. This view strikes me as pretty radical, but if we are going to reject it, it's worth asking how we know that it is false! This is an important question in the epistemology of possibility and necessity. But that important question is not going to be our focus here. We are going to focus on the metaphysics of possibility and necessity.

Let's get started. The first thing to do is to get clearer on the kind of possibility and necessity metaphysicians find most interesting to study, namely, *metaphysical possibility* and *metaphysical necessity*. As we will see, a good way to understand metaphysical possibility and metaphysical necessity is to contrast them with other kinds of possibility and necessity that we are already familiar with.

4.2 Different Kinds of Possibility and Necessity

Probably the easiest way to see that there are different kinds of possibility and necessity is to focus on different kinds of impossibility. Obviously, the notions of possibility, necessity, and impossibility are all connected. If something is possible, then it is not impossible; and if it isn't impossible, then it is not necessary that it not be. But if it is necessary that something be, then it can't not be, that is, it is not possible that it not be. This connection between possibility, necessity, and impossibility is easiest to see if we help ourselves to a few symbols. (And these symbols will be useful in the next section, so don't forget them.) Let's use "P," "Q," and other capital letters to stand for sentences. We will use the "not" symbol as an abbreviation for "It is not the case that." Finally, we will use "□" and "◇" as abbreviations for "it is necessary that" and "it is possible that" respectively. So, a sentence like "□Q" says "it is necessary that Q" and a sentence like "not ◇Q" says "it is not possible that Q." (That is, Q is impossible.) With these symbols, we can easily show necessity, possibility, and impossibility are related to each other:

For any sentence P: □P if and only if not (◇not P).[1]

Ok, now that we have this idea in the background, let's consider some different kinds of possibility and necessity. Consider each of the following speeches, which I am going to label so that we can easily refer to them later:

---

[1] The logic of possibility and necessity is called *modal logic*, and these are some of symbols modal logicians employ. This is a good place to start for more on modal logic: http://plato.stanford.edu/entries/logic-modal/

M1: "I can't speak French. I never bothered to learn it. I studied Spanish instead."

M2: "I can't speak French. I will have to study to learn it, but I'm good with languages, so picking it up won't be a problem for me. Just don't ask me to run a five-minute mile because there's nothing I can do to make that happen. I just wasn't born with the right body type."

M3: "It's physically possible for human beings to run five-minute miles; in fact, lots of them do this. There's nothing in the laws of physics, or biology, or anatomy to rule this out. So, there is a physically possible scenario in which I was born with the right body type and succeed in running a five-minute mile. In that sense, I can run a five-minute mile. But even in that sense, I can't run faster than the speed of light, because nothing can go faster than the speed of light."

M4: "The speed of light is about 186,000 miles per second, and because the speed of light has that speed, we can calculate how long it takes for light from distant stars to reach the planet Earth. But why is the speed of light about 186,000 miles per second? Couldn't it have been slightly faster or slightly slower? And what would have happened had the speed of light been different? The physical world would probably have been different in all sorts of amazing ways. But there are some limits to how different things could be. Even if the speed of light were faster, 7 + 5 would still have to equal 12. The truths of mathematics have to be what they are."

4.10   In each of M1–M4, different kinds of possibility and impossibility are brought into play. In M1, there is a kind of possibility that we might call *ability possibility*. Probably most of the time when we say that someone can do some action—that it is possible that they do this action—it is this kind of possibility that we have in mind. But it isn't always what we have in mind, as you can see by thinking about the kind of possibility that shows up in M2. We can call the kind of possibility that is being discussed in M2 *potentiality possibility*. When the army tells you to be all that you *can* be, it is potentiality possibility that is being discussed. When the army wants you to be all that you can be, they don't have in mind the possibility of you breaking the laws of physics. In M3, it is *physical possibility* that is being discussed. The idea there is that whatever isn't ruled out as impossible by some law of nature, such as a law of physics or chemistry, for example, is physically possible. Now some things can be physically possible that are highly unlikely to happen. It is highly unlikely that I will acquire surgically implanted bio-mechanical wings that will enable me to fly outside of an airplane, but as far I know nothing in the laws of nature rules this out.

Finally, in M4 we come to the widest notion of possibility, which meta- physicians call *absolute possibility* or *metaphysical* possibility. Notice how the kinds of possibility get progressively *weaker* as you move from M1 to M4. Here's what I mean by saying that the kinds of possibility get weaker. If something is ability possible, it follows that it is potentiality possible; but it doesn't follow from the fact that something is potentiality possible that it is ability possible; in fact, monologue M1 shows you why this doesn't follow. In short, ability possibility implies potentiality possibility, but the opposite is not true. In a similar way, potentiality possibility implies physical possi- bility, but physical possibility does not imply potentiality possibility. Finally, we come to metaphysical possibility: Every kind of possibility implies meta- physical possibility. This is why it is the weakest kind of possibility: If some- thing is genuinely possible in any way whatsoever, it is metaphysically possible, although something might be metaphysically possible without being physically possible, potentiality possible, or ability possible. [4.11]

Metaphysical impossibility is the opposite of metaphysical possibility. Metaphysical possibility is the *weakest* kind of genuine possibility but meta- physical impossibility is the *strongest* kind of genuine impossibility. What has ability impossibility can't happen given what my abilities are, but there is still some other way in which it could happen. And this is true for all the other kinds of impossibility except for metaphysical impossibility: what is metaphysically impossible is in no way genuinely possible. Similarly for metaphysical necessity: what is metaphysically necessary is absolutely guaranteed to happen. [4.12]

You probably noticed that I used the word "genuine" when talking about the kinds of possibility. There is a reason for that. We sometimes use the word "possible" and related words like "might" and "maybe" not to indicate that something could happen, but rather to indicate something about what we know or reasonably believe. Let me give you an example. Suppose Immanuel is trying to solve the math problem, "$x + 7 = 12$," and that he is struggling a bit with it because he only has ten fingers. He might say some- thing like this, "x can't be 3, because that would be too small. But maybe it is 4? It might be 5. I guess it could be 6. It can't be 7. I don't know." Given the situation that Immanuel is in, what he says is reasonable. Given his evidence and his mathematical abilities, he can rule out 3 and 7, but for all Immanuel knows, the answer might still be 4, or 5, or 6. The numbers 4, 5, 6 are what philosophers call *epistemically possible* answers to the question. More [4.13] generally, a proposition is epistemically possible for a person if and only if that person's evidence does not rule out that the proposition is true.

4.14   Epistemic possibility is not a kind of genuine possibility. The example involving Immanuel shows this. Although 4, 5, and 6 are each epistemically possible answers, 4 + 7 could not have equaled 12, and neither could 6 + 7. In other words, it is metaphysically impossible that 4 + 7 = 12 and it is metaphysically impossible that 6 + 7 = 12. It might be helpful to think of epistemic possibility as something like *alleged possibility*. Not all alleged criminals are really criminals, but some of them are. Similarly, not all epistemic possibilities are really possibilities, but some are. It is epistemically possible (for Immanuel) that 5 + 7 = 12, and moreover it is genuinely possible that 5 + 7 = 12, because it is actual that 5 + 7 = 12. In what follows, I will only discuss kinds of genuine possibility and I will ignore epistemic possibility pretty much altogether.

4.15   One other thing to mention: as the last sentence indicates, I don't use "actual" and "possible" as contraries. Anything that is actually true is therefore possibly true. ("It does happen" implies "it is possible that it happen.") The contrary to "actual" is not "possible," but rather "merely possible": a proposition is merely possible if and only if it is false but it is possible that it is true.

4.16   In this chapter, the kinds of genuine possibility, impossibility, and necessity we will focus on will be metaphysical possibility, impossibility, and necessity. But keep in mind the other kinds of genuine possibility, impossibility, and necessity just discussed, since part of the case for believing in possible worlds is that possible worlds help explain how these different kinds are related to one another. Let's turn now to a discussion of possible worlds.

4.3 The Idea of Possible Worlds

4.17 You might already believe in possible worlds, or at least may be heavily inclined to. I bet you didn't bat an eyelid earlier when I talked about possible situations, that is, situations that could have occurred. (A possible situation is *merely possible* if and only if it could have occurred but didn't actually occur; some possible situations aren't merely possible because they actually occur!) Remember that, in Chapter 3, the notion of a possible situation was explicitly used when formulating the Special Composition Question. Possible situations are homey little entities. *There are* several ways in which I could win this tennis match. That is, there are several possible situations in which I will win. (And many in which I will lose!)

A possible world is like a possible situation, only bigger and more com- 4.18 prehensive. Think of all the different ways in which your life could have gone: you could have read a different book instead of this one, you could have worn a red shirt rather than a blue shirt, you could have been a little taller, you could have died at the age of six, and so on. Each of these different ways your life could have gone corresponds to a possible situation in which your life does go that way. Think about a game you enjoy playing and now think about all the different ways in which you could win while playing that game: each of these different ways corresponds to a possible situation in which you play that game and win. Now think about everything that there is: not just everything in your immediate surroundings, but absolutely everything that exists. And now imagine all the different ways in which *that* totality of all that there is could have been different. Each of *these* different ways corresponds to what philosophers call *possible worlds*: a possible world is a *maximal* way that all of reality could have been. There is one possible world that corresponds to exactly how the world actually is. Metaphysicians call this unique world *the actual world.*

A possible world is a *maximal* way in which all of reality could have been. 4.19 Consider any claim *C*, say, for example, that Barack Obama was elected President of the United States in 2008. Metaphorically speaking, every possible world has an opinion on whether *C* is true, and what that literally means is that, at some possible worlds, *C* is true but at others *C* is false. At some possible worlds, *C* is false because Hilary Clinton beat Barack Obama in the Democratic party's primary, but at others *C* is false because John McCain beat Barack Obama in the general election; in some *C* is false because Barack Obama was never born and so couldn't become president, but in others *C* is false because Barack Obama never decided to run for office. And there are far more fanciful ways in which *C* could be false: in some possible worlds, *C* is false because the universe contracted moments after the Big Bang and so neither the United States nor Barack Obama ever existed. The point is that, *every possible world* says with respect to *any* given claim either that the claim is true or that the claim is false. To continue to use our earlier metaphor, a possible world has an opinion on any proposition whatsoever, and this is why I say that a possible world is a maximal way that all of reality could have been.

(There is potentially one important qualification. In Chapter 3, we consid- 4.20 ered the idea that there are propositions that are neither true nor false. If there are such propositions, then we need to be more careful: it would be better to say that every possible world says with respect to a given proposition that the proposition is either true, false, or neither true nor false. I'm going to ignore this epistemically(!) possible complication in what follows, but you should carefully consider the ways in which the passages to come will need to be re-thought if in fact there are propositions that are neither true nor false.)

4.21   Out of all the possible worlds, there is one world that gets every claim exactly right and gets none of them wrong. (If a possible world were both to agree and to disagree with a claim, then that world wouldn't really be a possible world, because contradictions are impossible.) This possible world that gets everything right and nothing wrong is the actual world: the actual world is that maximal possible situation that actually obtains.

4.22   We've now got a rough idea of what possible worlds are supposed to be, but this rough idea doesn't tell us what possible worlds are like, and it doesn't tell us whether we should believe in them. Let's discuss the question of whether we should believe in possible worlds first (in Section 4.4), and then turn to the question of what they are like (in Section 4.5).

4.4 A Case for Possible Worlds

4.23 One reason we've already touched on for believing in possible worlds is the following: There are possible situations, and some of these are more comprehensive than others, and possible worlds are nothing more than maximally comprehensive possible situations. So, if you believe in possible situations—ways in which things could have gone differently than they actually have gone—then there is no reason not to believe in possible worlds, since these are just maximal possible situations.

4.24   This argument is fine as far as it goes, but it doesn't go very far. It's true that, if you already believe in possible situations, then believing in possible worlds is not much more of an ontological commitment, but we are doing metaphysics here—and in this context, it is reasonable to wonder whether one should believe in possible situations of any sort, maximal or not.

4.25   So, let's see whether there is a better case for possible worlds. We will examine an argument that is based on the claim that possible worlds neatly explain various facts in a systematic way. Hence the case for possible worlds will be that we have a good reason to *posit* them: we should believe in possible worlds because theories that make use of them to explain various phenomena are successful theories.

The heart of the theory of possible worlds is that there is a deep connection 4.26
between possible worlds and possibility, which can be expressed in the following way: A proposition is possibly true if and only if it is true at some
possible world; a proposition is necessarily true if and only if it is true at every
possible world; a proposition is impossible if and only if it there is no possible
world at which it is true. In short, possibility, necessity, and impossibility
respectively are just truth at some, all, and no possibility worlds. (At some
point, we are going to need to get clearer on what it means to say that a proposition is true *at* a world; we'll come back to this issue in Sections 4.9 and 4.10.)

Remember that possible worlds are maximally opinionated: for any pos- 4.27
sible world and any proposition, either that possible world says that this
proposition is true, or that possible world says that it is false. If every possible world agrees that a proposition is a true, then it is necessarily true. If
every possible world agrees that a proposition is false, then it is necessarily
false, that is, impossible. But if at least one possible world says a proposition
is true, that is enough for it to be possibly true.

Let's now examine the claim that the theory of possible worlds explains 4.28
something that needs explaining.

First, the theory explains why the notions of necessity, possibility, and 4.29
impossibility are all inter-definable, an observation made at the beginning of this chapter. The explanation is straightforward. First, "some" /
"there is," "all" / "every," and "none" are inter-definable: "everything is F"
is true if and only if "nothing is not-F" is true; "something is an F" is true
if and only if "it is not the case that everything is not-F" is true. (Here are
some examples: some animals are cats is true if and only if not every animal is not a cat; no dog can breathe underwater is true if and only if every
dog can't breathe under water.) Second, on the possible worlds theory, as
mentioned earlier, possibility, necessity, and impossibility are just truth at
some, all, or no possible worlds. So the reason why "it is possible that P"
can be defined as "it is not the case that it is necessary that not P" is that
"it is possible that P" expresses the same fact as "there is a possible world
at which P is true." In general, the possible worlds theory tells us that the
reason why "possibility," "necessity," and "impossibility" are inter-definable
is that these notions mean the same thing as truth at some world, truth
at all worlds, and truth at no worlds, and "some," "all," and "none" are
inter-definable.

This is a neat result, but we can go further. The possible worlds theory 4.30
neatly explains how the various "senses" of "possible" are connected and
why it is that we easily move from one sense to another in a conversation:

the various "senses" of "possible" correspond to the various ways in which we can use words like "some" or "all."

4.31   Recall our discussion in Section 3.8 of the idea of restricted quantification. Whenever we use quantifiers, for example, words like "some" or "every," there is a domain of things that are relevant to the conversation we are in. In a given context, a sentence like "some F is G" is true if and only if at least one thing in that domain is both F and G. But, in ordinary contexts, we don't normally intend to be talking about absolutely everything. This is why we can truly say things like, "all the beer is in the fridge" even though there is beer that is not the fridge; in a context like this (like when we are at a party), beer really far away from us is not relevant, and is not included in the domain of things that we are talking about.

4.32   What does all this have to do with various senses of "possibility," "necessity," and "impossibility"? Well, remember that on the possible worlds theory, to say that something is possible is to say that *there is some* world at which it happens; to say that something is necessary is to say that *at all worlds* it happens; and to say that something is impossible is to say that *at no world* it happens. "Some," "all," and "none" are each quantifier phrases. So, if the possible worlds theory is true, there are as many different ways to use words like "possible," "necessary," and "impossible" as there are ways to use words like "some," "all," and "none."

4.33   And this is exactly what we find. When I say "I can't speak French. I never bothered to learn it. I studied Spanish instead," I say something true even though *it is metaphysically possible that I speak French*. When I say "I can't speak French," I say something true because I am not talking about absolutely all of the possibilities that there are but rather only some of them: I am talking about those worlds that are "in the immediate vicinity," that is, possible worlds that are not much different from the actual world. All the possible worlds that are very similar to the actual world, including with respect to the abilities I actually have, are ones in which I don't speak French. These are the worlds that correspond to what I called *ability possibility*; they are the ones, metaphorically speaking, "in my immediate vicinity," and are in the domain of quantification when I say, "I can't speak French."

4.34   Each of the different uses of "possible" corresponds to different domains for the quantifier phrase "some"; each of the different uses of "necessary" corresponds to different domains for the phrase "all" or "every"; and each of the different uses of "impossible" corresponds to different domains for the phrase "none." The possible worlds theory provides a very neat explanation for how there seem to be different uses of the words "possible," "necessary," and "impossible," how these seemingly different uses are connected to each other, and why it is that we can so easily switch between them. As we consider more and more of all of the possibilities that there are, what we can truthfully call "possible," "necessary," or "impossible" will change as well—although what is absolutely possible, absolutely necessary, or absolutely impossible does not change. Typically, the process of considering more and more possibilities involves considering some increasingly unlikely and increasingly stranger possibilities, in short, those that are "further" from reality. This is because what is metaphysically possible can be very different from what is actually the case. If you reexamine the speeches M1–M4, this seems to be exactly what occurs. In each succeeding speech, more and more possibilities are relevant to the speech being made, and correspondingly, the domain of quantification includes more and more possible worlds than it previously did.

The possible worlds theory has now scored two impressive points. But it 4.35 can go further. The possible worlds theory can also explain when *counterfactual conditionals* are true. A counterfactual conditional is a claim of the form "If P were the case, then Q would be the case." In general, a conditional is a claim that has an "if" part and a "then" part. There are different kinds of conditionals, and they don't all work in the same way. Here is an example that shows the difference between two different kinds of conditionals. Consider the difference between "If Mark Chapman didn't shoot John Lennon, then someone else did" and "If Mark Chapman hadn't shot John Lennon, then someone else would have." The first sentence is clearly true (since Lennon was shot), but the second is not very plausible. Many logicians treat sentences of the first kind (which are called "indicative conditionals") as being equivalent to disjunctions, that is, sentences containing "or." On their view, the first sentence just means the same thing as "Either Mark Chapman shot John Lennon or someone else did." But the second kind of sentence isn't equivalent to a disjunction. The second kind of sentence is called a *counterfactual conditional*.[2] I'll abbreviate and just say "counterfactual" in what follows.

The possible worlds theory provides the basis for a theory of counterfac- 4.36 tuals. We just discussed the idea that some worlds are more like the actual world than others; that is, that some worlds are "further" from reality than

---

[2] For more on counterfactual conditionals, see http://plato.stanford.edu/entries/conditionals/

others. Since we will use this idea when developing a theory of counterfactuals, let's convert this metaphor of one world being closer to the actual world than another into an explicit technical term: say that world w_1 is *closer* to the actual world *than* world w_2 if and only if w_1 is more like the actual world than w_2 is. (In general, w_1 is closer to world x than w_2 if and only if w_1 is more like world x than w_2 is like x.) A possible world in which there are unicorns and dragons is much more distant from the actual world than a possible world a lot like our world except that there is one fewer donkey in it.

4.37   We can now consider a very basic but still plausible theory of counterfactuals: a counterfactual of the form "If P were the case, then Q would be the case" is true if and only if at the closest world (to the actual world) in which P is true, Q is also true. In short, "If P were the case, then Q would be the case" means the same thing as "Take the world in which P is true that is most like the actual world. Q is also true at that world."[3]

4.38   This theory of counterfactuals does seem to nicely match up with the thoughts we usually have when we think about counterfactuals. Suppose we are wondering what would have happened had the United States never invaded Iraq in 2003. When we wonder about this, we don't consider really far-out possibilities, such as ones in which George Bush acquired telepathic powers and superhuman strength. Maybe that is metaphysically possible, but it isn't relevant to the question we are interested in. Instead, we consider only possibilities that are as similar to the actual world as you can get given the difference in question. So even though there is a very distant possible world in which we never invaded Iraq in 2003 and George Bush later acquires super powers, that there is a possible world like that just doesn't impact on what *would* have happened *had* we never invaded. It tells us something that *could* have happened (in some exceptionally weak use of "could") but not what *would* have happened—because this possible world is not very close to the actual world, and (more importantly) there are other worlds in which we never invaded Iraq in 2003 that are far closer to the actual world. This is why we will seriously consider whether it is true that had the United States never invaded Iraq in 2003, the United States would not have gone into a serious

---

[3] In a nutshell, this is the basis of the theory developed by Robert Stalnaker and refined by David Lewis. References to Stalnaker and Lewis's works can be found at http://plato.stanford.edu/entries/conditionals/

economic recession, but we won't seriously consider whether it is true that had the United States never invaded Iraq in 2003, George Bush would have acquired super powers.

This doesn't mean that we can always straightforwardly evaluate coun- 4.39 terfactuals in this way. Consider the following two counterfactuals:

C1: If Socrates and Confucius had been citizens of the same country, both of them would have been Greek.

C2: If Socrates and Confucius had been citizens of the same country, both of them would have been Chinese.

I have no idea which of these is true; maybe neither of them is. Thinking in terms of closeness of possible worlds doesn't seem by itself to help decide which is true. But the fact that the appeal to closeness isn't always helpful doesn't mean that it's not in general helpful, and it doesn't mean that the possible worlds theory of counterfactuals is objectionable.

Let's sum up what we've got so far. We've been examining the case for 4.40 believing in possible worlds. The basic idea is that, in general, you have a reason to believe in some things when they do a good job of explaining data that otherwise are hard to explain. We've been looking at various bits of data that possible worlds do a good job of explaining. Possible worlds explain why the notions of possibility, impossibility, and necessity can be defined in terms of each other. Possible worlds explain how the various kinds of possibility, impossibility, and necessity are all related to one another and why we can easily move from one kind of possibility to another within a conversation. And possible worlds provide the basis for an interesting and plausible theory of how counterfactual conditionals work. We don't yet have a better theory that explains all this data. Until we do, we have a reason to believe in possible worlds.

Now this reason might eventually be outweighed by arguments *against* 4.41 the existence of possible worlds. And this reason might be eliminated if we do produce a better theory that explains the data that possible worlds explain. The difference between a reason being outweighed and a reason being eliminated is roughly this: When a reason for some theory is outweighed by another reason against that same theory, the reason for the theory is still a reason you have to consider. Suppose an acquaintance tells you that he saw your romantic partner kissing someone else. You now have a reason to believe that your romantic partner kissed someone else. Suppose you confront your romantic partner about this, and your partner tells you he or she didn't do this. You now have a reason to believe that your romantic partner didn't kiss someone else. Given that you trust your romantic partner more than your acquaintance you will probably end up believing your partner instead of the acquaintance, but you will probably feel a little bit uncomfortable still—because even though your reason to believe that your partner kissed someone else was *outweighed* by a stronger reason, that reason to believe still exists.

4.42   When a reason is *eliminated* rather than *outweighed*, that reason ceases to exist altogether. Suppose we have a reason to believe in some entities because a theory that posits them is the best theory we have for explaining some phenomena; suppose also that this is our only reason for believing that theory. Suppose a while later we discover a new theory that does a better job of explaining those same phenomena, and this better theory does not posit the entities posited by the old theory. In this situation, we no longer have a reason at all to believe in the entities posited by the old theory. Our old reason to believe in them has not merely been outweighed. It has been eliminated.

4.43   The reasons for believing in possible worlds outlined earlier were, in a sense, linguistic reasons—the theory of possible worlds was advanced to explain various phenomena concerning language.[4] In this respect, the case for possible worlds developed so far parallels the case for properties considered in Sections 2.3 and 2.4. It would be nice to have some non-linguistic phenomena that the theory of possible worlds could explain. As we will see in the next section, whether there are such phenomena partly turns on how we answer the metaphysical question of what possible worlds are like.

4.5 Some Theories of the Nature of Possible Worlds

4.44 Let's start with the theory of possible worlds defended by David Lewis, which we will call *Lewisian Modal Realism*. According to Lewisian Modal Realism, possible worlds are entire physical universes that are completely disconnected from our own, but otherwise are fundamentally the same kind of thing as our own universe. Like our universe—which we call the

---

[4] And really, we've just scratched the surface. Linguists and philosophers of language have made major use of possible worlds and situations. An example is Angelika Kratzer, who is a very important philosopher and linguist. http://people.umass.edu/kratzer/

actual world—some other possible worlds contain people. Many of these people are much like us, and live lives similar to our own. But there is no way for us to visit them because there is no spatial or temporal link between them and us.

We can make this statement of Lewis's theory more precise by defining a   4.45
Lewis world (which is the kind of thing that David Lewis takes to be a possible world) in terms of two notions we are already familiar with: the notion of things being some distance from each other in either space or time and the notion of parthood. Lewis says that a possible world is a *maximal spatiotemporal whole*. A spatiotemporal whole is a composite object made out of parts that stand in some spatial or temporal distance to each other. What makes a spatiotemporal whole a *maximal* spatiotemporal whole is that it includes as a part anything that is some spatial or temporal distance from any of its other parts? It follows from this way of thinking of possible worlds that possible worlds are absolutely isolated from each other spatially and temporally. If there are two events such that one happens *before* the other, then both events are parts of the same possible world. If there are two people such that one person is ten feet from the other person, then both people are part of the same possible world. Objects that are parts of other possible worlds than our own are not merely infinitely far away from us in space and time—but rather there are literally no spatial and temporal relations between them and us. (Lewis's view of possible worlds seems to presuppose a view about time that we will discuss in Section 5.4; this view is called the "Static View.")

In Section 2.6, we discussed ontology. Recall that an *ontology* is a theory   4.46
of what there is that aims to provide a *comprehensive* and *exclusive* list of *fundamental categories* of what there is. A list of kinds of things is *comprehensive* if and only if every entity is a member of one of the kinds on the list, or built up out of entities that are each a member of one of the kinds on the list. A list of kinds of things is *exclusive* if and only if no entity belongs to more than one kind of thing on the list. The ontological category that Lewis's possible worlds belong to is *physical object*.

Remember that, in Section 2.6, I discussed what I called the   4.47
Commonsensical Ontological Theory, which had a number of distinct ontological categories: physical objects, properties, times, events, numbers, facts, and possibilities. (I also noted that we might want to add additional categories, such as the categories of places and propositions.) If Lewis's theory of possible worlds is correct, there is no need for an additional category of *possibilities* in our ontological system. Possible worlds exist, but as noted

earlier, they belong to the category of physical objects, which was already on our list. If Lewis's theory of possible worlds is correct, we have achieved a simpler ontological theory.

4.48   Moreover, as part of his case for his theory of possible worlds, Lewis shows how he can reduce the number of ontological categories to an even smaller base. In fact, Lewis's own ontological theory consists of exactly *two* categories: physical objects and sets. (He also considers whether to add places and times, although Lewis is not very committed to the last two categories.) It is hard to see how one could hope to defend an even more parsimonious theory. So how does Lewis shear the mane of ontological categories belonging to the Commonsensical Ontological Theory?

4.49   Let's start by talking about *sets*, since this category didn't appear in the Commonsensical Ontological Theory's list. You might have come across discussion of sets in a math class.[5] The basic idea is that a set is a collection or ensemble of things, which are called the *members* of the set. One might think that "set" is just another word for "composite object" or "whole" but this is not quite right, for a number of reasons.

4.50   First, the membership relation and the parthood relation work differently. For one thing, the parthood relation is *transitive* but the membership relation is not. (We discussed this difference in Section 3.9.) Remember that a relation R is *transitive* if and only if the following condition always holds: If x bears R to y and y bears R to z, then x bears R to z. Parthood is a transitive relation: If my finger is a part of my hand and my hand is a part of my body, then my finger is a part of my body. Membership is not a transitive relation: m can be a member of a set S and S in turn can be a member of a set T without m being a member of T. (An example to consider: I am a member of the set of human beings; the set of human beings is a member of the set of sets of animals; but I am not a member of the set of sets of animals, since its only members are sets, and I am not a set.)

4.51   A second and more striking difference is this. You can't make a new whole out of a single object: wholes always have more than on proper part. But there are plenty of sets that have exactly one member. These sets are called "unit sets." There is you—and then there is your unit set whose sole member is you. Even more striking: you can't make a whole out of nothing

---

[5] Or at the *Stanford Encyclopedia of Philosophy*: http://stanford.library.usyd.edu.au/entries/set-theory/

at all. But there is an empty set which has no members! Finally, most strik-ing of all: there is no guarantee that if one thing is part of another thing, there are infinitely many wholes, but in standard set theory, if there is one thing that is a member of a set, then there are infinitely many sets with members! For example, standard set theory says that given that your unit set exists, its unit set also exists, and so the unit set of its unit sets exists, and so on, to infinity and beyond!

Lewis does not offer arguments in favor of believing in sets besides 4.52 noting that mathematicians use them all the time when theorizing: they are up to their ears in set theory, because they use sets to formulate highly explanatory theories. Since these mathematical theories are highly explana-tory, Lewis thinks that there is sufficient reason to believe in sets. Lewis also thinks that it would absurd to not believe in sets because of philosophical unease when they have proved themselves so useful.

That said, it is one thing to believe in a bunch of entities, but it is another 4.53 logically more committal thesis that these entities form a fundamental ontological category. Lewis does hope that all the other kinds of mathemati-cal objects—such as numbers, functions, co-ordinate systems, and so forth—can be reduced to certain kinds of sets. (If this were a book on the philosophy of mathematics, we'd need to spend some time talking about the alleged centrality of set theory to mathematics.)

As I mentioned earlier, Lewis's ontological theory consists of two cate- 4.54 gories: physical object and set. (And maybe places and times, but as I said earlier, he is non-committal about these categories. I think he is non-committal because he suspects that material objects can be identified with regions of spacetime.) Possible situations are just parts of possible worlds, which are themselves just a special type of physical object: they are maxi-mal spatiotemporal wholes. The really impressive thing about Lewis's metaphysical system is how many of the other categories can be reduced—provided that there are the possible worlds that Lewis posits.

Let's start with the category of *properties*. According to Lewis, properties 4.55 are just sets of possible objects, that is, parts of possible worlds. So, for example, the property of being red is the set of all actual and merely possi-ble red things. Its members include things like stop signs, pints of blood, fire hydrants, and so on. The property of being a dog is the set of all actual and merely possible dogs. It includes Ranger and numerous other dogs that stand in no spatial or temporal relations to him. Since properties can be reduced to sets of physical objects, in Lewis's system, there is no need for an additional category of properties in his ontology.

4.56   (What about properties *of* properties? For example, the property of being a triangle and the property of being a square both have the property of being a geometrical property. Lewis would say that the property of being a triangle is the set of all actual and merely possible triangles, and the property of being a geometric property is the set of all actual and merely possible geometric properties. So, the set of all possible triangles is itself a member of the set of all possible geometric properties. In short, the property of being a geometrical property is itself a set that contains other sets.)

4.57   You might be wondering how much of a role Lewis's possible worlds played in the reduction of properties to sets. Couldn't anyone just identify properties with sets without also believing in that vast plentitude of physical universes that Lewis calls "possible worlds"? Perhaps, but not without some difficulty. Another interesting feature of sets is that they are *extensional* (that's the technical term set-theorists use), which means that two sets that have the same members are numerically identical sets. (You can't have two different sets that have the same members.) Suppose that as a matter of fact, every actual thing that has a kidney also has a heart, and vice versa. It follows that, if the only things that exist are actual things, the set of things with a kidney is identical with the set of things with a heart. And so, the property of having a heart would be identical with the property of having a kidney. And this seems wrong, since something *could* have a heart without having a kidney, and so the properties can't be identical. However, if in addition to merely the actual physical objects, there are other possible worlds that collectively contain vastly more things than there are in the actual world, then there are some creatures that have hearts that don't have kidneys. And so, the set of (actual *and merely possible*) things that have hearts is not identical with the set of (actual *and merely possible*) things that have kidneys. Given Lewisian Modal Realism, we might be able to reduce properties to sets. Without it, we can't.

4.58   Let's talk next about propositions. We briefly mentioned propositions in Section 2.6, where I said that propositions are the contents of beliefs and are what are expressed by declarative sentences. Propositions can be true or false, and a sentence is true (or false) *because* it expresses a true (or false) proposition. Similarly, a belief is true (or false) because the content of that belief—the proposition believed—is true (or false). So, propositions are neither sentences nor beliefs. Here are two arguments for these conclusions.

4.59   Argument one: Carrie says something. Hedwig says the same thing. But Carrie uttered an English sentence and Hedwig uttered a German sentence.

Carrie doesn't understand German and Hedwig doesn't understand English. Yet they still managed to say the same thing. Carrie said (in English) that dogs are friendly. Hedwig said (in German) that dogs are friendly. What they both said is *not* a sentence in a natural language, since if it were, it would either be a sentence in English (which Hedwig doesn't know) or a sentence in German (which Carrie doesn't know). So, what was said—the proposition that dogs are friendly—is not a sentence in any natural language, but rather is some other sort of entity.

Maybe it's a belief? Argument two: Carrie does not believe that it will 4.60 rain today. Hedwig hopes that it will rain today. What Hedwig hopes is what Carrie does not believe. So, what Hedwig hopes—the proposition that it will rain today—isn't identical with a belief of either hers or Carrie's. It is rather some other sort of entity. Propositions are not sentences of a natural language or mental entities like beliefs. So, what are they?

Perhaps propositions can't be reduced to anything else, but rather form a 4.61 fundamental ontological category. Perhaps, but this is not Lewis's position. Lewis instead offers a reductive theory of propositions. According to Lewis, propositions are sets of possible worlds. Remember that for Lewis possible worlds are just big physical objects. And remember that for Lewis properties are just sets of physical objects. So, basically, Lewis takes propositions to be a special kind of property: they are properties of whole worlds rather than parts of worlds. Remember that possible worlds are supposed to be maximally opinionated: for any proposition P and world w, either P is true at w or P is false at w. For Lewis, *truth* and *falsity at a world* can be explained in terms of the membership relation. A proposition is *true at a world* if and only if that world is a member of it; a proposition is *false at a world* if and only if that world is not a member of it. Lewis offers us not only a reductive theory of propositions but also an explanation of what truth and falsity at worlds are in terms of this reductive theory. Remember, earlier in Section 4.3, we talked about how possible worlds are maximally opinionated? This is how Lewis cashes this metaphor out: For any proposition and any possible world, either that possible world is a member of that proposition (in which case, the possible world "says" that the proposition is true) or that possible world is not a member of that proposition (in which case, the possible world "says" that the proposition is false).

According to Lewis's theory, a proposition just is the set of possible 4.62 worlds at which it is true. So, for example, the proposition that the speed of light is roughly 186,000 miles per second is identical with the set of all the possible worlds in which the speed of light is roughly 186,000 miles per second. Here's another example: The proposition that some dogs bark is identical with the set of worlds that each contain at least one barking dog.

4.63   Lewis's theory can reduce the categories of properties and propositions to the categories of physical objects and sets. Perhaps one reason to prefer theories that posit fewer kinds of things is that these theories are simpler theories. (Ockham's Razor shaves once again.)

4.64   There's a second reason to prefer theories that posit fewer categories. Theories with fewer categories also need less *ideology* to state them. The ideology of a theory consists in the *primitive expressions of the theory*. We encountered this idea in Section 2.10. Remember there I said that a *primitive expression of a theory* is some bit of vocabulary that is used to state the theory but is not given a definition in the context of giving that theory. And not every expression can be explicitly defined; those that cannot are *primitive* expressions full stop. Remember also the moralizing speech that I made in Section 2.10. There I said that you should feel a little squeamish about introducing a new primitive expression, because introducing one requires you to claim that there is the important concept you've discovered that can't be expressed using words that everyone understood before you discovered this concept. You take a kind of intellectual risk when you introduce a new primitive expression into discussion!

4.65   Consider Lewis's ontology and his ideology. Lewis's ontology consists of physical objects and sets. His ideology consists of the following expressions: "parthood," "spatiotemporal distance," and "membership." Lewis does not think he can give you definitions of these three expressions. (He'd love it though if it were possible.) But he does think that you understand these ideas prior to doing any metaphysics. If he is right, then Lewis is not taking that much of an intellectual risk by using these notions—or, at least, he's not taking more of a risk than everyone else who uses them outside of metaphysical discussions! But with this bit of primitive vocabulary Lewis can offer a lot of cool definitions. "Possibility" and "necessity," for example, are defined in terms of truth at some or all possible worlds, as discussed in Sections 4.3 and 4.4. And as we've just seen, "true at a world" and "false at a world" can be understood in terms of membership. We don't need to assume that we understand what these expressions mean, since Lewis can offer explicit definitions of them in terms we already understand quite well. If Lewis's theory is correct, this is a real intellectual gain.

4.66   As a general rule, ontological theories with more categories have more primitive expressions because, when stating the ontological theory, it's not enough to simply list the categories—we also need to say how the entities that belong to these categories are *related* to each other.

Consider a modification of the Commonsensical Ontological Theory that   4.67
has two additional categories: sets and propositions. This theory says that the ontological categories are physical objects, properties, times, numbers, possibilities, sets, and propositions. Ok, that's our list—but now we need to say how things belonging to items on the list relate to each other. Objects *have* properties. Can you give a *definition* of "have"? (Lewis believes that he can: an object has a property if and only if it is a member of that property. But someone who takes properties as an ontological category can't define "have.") Things are *in* time. Some possible situations *obtain*. Some things are *members* of sets. Propositions are *true in* some situations and not in others. Each of the words just italicized indicate relations between objects of different categories. If we can't give definitions of these words, we have to take them as primitive. But, if this theory has too many categories to begin with, we don't need as many primitive expressions as we thought we did. Reducing ontological categories allows us to also take fewer intellectual risks.

We've barely scratched the surface of Lewis's ingenious use of possible   4.68
worlds. Yet hopefully you've seen a positive case for Lewis's view of possible worlds. We'll now consider objections to Lewis's view.

The first objection is that, if Lewis is correct, then there are way more   4.69
physical objects than we previously thought that there were. There are infinitely many different ways things could have gone—and, on Lewis's view, each of these different ways is a distinct physical universe! If Lewis's theory is correct, there are infinitely many people, infinitely many dogs, infinitely many cats, and so on. A theory that posits so many physical objects is extremely non-parsimonious.

Lewis replies as follows: We should prefer explanations that posit fewer   4.70
fundamental *types* of things, but it is not clear that we should prefer theories that posit fewer *tokens* of things. But it's a good idea to distinguish two different ways in which a theory can be parsimonious—and Lewis thinks that it is better to have fewer types and more tokens of those types than vice versa. And, at rock bottom, Lewis only has two fundamental categories of things: physical object and set.

The second objection is that according to Lewis possible worlds are all   4.71
equally real—they are basically just big universes. So, something that exists in another possible world is just as real as something that exists in another country. In what sense then are these other worlds *merely possible*? Aren't they all equally *actual*?

4.72   Lewis replies to this worry by distinguishing *reality* from *actuality*. Everything that there is exists / is real. Not everything is actual though. So, what is actuality? According to Lewis, when some person says that some entity is actual, what that person says is true if and only if that entity is a part of the same world as that person. According to Lewis, "actual" basically means the same thing as "part of the same world as me." And "merely possible" basically means "not part of the same world as me." When a person says that something is merely possible, what that person says is true if and only if that thing is part of a world but not part of the same world as the person speaking.

4.73   On Lewis's view, "actual" works a lot like "here," and "merely possible" works a lot like "elsewhere." Here are some examples to consider. I'm currently in Syracuse, NY. When I say, "Ranger is here," I say something true. My mom is currently in Olympia, WA. When she says, "Ranger is not here," she also says something true. My mom and I are not contradicting each other. "Here" basically means the same thing as "at the same location I'm at." My mom can truthfully say, "Ranger is not in Olympia, WA. He is elsewhere." "Elsewhere" basically means "at some location other than the one I am at." When a merely possible person says, "I'm actual," she also says something true, even though she is merely possible. She says something true because she is part of the same world as herself, and I can truly say that she is merely possible because she is not part of the same world as me.

4.74   The final objection is that Lewis's theory—despite its impressive ability to provide ontological and ideological reductions—just is not a believable theory. Lewis calls this objection, "the incredulous stare."

4.75   There are two ways to take this objection. The first way to take it is as nothing more than a registration of a psychological inability. Imagine in other contexts saying, "the theory is great—it is simple, it is elegant, and it explains a lot of phenomena without positing new entities—but I can't bring myself to believe it." Ok, fine, you can't bring yourself to believe it—that's a fact about your psychology—but the interesting question is whether the theory is best supported by your evidence! The second way of taking this objection calls into question the methodology that has been used to defend the theory. If it is true that Lewisian Modal Realism is the best explanation of the phenomena it tries to explain, and yet we still shouldn't believe it, then it follows that *sometimes we shouldn't believe a theory of X even if it is the best theory of X we have.* But if we aren't entitled to believe in our theories when they are better than any of their competitors, then when are we allowed to believe in them?

Of course, Lewis's theory might not be better than its competitors. To 4.76
assess whether Lewisian Modal Realism is better than its competitors, we
need to examine the competition. So, let's now turn to this task.

4.6 An Alternative Theory of Possible Worlds: Propositions First

The first alternative to Lewis's theory says that propositions form an onto- 4.77
logical category and builds possible worlds out of propositions. Remember
that Lewis does not have propositions as an ontological category. Rather, for
Lewis, propositions are sets of worlds. But, on this alternative theory, which
I will call the *Propositions First Theory*, worlds are sets of propositions.

Ok, but is every set of propositions a possible world? No, because some 4.78
sets of propositions are *not* maximally opinionated in the way that possible
worlds must be maximally opinionated. Remember that we discussed the
metaphor that possible worlds are maximally opinionated in Section 4.3.
What we meant there was that, for any proposition P and possible world *w*,
either P is true at *w* or P is false at *w*. A possible world has an opinion on
whether P is true by either having P as a member or by having the negation
of P as a member. If possible, worlds are sets of propositions, then a set of
propositions is a possible world *only if* that set is *maximal* in the following
sense: for any proposition P, either P or not-P is a member of that set of
propositions.

Moreover, not every maximal set of propositions is a possible world. 4.79
Consider a maximal set that includes every proposition *and* that proposition's negation. This set is a maximally *inconsistent* set: its opinions are mas-
sively contradictory! This set is no possible world, since there is no possible
situation in which contradictions are true! So, at the very least, we need to
say that a set of propositions is a possible world *only if* that set is logically
consistent, that is, the set contains no logically inconsistent items.

Can we say that a possible world just is a maximal and logically consist- 4.80
ent set of propositions? Now we enter tricky territory. If every logically
consistent set of propositions is *absolutely* possible, then we can. But if a set
of propositions can be logically consistent and yet still impossible, then we
can't simply say that a possible world is a maximal and logically consistent
set of propositions—because some of these maximal and logically consistent sets of propositions might still be collectively metaphysically
impossible.

4.81   Not every formally logically consistent and maximal set of propositions is a possible world. Here's an exercise to see this. Consider the following (admittedly not maximal) set of propositions: {1. Kris is a bachelor; 2. It's not the case that Kris is a bachelor.} This is a logically inconsistent set of propositions: proposition 1 is of the form P and proposition 2 is of the form not-P. Any set that contains propositions 1 and 2 is definitely not a possible world. But now consider the following (admittedly not maximal) set of propositions: {3. Kris is a bachelor; 4. Kris has a spouse}. This set is strictly not *formally* logically inconsistent: it's not of the form P and not-P. Proposition 3 is of the form P and proposition 4 is of the form Q. In order to get a formal inconsistency, we need to introduce *definitions*. Since "bachelor" just means "unmarried, eligible to be married, adult human man" and "has a spouse" just means "is married to someone," by substituting the appropriate definitions we can replace propositions 3 and 4 with: {5. Kris is not married to anyone, is eligible to be married, and is an adult human male; 6. Kris is married to someone.} And 5 and 6 are formally logically inconsistent with each other.

4.82   So not every formally logically consistent and maximal set of propositions can be a possible world. But it also looks like the way forward is pretty straightforward—we require not merely that the sets be logically consistent as is but also that there is no logical inconsistency produced when we consider the correct definitions of our terms. There might be sets containing propositions 3 and 4 that are formally consistent but they are (in the sense just mentioned) rendered inconsistent when the correct definitions are introduced. Let's call this kind of inconsistency *informal inconsistency*. So, let's consider the view that any maximal, formally and *informally* consistent set of propositions is a possible world. Is this view of possible worlds ready acceptable?

4.83   Ok, now for something even harder. Consider the proposition that the number 2 is hungry. This proposition is absolutely impossible—there's just no way a number could be hungry! But, in order to show that the claim is *informally* logically contradictory, we'd need correct definitions of "number 2" and "hungry" that would generate the conclusion that the number 2 can't be hungry. Try to see if you can come up with these definitions! I doubt that an attempt to show that it is false *by definition* that the number 2 is hungry will succeed. This doesn't mean you shouldn't try!

4.84   If the proposition that the number 2 is hungry is informally consistent, then a set of propositions can fail to be a metaphysically possible set even if it is an informally consistent set. And so not every maximal and formally and informally consistent set of propositions is a possible world. I've just picked one example, but there are many such examples. (In fact, there are infinitely many problematic examples!) Consider the claim that Kris McDaniel is a pebble. Just to be clear, I'm not entertaining some weird metaphor. I mean consider the claim that I am literally a pebble, of the kind that you can find resting gently on a sandy beach. I can assure you that this claim is false—I am not a pebble—but the question now is whether it is absolutely impossible. Suppose that it is absolutely impossible: in no possible world am I a pebble. How can you derive a logical contradiction from the claim that I am a pebble? Is the claim that Kris McDaniel is a pebble informally inconsistent? What definitions of "Kris McDaniel" and "pebble" will yield a logical contradiction on the assumption that I am a pebble? I don't even think my name has a definition—instead, it's just a kind of tag or label used to refer to me. But, if my name does have a definition, then you should be able to produce it—and then you should be able to test whether the claim that Kris McDaniel is a pebble is informally inconsistent. (Note that we will return to the question of what you or I could have been like in Section 4.7.)

Metaphysical possibility isn't simply logical or informal consistency. A 4.85
proposition can be logically consistent, informally consistent, and absolutely impossible. If this is right, then the fan of the propositions first theory of possible worlds has two options. The first option is kind of heroic: it is to find some way of explicitly defining metaphysical possibility and then using that defined notion in the propositions first theory. In other words, this option requires you to find some way of filling in the following blank so that the result is a good theory of possible worlds: a possible world is a set of propositions that is (i) maximal, (ii) logically consistent, (iii) informally logically consistent, and (iv) _____. The second option is less heroic: it is to take this notion of possibility as a primitive. That is, someone who takes this second option assumes that we all understand this notion of absolute possibility, and uses it when giving her theory of possible worlds, but gives up on any attempt at providing a definition of "absolute possibility." People who take this second option add "absolutely possible" to their *ideology* in the sense described earlier in this section. For them, a possible world just is a maximal set of propositions that is absolutely possible.

I'll focus on the less heroic option, and evaluate the pros and the cons of 4.86
this version of the propositions first theory. One con, just noted, is that this less heroic option has to take the notion of absolute possibility as primitive,

and so accepting the theory as is requires us to take a bit of a gamble that we understand the notion of absolute possibility even if we can't give it a definition. Well, maybe we do understand it well enough—and if so, this might not be much of a con. But let's at least register it as a possible disadvantage. A second con, at least relative to Lewis's theory of possible worlds, is that we have to believe that propositions form an ontological category. On Lewisian Modal Realism, propositions are just sets of possible worlds, and possible worlds are just big physical objects. But, on the theory we are now considering, possible worlds are sets of propositions, and so propositions can't in turn be understood as sets of worlds. However, on the theory we are considering, there are still physical objects. So, the theory we are considering is committed to at least three ontological categories: physical objects, sets, and propositions, while Lewisian Modal Realism is only committed to physical objects and sets.

4.87   Remember, one nice thing about Lewis's theory of propositions is that it can explain what it is for a proposition to be true at a world. Consider the proposition that there are dogs. This is true at a world if and only if there are dogs at that world. So far, so good. But let's go deeper: in general, what is it for a proposition to be true at a world? Can we give an explanation of this notion? Or do we just have to take it for granted as well? Lewis's theory can explain what truth at a world is: truth, for Lewis, is just the special case of the more general membership relation. A proposition is true at a world if and only if it has that world as a member. And remember that for Lewis, properties are also just sets of physical objects. Really, the fully general account would be that a proposition is true at a world if and only if it has that world as a member and a property (such as the property of being a dog) is true of an object if and only if it has that object as a member. If we understand what "is a member of" means—and we understand a bunch of modern mathematics only if we do understand it—then we understand all we need to understand what truth is, at least if Lewis's theory is true. But if we give up on Lewis's theory, we give up on understanding truth in terms of membership. And so, we have to come face to face with the question of the nature of truth. In general terms, what makes a proposition true at a world?

4.88   None of these considerations amount to a decisive refutation to the propositions first theory individually or even collectively. In metaphysics, decisive refutations are rare! Rather, you should weigh up the collective pros and cons of a given theory and compare how that theory rates next to the others. And you should be open to new theories that we have yet to discover!

4.7 Another Alternative Theory of Possible Worlds: Primitive Possible Objects

The next theory that we will consider is one that takes the category of pos- 4.89
sible object as a primitive category. On this kind of theory, we should not
think of possible objects as being constructed out of or defined in terms of
other kinds of entities. So, they aren't physical objects like Lewis thought of
them and they aren't sets of propositions—or sets of any other kind of thing
for that matter. Possible objects are just a basic category of thing.

There are three versions of this theory. The first version takes the idea of 4.90
possible objects as basic and understands worlds as maximal wholes made
out of them. The second version takes possible situations as basic entities
and identifies possible worlds with maximally complex situations. The
third version takes *possible worlds* to be the basic entities and doesn't try to
build them up out of anything. I'm going to talk about each of these versions in turn.

The first version is the *possible objects first view*. On this theory, for every 4.91
actual kind of thing there is, there are possible instances of that kind. So, for
example, there are actual human beings, and there are merely possible
human beings. There are actual dogs and cats, and there are merely possible
dogs. There are actual planets and stars. And there are merely possible stars.
In addition, since there are more possibilities than actualities, there are also
possible things that have no actual counterparts. There aren't any actual
mile-wide spheres of gold. But there are possible mile-wide spheres of gold.
There aren't any actual winged horses. But there are possible winged horses.
I think you get the picture.

The possible objects first view sounds a lot like Lewis's view. So how is it 4.92
different? The big difference between this view and Lewis's view is how they
each characterize the difference between being actual and being merely
possible. Remember that Lewis thinks that the difference between being
actual and being merely possible is a lot like the difference between being
here and being elsewhere. According to Lewis, to be actual is just to be in
the same world as the world I am in, just as to be here is to be in the same
place as me. There's no important *metaphysical* difference between things
that are here and things that are there. I'm here in Syracuse, NY. I have no
idea where you are right now, but you probably aren't here with me. I am
sure that wherever you are though, you are not metaphysically different
from me simply because you aren't here. There aren't two fundamentally
different kinds of people, those that are here and those that are elsewhere.

There aren't two fundamentally different kinds of cats and dogs either, those dogs and cats that are here and those dogs and cats that are there.

4.93 However, on the possible objects first view, actuality is an absolute status rather than a merely relative status. Remember that for Lewis, to be actual is just to be in the same world as us. But for the possible objects first view, an object is either actual or merely possible full stop: actuality and mere possibility are intrinsic features of the objects that have them. This is an important difference from Lewis's view.

4.94 A second important difference concerns how this view handles statements about what is possible or necessary for particular objects, like me. Consider the statement that it is metaphysically possible that Kris McDaniel be six feet tall. (I'm not actually this tall.) A natural idea is that this is true if and only if there is a possible world in which I am six feet tall. If Lewis is correct about what possible worlds are, then this natural thought doesn't seem correct, since I am a part of exactly one world. (We'll have more to say about this line of thought in Section 4.9.) But, on the view we are now considering, I could in principle belong to more than possible world. Perhaps possible worlds are wholes made out of possible and actual objects.

4.95 So, there are some important differences between Lewis's theory and the possible objects first theory. There are some important similarities too. In fact, Lewis considers a view like the possible objects first view, which he calls *pictorial ersatzism,* and Lewis claims that pictorial ersatzism implies the existence of the same merely possible objects as his own modal realism. Both Lewis's modal realism and the possible objects first theory imply that there are, for example, talking donkeys. It is true that, according to the possible objects first theory, these talking donkeys do not belong to the same ontological category as actual talking donkeys. But they are still donkeys that talk.

4.96 Let's turn to the next theory, which I will call *the possible situations first theory.* On this view, we begin with the notion of a possible situation and build possible worlds out of them. The primitive entities used in this theory are *situations.* Situations either obtain or fail to obtain. Some of the situations that fail to obtain could obtain: they are the metaphysically possible situations. For example, the situation in which this book wins me the Nobel Prize for literature is really unlikely to obtain, but it is metaphysically possible that it obtains. (We take our solace where we can.) Some situations can obtain only if other situations obtain. For example, a situation in which Janice kicks a ball to David can obtain only if a situation in which Janice kicks a ball obtains. In general, let's say that situation A *requires* situation B if and only if it is not metaphysically possible for A to obtain without B also obtaining. And let's say that A is incompatible with B if and only if it is not metaphysically possible for both A and B to obtain. We now have the ideas we need in order to state the possible situations first theory of possible worlds. A possible world is a special kind of possible situation: Situation W is a possible world if and only if (i) W is a possible situation and (ii) any other situation S is such that either W requires S or W is incompatible with S. In short, possible worlds are maximally consistent situations.

There are clear analogies between the propositions first theory and the possible situations first theory. Both theories say that there is a primitive ontological category (propositions or situations) that possible worlds are constructed out of. Both theories take as an undefined the notion of metaphysical possibility and so give up on attempting to analyze this notion. It's hard to see how the possible situations first theory is an improvement on the propositions first theory. 4.97

Moreover, it's not clear whether propositions and situations are really different ontological categories. Propositions can be either true or false; situations can either obtain or fail to obtain. Propositions entail other propositions; situations require other situations. Propositions can be inconsistent with other propositions; situations can be incompatible with other situations. Maybe propositions just are the same entities as situations, in which case the propositions first theory and the possible situations first theory just are the same theory. If propositions are not situations, how are these kinds of entities different? Is there a reason why we should believe in both ontological categories if they are different? 4.98

The final theory we will consider takes possible worlds to be basic entities. This theory gives up on trying to explain them in terms of any other entities that we might have already believed in or felt we understood before we considered the metaphysics of possibility and necessity. Possible worlds on this view are not big physical objects, and they aren't constructed out of "smaller" or "less comprehensive" possible objects, possible situations, or propositions. They just are what they are. Let's call this theory *the primitive possible worlds theory.*[6] 4.99

---

[6] Robert Stalnaker defends a primitive possible worlds theory. See Stalnaker, R. (1976) "Possible Worlds," *Noûs* 10, 1: 65–75: https://philpapers.org/rec/STAPW

4.100   The friend of the primitive possible worlds theory does not need to take the notion of metaphysical possibility as undefined: she can say that a proposition is possible if and only if it is true at a possible world. But what is it for a proposition to be true at a world on this theory? Let's take a quick step back: What are propositions on this theory? Recall that on Lewis's theory, propositions are just sets of possible worlds. The friend of primitive possible worlds can parrot this claim: on her view, propositions just are sets of possible worlds. And so, what it is for proposition to be true at a world is just for that world to be a member of that proposition.

4.101   So, the friend of the primitive possible worlds theory does not need to add metaphysical possibility or necessity to her ideology, and she doesn't need to embrace a primitive ontological category of propositions. So far, her view has many of the strengths of Lewis's view. But it doesn't have all of them. She can't, for example, explain what properties are by saying that they are sets of possible objects. (The friend of the possible objects first theory could do this because she has possible objects in her ontology. The friend of primitive possible worlds theory doesn't believe in merely possible talking donkeys, for example, and so can't say that the property of being a talking donkey just is the set of all talking donkeys.) So, the primitive possible worlds theory can't offer some of the reductive definitions that Lewis can offer. In this respect, Lewis's theory has an advantage. How big of an advantage? I invite you to consider this question carefully.

4.102   One frustrating aspect of the primitive possible worlds theory is that there is not much we can say about the nature of possible worlds on this view. What are their intrinsic properties? How are they related to one another and to objects from other categories? One of them is actual, while the others are merely possible, and this is presumably because the physical universe we are in is the way it is rather than some other way. But what is it about the nature of possible worlds that ensures that this is the case? On the primitive possible worlds theory, it is really hard to see what the answers to these questions are.

4.8 Accidental and Essential Features

4.103 In the previous sections, the notions of necessity and possibility were discussed in depth. In this section, we will discuss some related ideas, specifically, the ideas of essential properties and accidental properties. Recall the definitions from Section 4.1: essential properties are properties that things must have in order to even exist; accidental properties are properties that things actually have, but could have existed without having. (An accidental property of you is your hair color: you could have existed but with a different hair color than the hair color that you actually have.) So, the notions of essential and accidental properties are intimately related to the notions of necessity and possibility that we discussed in Chapter 3. And since talk about necessity and possibility can be translated into talk about possible worlds, we should be able to understand the difference between essential and accidental properties by using possible worlds to think about them. And we can. We can say that an essential property of an object is one that it has in every possible world in which it exists, and that an accidental property is one that it has in some possible worlds (including the actual world) but not in every world in which it exists.

In this section, we are going to focus on two questions. The first question 4.104 we'll address is whether there are any properties that objects have essentially and, if there are any, what are they? We will focus on whether we have essential properties, as well as whether other ordinary physical objects like tables and chairs have essential properties. Along the way, we will examine two extreme positions, specifically the view that *every* property of every object is an essential property of it and the view that *no* (interesting) property of any object is an essential property of it. (Why we need to include a word like "interesting" will be made clear in a minute.)

The second question that we'll examine is what implications theories of 4.105 the nature of possible worlds have for our essential properties. Recall Lewisian Modal Realism. Remember that according to Lewisian Modal Realism, possible worlds are basically giant physical objects, and nothing is a part of more than one possible world. So, you are a part of exactly one possible world. We said earlier that an essential property is a property that an object has in every possible world in which it exists. According to Lewisian Modal Realism, you are part of exactly one world. So, it looks like any property that you actually have is a property that you essentially have. But then you couldn't have been any other way than the way that you actually are. There's no possible way your life could have been different. This seems like a bad consequence of Lewisian Modal Realism. We'll see whether someone who believes in Lewisian Modal Realism can get out of this objection, and in general, we will examine what different views about possible worlds imply about your essential and accidental features. We are going to discuss this more in Section 4.9.

4.106   Let's start with the question of whether you have any interesting essential properties. Here is why we need the qualification "interesting." There are some properties that, as a matter of necessity, everything must have. Here is one example. It is a law of logic that everything is identical with itself. Logical truths are necessarily true. So, there is no possible situation in which something fails to be identical with itself. So, for every possible situation you find yourself in, you are identical with yourself. So, you are essentially identical with yourself. This conclusion is clearly right, but it isn't very exciting. You have these kind of essential properties because the laws of logic are necessarily true. But everything has these essential properties, and so the conclusion that you have them is not very interesting. When metaphysicians ask whether you have any essential properties, they set aside these properties, because it is trivial that you have them. Are there any essential properties that you have but that not everything else has as well? Now that's an interesting question.

4.107   Suppose the answer to this question is "no." Then I assume that I also don't have any interesting essential properties. (Why would you be special in this way but not me?) So, suppose that neither of us have any interesting essential properties. Then our lives could have been very different indeed. I was born in 1976. I don't know what year you were born, but let's pretend it's 1995. If we have no interesting essential properties, you could have been born in 1976 and I could have been born in 1995. In fact, your life could have been just like mine and my life could have been just like yours. If you and I have no interesting essential properties, then it is not an essential property of you that you have the parents that you actually have. My parents could have been your parents. There is a possible world just like this one, in which you do everything I do in the actual world and in which I do everything you do in the actual world. Consider this allegedly possible world. In it, you are the one who wrote this book and I am the one reading it for the first time. In this world, your name is "Kris McDaniel" and my name is… whatever your name actually is. In that world, you look and act exactly like I actually do, while I look and act exactly like you actually do. This is a mind-boggling idea. If your motto is "no limits," this is the view for you: there are no interesting limits on how you could have been. Let's just call this view the *no limits view*.[7]

---

[7] Penelopie Mackie defends something like the no limits view in her book *How Things Might Have Been* (Oxford: Clarendon Press, 2006). For more of her work, go to her webpage at the University of Nottingham, where she is a professor of philosophy: http://www.nottingham.ac.uk/philosophy/people/penelope.mackie

The diametrically opposite view is the *all limits view*. On this view, 4.108
every property you have is an essential property. There is no possible way
for you to be different in any respect. Perhaps after considering this view,
you might actually find it consoling. Consider something that you did a
few years ago that you really regret doing. If the all limits view is correct,
there is no possible world in which you refrain from doing that action. In
other words, you essentially do that action at that time. So, there is no
point in wishing you had done something different than what you in fact
did, because you couldn't have done anything different. Don't you feel
better already?

Probably you don't, because probably you feel that your free will is jeop- 4.109
ardized by the all limits view. If you couldn't have done otherwise, how can
you be morally responsible for what you in fact do? This is an important
question, but we are going to table it for now. We will discuss this question
in Section 6.1.

The no limits view and the all limits view are polar opposites. Maybe the 4.110
truth lies somewhere in the middle. Maybe most objects have some (interesting) essential properties and a lot of accidental properties as well. Some
metaphysicians think that a thing's kind is an essential property of that
thing. On their view, a dog, for example, is essentially a dog. They are not
asserting the boring logical truth that it is necessarily true that all dogs are
dogs. Consider a particular dog, Fido. These metaphysicians say that Fido
is a dog in every possible world in which Fido exists. If they are mistaken,
there is a possible world in which Fido isn't a dog, but is something else,
such as a cat. Other metaphysicians think that an object's origin is essential
to it. Consider a particular loaf of bread, baked from a particular set of
ingredients at a particular moment. If this loaf's origin is essential to it, it
couldn't have existed had not these ingredients been used at that time. (Or
at least most of the ingredients—but we'll see in Section 4.9 that qualifying
this claim in this way can lead to trouble.)

It is commonsensical that we could have been different in a lot of ways, 4.111
but not in every way. But there's a puzzle awaiting us if we simply follow
commonsense about what properties are essential. We already encountered
this puzzle in Section 3.7, but I'll remind you of it now.

Remember that lump of my kids' playdough from which I made a 4.112
beautiful work of art, the statue Little David? Remember the evil people
who squished him flat? Little David was destroyed by being squashed.
This is because Little David was a statue, and statues are destroyed when
they are squashed. All that remains is a flattened splat of playdough. Ok,

let's be explicit about what I am relying on when I make this judgment: I am relying on the commonsensical idea that works of art like Little David have as an essential property that they are shaped roughly in the same way that they actually are. Probably Little David could survive some deformation—works of art, like many physical things, can subtly expand and contract as the temperature changes—but Little David is essentially not shaped like a pancake. These seem to be the verdicts of commonsense.

4.113   Little David is no longer with us, but a flattened lump of playdough is with us, Lumpy. A lump of playdough does not have its shape essentially but instead has its shape merely accidentally. So Lumpy can survive being stretched or flattened. In fact, Lumpy can even survive being shaped like a statue of David Lewis. The important upshot discussed in Section 3.7 was that, if we just follow commonsense judgments, we should conclude that Lumpy does not go out of existence when Little David comes into existence. So, there are two things that are in the same space at the same time! Commonsense leads to a conclusion that is not very commonsensical. To some philosophers, this is too extreme of a revision to their views of how material objects behave. (We'll see in Section 4.9 one way in which Lewisian Modal Realists respond to this argument.)

4.114   The general moral to draw is that, if we trust commonsense about which properties things have essentially, we risk ending up committed to a lot more things than we might have initially thought. The case of Little David and Lumpy is one of many, as we also discussed in Section 3.7. But maybe this is ok. Recall our discussion of Lynne Rudder Baker (in Section 3.7), who stresses that it is an advantage of her view that it better fits with our ordinary beliefs about the important differences not only between lumps of clay and statues, but also between dollar bills and the pieces of paper that constitute them, people and the bodies that constitute them, and so on. On Baker's view, our particular beliefs about particular cases of constitution demand more respect than abstract general principles such as "two material objects cannot occupy the same space at the same time" or "two material objects can't be made of the same parts at the same time."

4.115   However, my point here is not to argue for or against trusting commonsense about these things but rather to illustrate the puzzles that trusting commonsense can generate.

4.9 Theories of Possible Worlds and Theories of Essential Features

We'll now explore the connection between theories of possible worlds and 4.116
theories of essential properties.

Let's start with Lewisian Modal Realism. Recall that on Lewis's view of 4.117
possible worlds, every object is a part of exactly one possible world. You are
a part of exactly one possible world. There is no other world that has you as
a part. Same with me, and everything else we see. These simple consequences of Lewisian Modal Realism might seem very problematic. Here's
why. I'm actually 69 inches tall, but I could have been 72 inches tall. But
there is no possible world in which I am 72 inches tall—there is only one
world that has me as a part, and I am 69 inches tall in it. So, it looks like
Lewisian Modal Realism implies that every property that I actually have is
a property I essentially have. Since I have some accidental properties,
Lewisian Modal Realism must be false.

This seems like a devastating objection to Lewisian Modal Realism, but 4.118
Lewis has a response to it. We are not forced to say that in order for you to
possibly be different than you actually are, you have to be a part of more
than one possible world. Instead, according to Lewis, what must be the case
is that there is someone sufficiently like you in other respects who is a part
of a different possible world. In short, Lewis proposes a *counterpart theory*
of essential and accidental properties. According to counterpart theory, x
could have been F if and only if there is a possible object y that is a *counterpart* of x and y is F. On this counterpart theory, I could have been 72 inches
tall because there is a merely possible person who is my counterpart and
who is 72 inches tall.

Something is a counterpart of me only if it is sufficiently similar to me in 4.119
various respects. In what respects? The counterpart theorist typically thinks
that there is no absolute answer to this question. In most situations, we
won't count something as being sufficiently like me unless it has a similar
history to me and has similar intrinsic properties. So, in most situations,
something can count as a counterpart of me only if it is also a human being
whose parents are sufficiently like my parents (sufficient enough for his
parents to be counterparts of my parents) and so on. But perhaps in other
situations we will be willing to count things as counterparts of me even if
they are very different from me. Could I have been, for example, a robot

rather than a human being? There are possible robots who think and act a lot like how I actually act. This is a really important way in which these robots are similar to me. Should I count them as counterparts of me? Why or why not?

4.120   Our standards for when one thing counts as similar to another are both vague and context sensitive. Suppose that Sara and I are going shopping and we see a bronze statue of David Lewis in the window. I say to Sara that I really wish I had something like that. Sara knows that my birthday is coming up and is determined to get me something a lot like that statue. My birthday comes around, and Sara gives me a ball of bronze and tells me that it is a lot like the statue. Sara's reason for saying this is that the ball of bronze is made up of the same stuff as the statue, and moreover has exactly the same weight as the statue. Both the ball and the statue are a lot alike: they are solid chunks of bronze. So, when Sara says that the ball and the statue are a lot alike, what she says is true. Daniel is also at my birthday party, and he gives me something that he knitted himself: a "statue" of David Lewis made entirely out of yarn. He also tells me that his birthday present is a lot like the statue, and it seems that what he says is true too. Is either the bronze ball or the knitted statue more like the bronze statue than the other? Why? To a chemist, the bronze ball is more like the bronze statue, but to an artist, the knitted statue is more like the bronze statue. Who is right? (The connections between this question and the issues about "belonging with" that we talked about in Chapter 1 are worth thinking about.) It seems that in one context you can say that one is more like the statue than the other because in that context what you care about most is a certain set of properties, but in the other context you care more about a different set of properties.

4.121   If in most cases there aren't absolute facts about when objects are sufficiently similar, then there won't be absolute facts about when objects are counterparts of each other. And given the counterpart theory of essential properties, there won't be absolute facts about the essential properties of objects. Is this a problem for Lewisian Modal Realism? Perhaps it's an advantage. Remember the kinds of examples that motivate philosophers like Lynne Rudder Baker to claim that the statue is a different entity than the lump that constitutes it. A statue made of playdough can't survive being flattened but the lump of playdough can survive being flattened. Since the two objects have different essential properties, they must really be two objects. This is the argument we discussed at the end of Section 4.8. But now we can see how the Lewisian could respond to this argument. According to the Lewisian, there is just one entity there, which we can describe with equal accuracy as either being a statue or as being a lump. In some contexts, such as ones in which what we care about is the chemical properties, we count a flattened lump of playdough as sufficiently similar to our statue-shaped lump. In those contexts, we can truthfully say of the statue-shaped lump that it could survive being squished. In other contexts, such as ones in which what we care about are the aesthetic properties, we are not willing to count a flattened lump of playdough as being sufficiently similar to our statue made out of playdough. In those contexts, we can't truthfully say that the statue made out of playdough could survive being squished. There is only one thing there, which is both a lump of clay and a statue—but there are two distinct standards for counting something as being similar to that one thing there.

An interesting feature of counterpart theory is that the counterpart rela- 4.122 tion is not transitive, since the counterpart relation is a relation of less than perfect similarity, and, in general, less than perfect similarity is also not transitive. Here are two examples to illustrate that less than perfect similarity is not transitive. A six-feet-tall person is similar in height to a five-feet-eleven-inch-tall person, who in turn is similar in height to a five-feet-ten-inch-tall person, and so on, and so on. But a six feet tall person is not similar in height to a four-feet-tall person. On a color wheel, adjacent shades are very similar to each other, but non-adjacent ones needn't be.

So, the counterpart relation is not transitive. This fact might enable 4.123 counterpart theory to solve some metaphysical puzzles.

Here's one such puzzle. Consider the first moment of an ordinary com- 4.124 posite object's existence. At that moment, the composite object is made of many parts. But it could have existed at that moment with slightly different parts. This is because, in general, ordinary composite objects do not essentially have all of their parts that they initially have. Let's say that the *initial parts* of an object are just those parts that it has at the first moment of its existence. Consider the following scenario. Laurie finishes assembling a log cabin at noon; call this log cabin "Loggy." Laurie used a lot of logs, and posts, and thick screws, and nails, and roof shakes, and so on. These are the initial parts of Loggy. But Laurie could have used a different nail than any of the ones she actually used—she still has a whole box of them left over—and Loggy would have still existed. Loggy didn't have to be made with exactly those initial parts. On the other hand, Loggy couldn't have been created with entirely different initial parts—had Laurie used none of the parts she actually used when she made her log cabin, she would have created a different log cabin than Loggy.

4.125   Here is a principle we might extract from thinking about this case: In any possible world in which an ordinary composite object is created, that very same object could have been created with slightly different initial parts. Here is a second principle we might also extract: An ordinary composite object could not have been created with totally different initial parts. Both principles are plausible.

4.126   But they are also in tension with each other. Start with an ordinary composite object; consider a possible world w_1 in which that object is created with most of the same initial parts, say 95%. In w_1, that object could have been made with slightly different initial parts. So, consider another possible world, w_2, in which that object has only 95% of the same initial parts as it has in w_1. If we keep applying this principle, we will eventually end up with a possible world in which the composite object we started with is composed of wholly different initial parts than it is in the actual world. And the second principle says that this is not possible.

4.127   This puzzle arises because we are talking in terms of numerically the same object in different possible worlds. And numerical identity is a transitive relation.

4.128   Here's how counterpart theory solves this puzzle. First, if counterpart theory is true, we need to formulate those two principles in terms of counterparts. Here's how to do this. If counterpart theory is true, the first principle should be formulated roughly as follows: Every ordinary object has a counterpart that is created with slightly different initial parts. (This is just a rough formulation, for really we should say that every ordinary object has a counterpart that is composed of initial parts that are mostly but not totally counterparts of the initial parts the original object actually has. That's a more careful statement, but it's also a mouthful, so I am going to use the rougher formulation in what follows.) And if counterpart theory is true, the second principle should be formulated roughly as follows: No ordinary composite object has a counterpart that, at the moment it is created, is composed of totally different initial parts than the ordinary object's initial parts. (This is also a rough formulation. The more precise one is this: No ordinary composite object has a counterpart that has no initial parts that are counterparts of initial parts of that object. Also a mouthful, and also will be ignored in what follows.)

4.129   The important thing is that, if counterpart theory is true, these two principles are consistent. This is because the counterpart relation is not transitive: just because x is a counterpart of y, and y is a counterpart of z, it does not follow that x is a counterpart of z. In short, the counterpart relation, unlike the relation of identity, is not transitive. Once we adopt counterpart theory, instead of thinking of accidental and essential properties in terms of the identity of objects in different possible worlds, the puzzle evaporates.

We've talked about what Lewisian Modal Realism implies about our acci- 4.130
dental and essential properties. Do the other views about possible worlds we've discussed also have interesting implications?

This is harder to assess. Start with the possible worlds first view. On this 4.131
view, possible worlds aren't reduced to anything else. But still we exist at some but not all possible worlds, and have different properties at different worlds. For the possible worlds first view, what does this amount to? I suspect that the fan of the possible worlds first view can't give an answer to this question, and instead has to take "exists at" and "has property F at" as primitive in her theory. It's not clear to me that anything in this metaphysics constrains what our essential or accidental features might be, or gives us any guidance about this.

Let's turn to the propositions first theory. On this theory, you exist at a world 4.132
if and only if there is a proposition that is about you that is an element of that world. (So, I exist at world *w* because *w* is a set that contains a proposition about me, such as the proposition that Kris McDaniel works at ACME Paper Company.) On the propositions first theory, I exist at more than one possible world. And on the propositions first theory, for me to have a property at a world *w* is for *w* to contain a proposition that says that I have that property. It looks as though, if the propositions first theory is true, nothing like Lewis's counterpart theory of accidental and essential properties could be true.

Finally, let's turn to the possible objects first theory. It seems to me that 4.133
the fan of this theory has a choice to make: when building possible worlds out of possible objects, should we allow a possible object to be literally a part of more than possible world, or should we insist that every possible object is a part of exactly one possible world? If we take the former route, it looks like counterpart theory is out of the question, but if we take the latter route, it looks like counterpart theory is mandatory, unless we want to say that every object has all of its properties essentially.

4.10 Doing Metaphysics

If "possible" and "can" can't be defined in terms of truth at some possible
world, how can we make sense of the different ways of using the words
"possible" and "can"?

We talked about how to understand counterfactual conditionals, that is, conditionals of the form "If P were the case, then Q would have been the case." But what do indicative conditionals mean? An indicative conditional is just of the form "If P is the case, then Q is the case." And what about conditionals like "If P were the case, then Q might be the case"?

Can someone reasonably accept parts of David Lewis's modal realism without accepting all of it? Which parts can be separately accepted?

What other theories of possible worlds are worth considering?

How do we know when a property of a thing is essential to that thing? What is our evidence for claims about essences?

Further Reading

Angelika Kratzer (2012) *Modals and Conditionals: New and Revised Perspectives*, Oxford: Oxford University Press.

An important of discussion of modality and conditionals from a linguistic perspective.

David Lewis (2001) *Counterfactuals* 2nd edition, Oxford: Wiley-Blackwell.

Discusses Lewis's theory of counterfactuals as well as presents a classic argument for the existence of possible worlds.

Penelopie Mackie (2009) *How Things Might Have Been: Individuals, Kinds, and Essential Properties*, Oxford: Oxford University Press.

An important discussion of the extent to which we have interesting essential properties.

5

TIME

5.1 Introduction to the Philosophy of Time

Time is amazing. We worry about wasting our time and often do. Sometimes _{5.1} time seems to rush by, and sometimes time seems to drag on forever. We live and die in time. We also don't really understand it very well: time is a source of a variety of philosophical question and puzzles.

In this chapter, we are going to discuss several metaphysical questions _{5.2} about time. The first question we will examine is really a meta-metaphysical question about the methodology of philosophy of time. This will be the focus of Section 5.2.

The second question we will discuss is whether time is a thing in its _{5.3} own right. This question will be focus of Section 5.3. On one view about the nature of time, which I will call *the container view*, time itself is a whole that is made out of smaller bits, which are called "times." On the container view, times belong to their own distinctive ontological category. Physical objects are *in* times; this is why the container view is called "the container view." The container view is plausible, and fits well with how we talk and think. For example, we often measure intervals of time and assign them temporal lengths (such as an hour) in much the same way that we sometimes measure the width of a barrel and assign it a spatial length (such as 2 feet). In both cases, there seems to be some entity that we are measuring.

An opposing view is the *relationalist view*. According to the relationalist _{5.4} view, strictly speaking there aren't any times. There are, however, temporal

This Is Metaphysics: An Introduction, First Edition. Kris McDaniel.
© 2020 John Wiley & Sons, Inc. Published 2020 by John Wiley & Sons, Inc.

relations between physical objects and events. So, although there are no such entities as time or times, it is still true that World War I happened *before* World War II. We'll discuss some reasons for and against both the container view and the relationalist view in Section 5.3.

5.5   Changes occur to things *in* time. My two children are relentless markers of the passage of time, because they change so quickly from week to week. Things in time undergo change. But does time itself change? This will be the third metaphysical question we will address; it will be discussed in Section 5.4.

5.6   If time changes, it doesn't change by getting taller, or by losing hair, or by gaining wisdom. So, if time can change, how does it change? Perhaps this is how time changes: right now, a specific moment is the present moment. But that moment wasn't always the present moment. Instead, it used to be a moment that belonged to the future. In another moment, that moment that we've been talking about will not be present, but will instead belong to the past. I guess this change probably happened midway through reading this paragraph. So, here's one way in which time seems to change: parts of it cease to be parts of the future, become present, and then become parts of the past.

5.7   Perhaps our belief that time changes in this way is why we think in terms of the *flow* of time or say things like, "time keeps on slipping into the future." In Section 5.4, we'll discuss whether time changes in this way. We will look at some different metaphysical theories that each imply that time changes, but which disagree with each other on how to explain the way that time changes. We'll also examine a view that says that time does *not* change in this way. According to this view, which I will call *the Static View*, things in time change, but time itself doesn't change.

5.8   On the Static View, there is a difference between the past, the present, and the future, but this difference is a merely relative difference, in the same way that the difference between here and elsewhere is a merely relative difference. There's a difference between here and elsewhere: I'm here, not there! My car is here with me in South Bend, IN, not elsewhere in Washington State, with my parents. And my kids are with me right now, not with my grandparents during World War II. On the Static View, when I say that my kids are with me right now, what I mean is that my kids are at the same place where I am speaking and are at the same time that I am speaking. When I use the word "here," I refer to the place that I am at. When I use the word "now," I refer to the time that I am at. On the Static View, just as all places are equally real—there is no metaphysical difference between Washington State and myself simply because it is not here but I am here—so too are all times equally real. We can truthfully say that this is the present year because it is the year in which we are talking. But in 1861, Abraham Lincoln can truthfully say that 1861 is the present year. On the Static View, there isn't any sense in which we are right and Abraham Lincoln is wrong. On the Static View, other times are just like other places, and people in other times are just like other people in other places. My parents are just as real as I am even though I am here and they are there. Abraham Lincoln is just as real as I am even though I am now and he is then. So, on the Static View, since what is "now" for Abraham Lincoln needn't be "now" for me, there is not an absolute difference between past, present, and future.

According to the Static View, future objects and events are just as real as 5.9 present ones. Your birth and your death are just as real as your currently reading this chapter. Your future decisions and actions are just as real as your present decisions and actions. People tend to think that the past is closed and the future is open. But if the future and the past are both just as real as the present, in what sense is the past closed and the future open? There are facts about what did happen. There are also facts about what will happen, including facts about what you will do tomorrow. What are the implications of the Static View for free will? We will discuss this question in Chapter 6 (specifically, in Section 6.2), which is focused on metaphysical questions about freedom.

But independently of concerns about free will, one might wonder 5.10 whether the Static View is incompatible with our reasonably reacting differently to past and future objects. On the Static View, a past pain is just as real as a present pain, and both are just as real as a future pain. If they are all equally real, why does it make sense to prefer that my pains be in the past rather than in the future?

The final question we will focus on in this chapter is how things per- 5.11 sist through time. This will be discussed in Section 5.6. Consider first how an ordinary physical object is spread throughout space. A table is spread through space by having smaller parts: it has a left half and a right half, or a table top and legs, for example. You are extended along three spatial dimensions because you are made up of tinier things that are also distributed in these three dimensions. In short, it seems that whenever an object is extended in space, it is because that object has parts that correspond to the parts of the space in which it is extended. You have a left half and a bottom half, and a top half and a bottom half.

5.12   (Well, maybe. A lot of what was just said is false if certain answers to the Special Composition Question are true. Your top half is not a living thing; so, Life implies it does not exist. Compositional nihilism implies that none of the items mentioned in the previous paragraphs are composite objects. Conversely, some answers to the Special Composition Question imply that you have a left half and a top half: compositional universalism most clearly does, but the sufficiently stuck together theory (SSTT) seems too as well.)

5.13   Do we persist through time in the same way that we are spread out in space? Just as we have a left half and a bottom half, do we also have an earlier half and a later half? Some metaphysicians think that we do. These metaphysicians say that, in addition to having spatial parts such as hands, eyes, or feet, we also have *temporal parts*. The view that we have temporal parts is called *perdurantism*. Here is an example to help you understand perdurantism. I was born in 1976; it was a time of great national unrest and disco. Let us assume that I will die in 2076. According to the theory we are considering, there is something that is a part of me that comes into existence in 1976 and goes out of existence in 2026, when I am 50 years old. This is my early half, just as the part of me that begins around my belly button and ends at the top of my head is my top half. My early half is literally a part of me, just as my top half is literally a part of me.

5.14   Let me be clear: I'm not talking about the first half of my life, but rather the first half of me. My life is a complex event in which a bunch of other events happen: my birth, various growth spurts, naps, ingestions of food, catastrophic injuries, and so on. A nap is an event in my life; it is not a part of me, even if perdurantism is true. In general, metaphysicians don't fight much about whether events have temporal parts. A football game is a long, drawn out event with a first half and a second half.

5.15   That said, if physical objects have temporal parts, we are a lot more like events than we might have previously thought. In Section 5.6, we will explore the question of whether we have temporal parts while examining the more general question of how we persist through time.

5.2 Methodological Issues in the Philosophy of Time

5.16   Before we get to the metaphysical questions, though, a few remarks on methodology are in order, specifically, about how the questions in the philosophy of time are related to scientific questions about time. And these questions are connected to more general questions about how science and philosophy should interact with each other.

One can't hope to discover the correct metaphysical view about the nature of time if one completely ignores the important discoveries about time made by people working in physics departments. One can't have a comprehensive theory of the nature of time without giving a lot of consideration to how we perceive time, and this means that an adequate philosophy of time should also take into account the discoveries made by people working in psychology departments. The issues that metaphysicians are interested in are too interconnected with issues that physicists and psychologists are interested in, so their input has to be taken into account. But we can't discover the true philosophy of time only by doing physics and psychology. We'll have to do some philosophy too. 5.17

That said, in what follows, I am going to avoid discussing any heavy-duty physics or psychology. I will briefly discuss some purported consequences of the special theory of relativity for the metaphysics of time in Section 5.4, but that's about it. I'm going to focus on the philosophical puzzles that confront us as we think about our ordinary ideas of what time is like. Here's why I think this procedure is reasonable, despite what I just wrote in the previous paragraph. This book is an introduction to metaphysics, rather than a book that decisively presents and defends the absolutely true metaphysical theory of the world. So the goals of this book are relatively modest: I want to help you understand some metaphysical questions, to guide you as you think through them, and to put you in a position to think further about them on your own or in a setting with others, such as in a classroom or reading group. These are modest goals, but appropriate ones for an introduction to metaphysics. In fact, I think it would be absurd to try to decisively present and defend the absolutely true metaphysical theory of the world in an introductory book. Let me briefly explain why I think this, since it will also shed light on why I'm going to focus on the philosophical puzzles that confront our ordinary conception of time here. 5.18

Here's what a typical introduction to physics class is like. For better or for worse, during a large portion of such a class—often a very large portion— the professor teaches the students basic mathematical techniques for solving a variety of physics problems. The professor will need to spend some time getting her students to understand the concepts involved in the class, so she will need to, for example, teach her students the difference between momentum, kinetic energy, and force. But the amount of philosophical reflection about these concepts she will require of her students will be 5.19

minimal, even though it took her scientific ancestors a tremendous amount of philosophical reflection to come up with and carefully distinguish the concepts of momentum, kinetic energy, and force.[1] In an introduction to physics class, the job of a physics professor is not to teach the philosophy of physics, but rather to get the students to be able to apply mathematical equations to physical problems. It's someone else's job to get the students to engage in philosophical reflection.

5.20   It is the philosopher's job. In a college or a university, there is a division of intellectual labor. We are all working together to try to build something that will stand the test of time: an interconnected, comprehensive body of knowledge. This body of knowledge isn't like a building made out of bricks, where anyone can just stack one piece of knowledge on top of another. Instead, what we are aiming for is more like a very complicated machine or living body: each of us contributes our own specialized knowledge and we all try to see how what we all contribute fits together into a coherent whole. Since it is very hard for any single one of us to really excel at more than one thing, we need a bunch of different people excelling at different things, learning different things and developing different skills, and then coming together into what we hope will be a fruitful dialog with each other in order to build something wonderful. This is the fundamental reason we need to have something like universities.

5.21   But, in order for the division of intellectual labor to work, philosophers need to develop special skills of their own, such as the ability to carefully reflect on philosophical puzzles, the ability to come up with creative solutions to these puzzles, and the ability to logically argue for and against purported solutions to these puzzles. And philosophers need to have specialized knowledge of their own as well, and this knowledge comes partly through seeing the puzzles that arise for our ordinary ways of thinking about the world and figuring out how to confront these puzzles. Then we can hopefully apply that philosophical knowledge to what the physicists (and psychologists, and chemists, and so on) tell us about the world. One of the jobs of this book is to help you develop these skills and acquire the knowledge base necessary to do this.

5.22   I said a few paragraphs back that I thought it would be absurd to try to decisively present and defend the absolutely true metaphysical theory of the

---

[1] On force, see http://materias.df.uba.ar/f1ba2014c1/files/2012/07/1994-storyofforce.pdf

world in an introductory book. You've seen one reason why this would be absurd—such a theory would have to draw on a variety of specialized knowledge you and I probably don't have, because no single one of us has it. But here's a second reason to consider that is somewhat independent of the first one I gave you. Think back again to what happens in a typical introduction to physics class. Some of the things that you learn are a bunch of mathematical equations that you use to solve various physics problems. However, it is worth stressing here that the equations that are taught in introduction to physics classes *are not the correct equations*. Let me give you a simple example. Suppose a boat is traveling away from a point at a stationary beach at a constant velocity of 10 miles an hour. Suppose a bird is flying away from the boat, and the bird and the point on the beach form a straight line that the boat is traveling along, as demonstrated in this diagram:

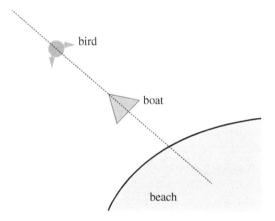

Suppose now that the boat measures the bird as traveling at a constant 5.23 velocity of 5 miles an hour. In one hour, how much further from the beach will the bird be? Here's how you will be told to solve this problem in an introductory physics class. First, simply add the velocity of the bird relative the boat to the velocity of the boat relative to the beach, and then solve for distance. What we get is that, relative to the beach, the bird is moving at a constant 15 miles per hour, and so in one hour, will be 15 miles further from the beach. This answer of course seems very plausible, and it is *approximately* correct. But it is not correct. And your physics professor knows that she is teaching you something that is merely approximately correct. Sometimes the physics teacher will even explicitly say that she is teaching you something that is merely approximately true but not actually true. Why doesn't she just teach you the true equations? Two reasons—she doesn't know exactly what they are (because *no one* knows exactly what they are, as of yet, although what she knows will give her a much better approximation). And second, even if she did know exactly what they are, it would be unreasonable to try to teach them in an introductory physics class. This is because the true equations are going to be much more complicated than the ones she is trying to teach her students, and many of her students are going to struggle with the merely approximately true equations as it is. In an introductory physics class, she will teach things that are kind of like what is true but are simpler and easier to learn than the true equations *because the students need to develop the skills and knowledge base first* before they are ready to tackle the harder stuff that comes in later physics classes.[2]

5.24   The same is true for metaphysics. By getting you to work through the philosophical problems that arise just for our ordinary way of thinking about time, I hope that you will acquire the knowledge base and skills necessary for tackling the philosophical puzzles that arise for a scientifically informed view about the nature of time. As I mentioned, we will see a bit of the interface of physics and metaphysics in Section 5.3, but for the most part, I plan to focus on the simpler stuff that we need to get a hold of first. Many of the positions that we will discuss have "scientifically sophisticated" analogs. You can think of working through these positions as doing something analogous to learning how to solve physics equations with the simpler equations you learn in introduction to physics.

5.25   There might be one important respect in which introduction to physics and introduction to philosophy are not alike. In introduction to physics, you learn claims that are false but in some sense are approximately true. And the approximations are serviceable: bridges won't break even if you used the false equations when you made them. Maybe it is more of an open question whether introduction to philosophy presents material that is approximately true. I suspect that it is, at least in the respect that most of the positions discussed here have more sophisticated analogs that take into

---

[2] Here is the equation for adding velocities in Newtonian physics and the somewhat more complicated equation for Special Relativity: http://www.pa.msu.edu/courses/2000fall/phy232/lectures/relativity/vel_add.html See also http://math.ucr.edu/home/baez/physics/Relativity/SR/velocity.html

account the more sophisticated science. Is introduction to philosophy also serviceable? That partly depends on whether philosophy in general can be serviceable, and we'll discuss that question in Section 7.5.

5.3 The Container View vs. the Relationalist View

The first metaphysical questions about time we will delve into are about 5.26 whether times belong to their own ontological category and whether our ordinary way of talking about time is appropriate or misleading given what kind of entity time ends up being. Is time something like a container in which physical objects can be placed? Are individual times (moments, seconds, hours, and so on) parts of this big container? The Container View says "yes": time is itself a thing that has times as parts and that contains things in time.

The relationalist view denies that either time or times are ontological 5.27 categories. According to the relationalist view, there are temporal relations, such as being one year apart, being five minutes after, being a hundred years earlier, and so on. But these are relations that objects bear to one another directly. There are no times that are one year apart, and there are no pairs of times such that one of them is five minutes after the other. Objects can be temporally distant from each without being *in* a temporal container that is distinct from them. On the relationalist view, there are only objects and the temporal relations between them—hence the name, "the relationalist view."

Should the advocate of the container view of time also believe in a con- 5.28 tainer view of space? It would be logically consistent to believe the container view of time without believing a container view of space, and vice versa. But the arguments for and against the container view of time have analogous arguments that seem equally plausible as those for and against the container of space. I suggest that, as you read through this section, when it's time to evaluate an argument for or against the container view of time, you check whether you think the analogous argument for the container view of space is just as plausible. It would be interesting to see whether there are differences in how plausible they are. We are going to consider an argument for the container view of time and an analogous argument for the container view of space in a moment.

Let's now consider an argument for the container view of time. The first 5.29 premise is that there are highly general patterns about how objects are temporally related to each other, and these highly general patterns are not merely accidental regularities, but rather are the result of something that explains these patterns. The second premise is that the best candidate for being what explains these patterns is that there is an entity, namely time, and the structure of this entity governs how objects in it can be arranged. And so, provided that we are justified in believing that something exists when it is the best explanation for a phenomenon that needs explanation, we are justified in believing that time itself exists and that it contains the objects that are in time.

5.30   There is a parallel argument for the container view of space. Since I think that it might be easier to understand than the argument for the container view of time, I am going to explain it first. Hopefully, this will help me clearly explain the argument for the container view of time. The parallel argument for the container view of space is this. The first premise is that there are highly general patterns about how objects are spatially related to each other, and these highly general patterns are not merely accidental regularities, but rather are the result of something that explains these patterns. The second premise is that the best candidate for being what explains these patterns is that there is an entity, namely space, and the structure of this entity governs how objects in it can be arranged. And so, provided that we are justified in believing that something exists when it is the best explanation for a phenomenon that needs explanation, we are justified in believing that space itself exists and that it contains the objects that are in space.

5.31   Let's first think about the first premises of these arguments, starting with the argument for the container view of space. I will work my way up to eliciting a highly general pattern about objects in space. First, consider these two-dimensional objects:

These objects have the same intrinsic properties. They differ only in how they are oriented, and even that difference would be eliminated by simply rotating the figure on the right by 180 degrees. Moreover, that figure can be rotated without lifting it off the page—it can simply be "spun" on the two-dimensional plane that both figures are on, and if you did this, here's what you'd see:

Consider now two other asymmetric objects that are mirror images of 5.32
each other, such as the two triangles shown here:

There is no way to spin one of these two objects on the same two-dimensional
plane so that they are both pointing the same way. However, these two-
dimensional objects can be rotated through a third dimension, and there is
a way to rotate them so that the difference in how they are oriented would
be eliminated.

Finally, consider a pair of three-dimensional gloves, one of which is left- 5.33
handed and the other right-handed. The gloves might be perfect duplicates
of each other, but they nonetheless differ in how they are oriented. And
there is no further dimension along which they can be rotated.

So here is a highly general pattern that is illustrated by these examples: If 5.34
two duplicates are either one-dimensional and two-dimensional objects,
they can always be rotated in three-dimensional space so that they are oriented in the same way, but it is not the case that three-dimensional objects
that are duplicates of one another can always be rotated in three-dimensional
space so that they are oriented in the same way. There is a pattern of possibilities and constraints.

This pattern doesn't seem to be an accidental regularity. An accidental 5.35
regularity is a pattern for which there isn't a single explanation for why it
occurs but rather different elements of the pattern are explained in different, largely unrelated ways. For example, suppose it turns out that every
philosopher has an odd number of hairs on her head. (That is, one hair, or
three hairs, or five hairs, and so on) That would be surprising, but it would
also just be a funny coincidence. There's no deep connection between being
a philosopher and having an odd number of hairs; that's just how things
turned out. The highly general pattern about how objects can be oriented
isn't like that; it is not a coincidence that all objects fall into this pattern.
And so, there should be a uniform explanation of why they do.

One uniform explanation for this pattern is that there is a thing, space, 5.36
that has a fixed number of dimensions, namely three, and this fact about
space constrains the ways in which objects can be spatially related to one

another. A three-dimensional left-handed glove can't be rotated so that it fits perfectly on a right hand because space doesn't have a fourth dimension through which it could be rotated. It is hard to see what other uniform explanation could explain this phenomenon, and if there isn't one, an explanation involving space as a container is the best explanation by default.

5.37   The case for the container view of time is similar. The first premise is that there are highly general patterns about how objects are temporally related to each other, and these highly general patterns are not merely accidental regularities, but rather are the result of something that explains these patterns. Certain relations between things in time are possible, but others are not. More specifically, the following claims are true about how objects are related to each other in time. First, the relation of *occurring after* is *asymmetric*. A relation R is asymmetric if and only if, if x bears R to y, then y does *not* bear R to x. An example of an asymmetric relation is the relation of being taller than: if I am taller than you, then you definitely are not taller than me. Since President Obama's time in office occurs after President Bush II's time in office, it follows that President Bush II's time in office does not occur after President Obama's time in office.

5.38   Second, the relation of *occurring after* is transitive: if z occurs after y, and y occurs after x, then z occurs after x. For example, if President Obama's time in office is after President Bush II's time in office, and President Bush II's time in office is after President Clinton's time in office, then President Obama's time in office is after President Clinton's time in office. Third, for any two things in time, either the first occurs before the second, or the second occurs before the first, or they both occur simultaneously.

5.39   These three patterns about how objects can and must be temporally related to each other are highly general, and they do not seem to be accidental. These patterns can be summed up together by noting that temporally related objects always can be represented as falling on a line.

5.40   What explains this fact about how objects can and must be temporally related? One explanation is that temporally objects can always be represented as forming a line because they are in a container, time, that has a linear structure and so the objects in that container must conform to that structure. And time itself has the structure of a line—it is a one-dimensional container. The reason that my death can't happen both before and after my birth is that both my death and my birth are located in a linear one-dimensional time. Similarly, the reason that for any two events you pick, they are either simultaneous or one happens before the other is that these events are located in a linear one-dimensional time. It's not just dumb luck or a weird coincidence that events line up neatly along a line—that they do is explained by the container view.

Note that, on the relationalist view, there is no container to constrain the arrangement of things in this way, and so it is not at all clear what could explain why it is that events are all arranged so as to form a single temporal line. If the container doesn't keep these events in line, so to speak, what does? 5.41

Perhaps someone who believes the relationalist view could respond that what imposes a linear order on objects in time isn't time itself but rather the laws of nature that govern how the things in the world undergo change. This would be an alternative explanation to the explanation offered by the container view, and it is worth thinking about which of these explanations is better. Note that, for this response to succeed, the laws of nature can't themselves be mere regularities, but should explain the patterns of events that they govern. We will return to a discussion of the laws of nature in Section 6.7. 5.42

I've been talking about constraints, but there's a parallel question about freedom from constraints. Suppose for a second, just so you can see the sort of issue I'm interested in, that there is a first event and a last event. (Maybe the first event is the big bang and the last event is the so-called big crunch.[3]) Suppose that these events are at a finite but incredibly large temporal distance apart. Could they have been even further apart than they actually are? This is a tough question to answer, but the container view might provide some light on what the answer could be: it partially depends on the shape of the container. If time is infinitely extended rather than a line of a finite length, then there is room for the two events to spread apart, so to speak. However, if these two events are each occupying the beginning and end of time itself, as it were, then there is no further "place" for them to spread out: there is no moment after the last moment of time and there is no moment prior to the first moment of time. (Maybe they could be closer together by no longer being the first and last events, but set that aside and hold fixed that they are the first and last events respectively.) 5.43

I've presented a case for the container view of time. Now we will consider an objection to the container view. This objection is interesting in that it attempts to use the greatest strength of the container view against it. Consider all the events that ever have happened, are happening, or will happen. Each of these events is located at some part of time or other. Given the 5.44

---

[3] http://science.nasa.gov/astrophysics/focus-areas/what-powered-the-big-bang/

container view of time, there is another possible world just like this one in which all of these events occur exactly one year earlier than they actually occur. So, for example, in the actual world I am born in 1976 and I die in 2076, but in this possible world I am born in 1975 and die in 2075. In the actual world, World War II began in 1939 and ended in 1945. In this other possible world, World War II began in 1938 and ended in 1944. In other words, all the events that happen in the actual world happen in this other world, but they are each shifted to a time that is exactly one year earlier.

5.45   Note that, if these two allegedly different possible worlds really are different from each other, then there is no way for us to say which of them is actually the actual world. What kind of test could we use to determine which of them we are in? Any test we conduct will occur in time, and will yield a result that will occur in time. Suppose we begin our test and then an hour later we finish our test. Satisfied with our results, we order in some pizza and watch re-runs of the cooking show *Chopped*. In the other possible world, a test also is begun and then an hour later it is finished. Afterwards, the testers are satisfied with their results, order in some pizza and watch re-runs of the cooking show *Chopped*. It's not clear then why anybody should be satisfied with whatever results they got from their tests, since our buddies in the other possible world got the same results, only a year earlier. Of course, they also started the test a year earlier. But whatever their lab equipment said a year ago in their world, our lab equipment will say the same thing now. If these two possible worlds really are different, no observation will tell us which one we are in. The difference between them will be completely undetectable.

5.46   The background assumption driving this thought experiment is that time itself is homogenous. That is, every instant of time is exactly like every other instant of time, at least intrinsically. Two moments might differ from each other extrinsically, because they have different sorts of events happening in them, but these two moments are themselves intrinsic duplicates of each other. And, on this background assumption, the same is true for longer stretches of time: every hour-long length of time has exactly the same intrinsic properties as any other hour-long length of time, every year-long length of time is an intrinsic duplicate of any other year-long length of time, and so on. Because time is homogenous in this way, simply uniformly shifting all the actual events up or down the timeline can make no difference to how those events play out.

5.47   What this thought experiment tells us is that an event's absolute location in homogenous time is completely undetectable to us. What we can detect are the relations between one event and another. Although we can't say which moments the respective events are in, we can figure out that one event takes place an hour later than the other event. The facts that we can detect are facts about the temporal relations between objects, but not the relations between objects and time itself. In other words, the facts that we can actually detect are the facts that the relationalist view of time accepts. According to the relationalist view of time, once you have figured out all the events that occur and figure out how those events are temporally related to one another—are they simultaneous? Three minutes apart? Does this one come after that one?—then you have figured out everything that there is to figure out about time. According to the container view, there is still a further fact concerning where in the container each is located. But the relationalist will object that this further fact is completely unknowable.

Moreover, the relationalist will charge that, in addition to being completely unknowable, the facts about where objects are in time seem to be in principle completely unexplainable. What possible cause could there be for the first event to occur at one moment in time rather than a slightly earlier or slightly later moment of time? It's hard to see how there could be any natural explanation for why the events are distributed where they are in the container rather than further up or further down the timeline. (Unless of course the container is exactly as wide as the distribution of events in it. The thought experiment we've been considering also seems to presuppose that the container is bigger than all of the things that it contains, and that is why there is "room for things to slide up and down." We'll discuss this more in a second.) 5.48

So, if there can't be a natural explanation for why events are located where they are in the container, perhaps there is some supernatural explanation? But what would it be? Suppose God is trying to decide which of the two abovementioned worlds to create, and God turns to you for advice. What possible reason could you have for favoring one world rather than another? The choice between the two seems completely arbitrary; there's no reason to pick one rather than the other. God might as well flip a coin. 5.49

So, it looks like the container view of time is committed to facts that we can't know and that cannot possibly be explained. The container view might explain important patterns, but it also generates facts that do not themselves seem to be explainable. Given this, should we believe the container view? 5.50

As I noted earlier, the relationalist's objection seems to employ two assumptions that might be false, namely that time is homogenous and that time is bigger than the events contained in it. We've discussed the first 5.51

assumption, so let's turn to the second one. When I say that "the container is bigger than the events it contains" I mean this: the container contains as a part some time that is either earlier than any time in which an event occurs or later than any time in which an event occurs.

5.52   But actually, this way of stating the second assumption is stronger than needed. There are two ways in which events in time could move up or down the timeline, and one of those ways is that the container is bigger than the events within it. The other way is for the container to be infinitely extended and for there to be infinitely many events in it.

5.53   To see this, let's consider a famous thought experiment called "Hilbert's Hotel."[4] Hilbert's Hotel is a really big hotel. In fact, it has infinitely many rooms! Each room has a unique number: you can stay in room 1 or room 2,000 or room 5,667,890 or—well—any number you want, and there are infinitely many of them! For any natural number, Hilbert's Hotel has a room with that number inscribed on it. Now you arrive at Hilbert's Hotel and are excited to stay there. But your excitement turns to ashes when you learn that Hilbert's Hotel is fully occupied: each room in the hotel already has someone staying it. There are no vacancies and infinitely many guests already checked in.

5.54   Will you sleep in the cold tonight? Is your vacation ruined? No. The management is not prepared to kick anyone out of the hotel to accommodate you, but the management is prepared to ask everyone to change rooms. The person currently in room 1 will move to room 2. The person currently in room 2 will move to room 3. The person currently in room 3 will move to room 4. The person currently in room 4 will move to room 5. In general, the person currently in room n will move to room $n + 1$. Everyone currently in the hotel will still have a room, but now room 1 has opened up for you.

5.55   Suppose time is like Hilbert's Hotel. Every moment of time is currently occupied by some event. That is, each event happens at a unique moment. Still, on the container view, there is a distinct possible world in which each event is shifted up a minute, *even though the container is not bigger than the events that it contains.* So, the relationalist's objection to the container view does not require that time be strictly bigger than the events it contains in order for the objection to work against the container view.

---

[4] http://www.youtube.com/watch?v=faQBrAQ87l4. For a discussion of Hilbert's philosophy of mathematics, go here: http://plato.stanford.edu/entries/hilbert-program/

However, if it turns out that time is finite rather than infinite *and* time is not bigger than the events that it contains, then the relationalist's objection won't work, because there won't be any room for events "to slide up or down the timeline." If time is like this, then time is very different from how we ordinarily think it is, but maybe time is different than how we ordinarily think it is. This is one place among many where we should expect that input from the sciences would be helpful for our philosophizing. 5.56

5.4 Does Time Itself Change?

As mentioned in Section 5.1, there are a number of metaphors we use to convey the idea that time in some way changes. We talk about time passing. The moment that is currently present is about to recede into the past. The future is a river rushing towards us. 5.57

I'm going to try to do two things in this section. First, I am going to discuss some theories about the metaphysics behind the metaphors. These theories all agree with each other that time changes, but they disagree on what that change amounts to. Once we get these theories on the table, well look at some reasons for and against them. I'm going to follow convention here and call these theories of time "A-theories" of time. 5.58

Because the A-theories of time all agree that time changes, they are "dynamic" theories of time. We'll discuss one theory, the Static View of Time, which denies that time itself changes. If the Static View is true, every A-theory is false. 5.59

The label "A-theory of time" is one you are definitely going to come across if you do further readings on the philosophy of time, so you might as well get introduced to it now. The reason for this label is surprisingly boring, however. (The label has nothing to do with the A-Team, who are an ex-military unit accused of a crime that they didn't commit.) In the early 20th century, a philosopher named J.M.E. McTaggart (guess what the "M" stands for) wrote an article called "The Unreality of Time" in which he distinguished between two ways of ordering times or events in time.[5] One way of ordering them uses the relations of before and after, and this way tells us simply which events come before or after each other. McTaggart calls this order "the B-series." For example, the start of World War I is before the start 5.60

---

[5] For more on McTaggart, go here: http://plato.stanford.edu/entries/mctaggart/

of World War II, the start of World War II is before Ronald Reagan's first moment as President of the United States, and so on. The other way of ordering times or events in times adds information about which moments or events are past, present, and future. For example, the start of World War I is a past event, your reading this page is a present event, and the heat death of the universe is a future event. McTaggart calls this order "the A-series." Philosophers who think that time passes think that there are important metaphysical differences between the past, present, and the future. So, they think the A-series is metaphysically important; hence they got called "A-theorists" and the theories they ended up using to explain how the present, past, and future differ from each other all got called "A-theories."

5.61   The first A-theory I'll discuss is *presentism*. Presentism is the view that the only things that exist are the things that exist now. For the presentist, there is a really important distinction between past and future objects and present objects: there are present objects, but there aren't any past and future objects. There are objects that are not here but there, but there aren't any objects that aren't now but then. On the presentist theory, to be is to be now. You sometimes hear the expression, "live in the now!" For the presentist, it is especially important to live in the now. Since the only time that exists is the time that is now, if you don't live in the now, you don't live at all. But for this reason, it is also really easy to live in the now: everything there is exists in the now, every living thing lives in the present moment.

5.62   I invite you to write down what you take to be a representative sample of what there is. Did you mention dinosaurs on your list? Or self-aware robots? If you didn't, is this because you didn't think of things relevantly like them— that is, past things or future things—when you wrote your list? Or did you neglect to mention them because you don't think such things exist? If so, you might implicitly believe presentism; presentism implies that there are no dinosaurs or self-aware robots.

5.63   According to the Static View, there are dinosaurs. None of them is located in the times that we are located in. But they exist nonetheless. (Just as the moon is not located in any of the places that we are located in, but it exists nonetheless.) And, assuming that the Static View is true, if self-aware robots are in our future, there are self-aware robots, even though they are not located when we are located.

5.64   Part of the reason why presentism might seem so plausible to us, at least when we first think about it, is the way in which English (and many other natural languages) works. Many natural languages have *tenses* to indicate temporal differences.[6] Compare the difference between: "Jane ran," "Jane will run," and "Jane runs." Every verb in English can be changed by changing its tense, including verbs like "is" and "exists"! Now consider the difference between "there were dinosaurs," "there will be dinosaurs," and "there are dinosaurs." Even the presentist believes that there were dinosaurs, and that, given time, money, and suitable advances in cloning technology, there will be dinosaurs. But, of course, there aren't any dinosaurs right now. So, isn't presentism just the obviously, boringly, trivially true claim that everything that there is (as opposed to "was" or "will be") exists in the present moment?

Here is where we need to be careful. In English, if you are going to use a verb, that verb has got to be written or spoken with some sort of tense. But the fact that we use the present tense doesn't always convey that we are talking about what is happening at the present moment. Let me give you some examples of sentences in which verbs are used in the present tense but that don't commit the speaker of the sentence to anything about the present moment. First, suppose I want to describe to you what happens in a purely fictional story. I might say something like this: "First, Peter Parker gets bitten by a radioactive spider. A short time later, he decides to wrestle semi-professionally for money. Soon after, he fails to prevent a burglar from escaping. The next day, the burglar robs Peter Parker's house and shoots his Uncle Ben. Peter Parker is filled with grief and regret and vows to fight crime as Spider-Man." I want you to notice a few things about this story. Almost every single verb used in this story is used in the present tense even though the story describes a bunch of events that happen at different times (in the story). If the mere fact that a verb is presently tensed in a sentence communicated that the events described in that sentence are all presently occurring events, then in my retelling of the Spider-Man story, we would have to conclude that Peter Parker gets bitten by the radioactive spider at the same moment that Uncle Ben gets shot. We shouldn't conclude that; that's not what the story says. Second, in my retelling of the Spider-Man story, I never actually say which things in the story are happening right now even though pretty much every verb is presently tensed.

Ok, here's a second example. Suppose I tell you that two plus three equals five. I'm not saying that two plus three equals five *right now*. What would be the point of adding that qualification to the sentence? It's not like two plus

5.65

5.66

---

[6] https://www.princeton.edu/~achaney/tmve/wiki100k/docs/Grammatical_tense. html

three will equal some other number at some point in the future. I'm not even sure that numbers are in time at all. It makes sense to wonder whether numbers are in or outside of time; this is something we could have an interesting metaphysical debate about. So, consider the theory that numbers exist but are not in time. Notice that I have to use a present-tensed word—specifically, the word "are"—to even state the theory. But that doesn't mean that the theory is incoherent. The theory would be incoherent if the use of the present tense always indicates that the things we are talking about are things in the present moment.

5.67   Here is a third example. In the philosophy of religion, there is a long-standing dispute among philosophers who believe in God concerning whether God is in time or outside of time. This is an important debate to these philosophers.[7] But it would be odd to settle the debate by saying that, if God exists, then God must be in time, because "exists" is a present-tensed verb.

5.68   In general, if time is a container, why should we think that it must contain everything? If relationalism is true, why should we think that everything must be related by temporal relations? An appeal to the grammar of English language seems inapt here. What these observations suggest is that we can use words like "exists" and "is" without committing ourselves to the claim that *as a matter of definition* everything presently exists. Presentism is a metaphysical thesis that is not settled by observations about grammar.

5.69   Does presentism seem as plausible now that we have made these observations about language? It is true by definition that the only things that *exist now* are those that are located in the present. But is it as clear that the only things that exist are located in the present?

5.70   Let's turn to some reasons to worry that presentism is false. First reason: If presentism is true, then there are no past or future objects. So, Abraham Lincoln in no sense exists. But then how are we able to think about Abraham Lincoln? How can "Abraham Lincoln" refer to Abraham Lincoln, if there is no Abraham Lincoln to be named? In general, how can we think about or refer to things that don't exist?

5.71   Second reason: Abraham Lincoln was a better president than George Bush II. But how can that be true if only George Bush II exists but Lincoln doesn't? (You would have to be a pretty terrible president to be worse than a non-existent president!) In general, how can things that don't exist have properties or stand in relations to things that do exist?

---

[7] For example, see here: http://www.iep.utm.edu/god-time/

When you read a history book, you read about real people and real events 5.72
that happened, that is, that take place sometime in the past. You learn about
the properties these people have and about the relations they stand in.
When you read about Spider-Man, you don't read about a real person or
real events that happen. (In Section 7.3, we will further discuss the
metaphysics of fictional objects.) You might enjoy the stories, but you
strictly speaking aren't learning anything about Spider-Man, because there
is no such thing as Spider-Man, not in reality. Presentism is a view on which
Abraham Lincoln is basically like Spider-Man: in neither case is there such
a person. That seems kind of weird. So, here is the third reason to worry
that presentism might be false: Does presentism make history a study of
fiction? It is hard to see how on the presentist's view, there can be true
historical claims. Consider the proposition that George Washington had
blue eyes. That's true. What makes it true? The proposition that I have
hazel eyes is made true by existing facts about me and my eyes. (Remember
Section 2.8 in which we discussed truth makers.) But if presentism is true,
neither George Washington nor his eyes exist. So, how can there be facts
about them?

Here is a more theoretical version of the third reason to worry. In the 5.73
previous section, we discussed an argument for the container view of time
that had as a central premise that there are general patterns in time that
require explanation. But if presentism is true, how can there be general patterns in time, since the only time that there is, is the present moment?

The next A-theory we will talk about is the *Growing Block View*. 5.74
According to the Growing Block View, there are both past and present
objects, but there are no future objects. So, if the fan of the Growing Block
View were to try to write down a list of all that there is, she would have to
include on her list human beings and dinosaurs. But she would not include
on her list self-aware robots. Here's why the view is called the Growing
Block View. Think of reality as a four-dimensional block consisting of
three spatial dimensions (height, width, and depth) and one temporal
dimension. According to the Growing Block View, time itself changes by
getting bigger: every time that time changes (so to speak), this four-
dimensional block gets a little longer along its temporal dimension. As the
block gets bigger, new events and objects come into existence. And the
block just keeps on growing.

The Growing Block View can handle the problems concerning his- 5.75
tory that the presentist faced. According to the Growing Block View,
Abraham Lincoln and George Bush II are both real, and so we can make

comparisons between them. So, we can truthfully say that Abraham Lincoln was a better president than George Bush II. We can think about both of them and refer to both them, since both of them exist. Since they both exist and can strand in relations to each other, there are truths about them. On the Growing Block View, there are facts about what eye color George Washington had, and that's why the proposition that George Washington had blue eyes is true. The Growing Block View doesn't treat studying history like reading fiction: on the Growing Block View, history is just as much about real things as the nightly news is about current events.

5.76   So, the Growing Block View does not face objections concerning the truth of historical claims. But maybe there is an objection concerning predictions. Suppose I predict that the president of the United States in 2021 will be a woman. My prediction is either true or false. Suppose it is true. What makes it true? According to the Static View, my prediction is true because there is a future object that is a certain way: specifically, there is some woman who is located in 2021, and who is the president of the United States at the time that she is located. But no such person exists if the Growing Block View is true.

5.77   Perhaps the friend of the Growing Block View will be unmoved by this worry. Maybe it is ok if my prediction about the future is neither true nor false. But it is horrible if claims about Abraham Lincoln are neither true nor false—and so, in this respect at least, the Growing Block View is more plausible than presentism.

5.78   Let us turn now to a discussion of the Static View. One interesting argument for the Static View comes from considerations of the special theory of relativity. We'll discuss this argument here.

5.79   The basic idea is that, given special relativity, there aren't absolute facts about whether events happen simultaneously: there is no such thing as absolute simultaneity. Instead, simultaneity is relative to a reference frame.[8] Here's a place where it actually would be a great idea to pause and examine the cool physics discussion in the attached link.[9]

---

[8] This is a helpful but at times very technical discussion of this idea from the *Stanford Encyclopedia of Philosophy*: http://plato.stanford.edu/entries/spacetime-iframes/#SpeRelLorInv

[9] See here for a comprehensive discussion: http://www.phys.unsw.edu.au/einsteinlight/jw/module4_time_dilation.htm

The relativity of simultaneity is problematic for presentism and the 5.80 Growing Block Views. Both views imply that there is such a thing as absolute simultaneity. Start with presentism. If presentism is true, to be is to be present. Everything that there is must exist simultaneously with everything else. But if simultaneity is relative, then being present is relative. And so, existence is itself relative. How can something exist relative to one reference frame but not another? Does this even make sense? A similar problem faces the growing block theory. To be present is to be on the outer "surface" of the four-dimensional block. Every object on this outer surface is simultaneous with each other. So, it looks like the Growing Block View also implies that simultaneity must be absolute.

If both presentism and the Growing Block Theory are refuted by special 5.81 relativity, then only the Static View is left standing.[10]

5.5 Time and Reasonable Emotions

Should metaphysical beliefs about the nature of time affect how we feel 5.82 about events in our lives? Are some emotions reasonable only if certain views about the metaphysics of time are correct? These are the big questions we'll address in this section.

These questions presuppose that emotions are the sort of thing that can 5.83 be reasonable or unreasonable. Whether this presupposition is correct is an important question in ethics. Here's one reason to believe it's correct. Consider a man who is terrified of a blade of grass. He is not allergic to grass; he has no reason to believe that the grass poses any danger to him; and he knows all of this. His fear is unreasonable: it is an inherently inappropriate reaction to something that is no threat to him, and he has no evidence that it is a threat to balance out the inherent inappropriateness of his reaction.

Let's begin our discussion of these big questions by assessing whether the 5.84 Static View of time should lead us to rethink our views about the rationality of treating the past and future differently.

Here is a possible situation to think about. Suppose that you are in a car 5.85 accident and are knocked out. While in the hospital, you drift in and out of

---

[10] There is a large literature on these issues. A good place to start is the *Stanford Encyclopedia of Philosophy*: http://plato.stanford.edu/entries/spacetime-bebecome/

consciousness. This has been going on for a while; you currently have no idea how long you have been in the hospital. You don't even know what day it is. You look at the chart posted near your bed. It says on the chart that on Monday you are scheduled to have a painful procedure. Is Monday in the future or in the past? You don't know. The thought that the painful procedure is in the future fills you with dread. Your hands get sweaty and your throat gets dry. The thought that the procedure is in the past on the other hand is nowhere near as troubling. In fact, you strongly prefer that the procedure is in the past rather than the future.[11]

5.86   If the Static View of time is correct, then regardless of where in time the painful procedure is located, the painful procedure is fully real—and fully painful. At some point in your life, you undergo the procedure, and it is a painful experience. What justifies you in treating the experience differently on the basis of where it occurs in time? In general, how can this bias towards the future be rational given the Static View of time?

5.87   For a much more dramatic example of how deeply we treat the difference between past and future, consider our differing attitudes towards our coming into existence and our going out of existence, that is, our deaths. Many people believe that they will not continue to exist after the destruction of their physical bodies. On their view, we are living animals, and the moments of our deaths are our final moments. Frankly, this possibility terrifies me. There have been nights in which I have almost been asleep, about to drift off, but then suddenly the thought that one day I will die pops into my head and then—BOOM!!—I am wide awake and unable to fall asleep. I'm not alone in having had this experience. Perhaps you have too. Perhaps now that I have put these thoughts in your head, you will have this sort of experience later tonight. If so, I apologize.

5.88   But apologies aside, there is an interesting philosophical issue here. Given the Static View of time, is my attitude towards my death a rational attitude? According to the Static View of time, Abraham Lincoln is just as real as I am; he's just not here at this present moment, but rather is temporally located at an earlier place in the timeline. So, on the Static View, when someone dies, he or she does not go "out of existence." Rather, he or she simply ceases to be located at any later times in the timeline. Why should it bother me that the extent of my timeline isn't longer than it actually will be?

---

[11] http://www.logicmuseum.com/time/thankgoodness.htm. See also Parfit, D. *Reasons and Persons* (Oxford: Oxford University Press, 1984), p. 214.

There is a plausible answer to this question, but as we'll see in a second, 5.89 this plausible answer doesn't address an even deeper, harder to answer question. Here's the plausible answer: In general, a life goes well for the person living it to the extent that this life is filled with things that are intrinsically good to have and is empty of those things that are intrinsically bad to have. I'll assume for now that among the intrinsically good things to have in one's life are pleasure, knowledge, achievements, and loving relationships. (We'll return to the question of which things in life make a life go better or worse in Section 7.5, when we discuss the value of doing metaphysics.) I'll also assume that a life that has more intrinsically good things in it is a better life than a life with fewer intrinsically good things in it, all else being equal. If these assumptions are true, then with the possibility of a longer life comes the possibility of a better life: if I live longer, then I will have the opportunity to have more intrinsically valuable things in my life. Of course, I also run the risk of having more intrinsically *bad* things happen in my life as well, and so there are risks to living longer as well. If your life is going well for you, it is clear why you would like your life to continue, at least given that it will continue to be a good life. Death then is to be feared for what it possibly deprives us of: the things in life that make a life worth living.

This is a plausible answer. But now for the deeper question. Why should 5.90 we treat the moment of our death differently than the moment of our coming into existence? Both moments mark endpoints of our timeline. And, of course, for any line segment, there are *two* directions in which that line segment could conceivably be lengthened. Why then am I terrified of my death but completely indifferent to the fact that I have not always existed? What justifies or grounds this absolute difference between moments that are, from the perspective of the Static View, completely equivalent? Had I existed earlier and still died at the time I will actually die, then I also would have more opportunities for good things in my life. My life would have been longer by being lengthened in the earlier direction.

Granted, it is not obvious that you could have existed earlier, while it 5.91 does seem that a later death is possible. Maybe one of your essential properties is coming into existence when you in fact did. Maybe. But consider someone who comes into existence as the result of artificial insemination. Suppose that person developed from previously frozen sperm and egg cells. As a matter of fact, these cells were defrosted and then brought together at 12:00 P.M. on a Tuesday, but they could have been defrosted and joined earlier. There's a case to be made that it would have been the same person who would then have been created at an earlier moment than the moment he actually was. Or consider what would have happened had the same sperm and egg pair that you originated from been united just a bit earlier than when they actually joined; would you not have existed had that happened?

5.92   Keep in mind that I not talking about a simple preference for a later death instead of an earlier life. If our attitudes towards later death and earlier life were simple preferences—like the preference for blueberry muffins over poppy seed muffins—then the question of what justifies this preference would not be so pressing. Maybe we just like one a bit more. But people fear death—as noted it earlier, it terrifies them. And they are largely indifferent to earlier creation. That's different than just simply preferring later death to earlier life.

5.93   We've talked about whether the Static View implies that our fear of death is unreasonable. However, even if it is unreasonable, it doesn't follow that our deaths are not bad for us. Maybe our death is bad for us only if the Static View is true. We'll close this section with a discussion of this argument, which is plausibly attributed to Epicurus, a philosopher who lived in ancient Greece.[12]

5.94   Here is the argument. In general, something is bad for someone only if that person exists; nothing can be bad for someone who does not exist. But when you die, you cease to exist. And so, your death cannot be bad for you, since you do not exist when you die. Your dying might be bad for you—it might be painful or distressing—but your dying is the process leading up to your death, not your death itself. As long as you are dying, you still exist. You do not exist anymore when you die.

5.95   One might challenge the second premise by denying that we are physical things who go out of existence when we die. Perhaps we are souls or some other kind of spiritual being. Epicurus rejects this challenge, but we won't pursue his reasons for rejecting it here. (Although recall the argument in Section 3.3 for the conclusion that we are physical objects.)

5.96   Instead, we are going to look at a different challenge to the second premise. Note that the epicurean argument that death is not bad for you implicitly presupposes presentism. If presentism is true, then you do go out of existence when you die. This is because, once you die, you will not be located at the present moment ever again. And since presentism says that

---

[12] See https://plato.stanford.edu/entries/epicurus/ See especially section 4 of this entry.

the only things that exist are present things, and you will never be a present thing after you die, after death, you cease to exist altogether. But there are other views on the nature of time, specifically, the Growing Block View and the Static View, both of which imply that, in addition to presently existing objects, there are objects (such as Abraham Lincoln) that are located in past times. On these views, ceasing to be presently located does not imply ceasing to exist.

5.6 How Do Things Persist through Time?

All this talk of life and death naturally leads to a related set of questions   5.97
about how we persist through time. Let's not worry only about the endpoints of our lives. Let's also consider what happens in the middle!

As I mentioned in Section 5.1, there are, broadly speaking, two competing   5.98
views about the nature of persistence over time that we will consider. Both of them have a variety of names in the literature on persistence through time. I'm going to use two of the uglier names: *perdurantism* and *endurantism*.

According to perdurantism, you persist through time in the same way   5.99
that you are spread out through space. Consider a table. A table has a number of parts: it's made out of four table legs and a table top. Suppose the table is between two rooms: it's partly in the kitchen, and it's partly in the dining room. (Not the best place to leave a table, but bear with me.) So, in a sense, the table has two locations: a *part* of it is in the kitchen (say the front half of the table) and a different *part* of it is in the dining room (say the back half of the table). This table is just one physical object hanging out in space, but there is a general view we can formulate: in general, when an object is spread out in space, it occupies different regions in space by having parts at those different regions. The perdurantist says that this is exactly how it is that objects are spread out through time. According to the perdurantist, I am partly in the 20th century and I am partly in the 21st century. That is, according to the perdurantist, I literally have a part that is located in the 20th century—it's my "earlier part" if you like, or my first 25 years part—and I literally have a different part that is located in the 21st century. I am spread out in time in the same way that the table is spread out in space: just as the table is in two spatial locations by having parts in each of those locations, I am in two temporal locations by having temporal parts in those locations. The perdurantist calls these parts *temporal parts*.

5.100   Given perdurantism, there are numerous short-lived objects. Any time an object lasts for longer than a minute, it has a truckload of temporal parts, each of which last no more than a second.

5.101   The endurantist disagrees. According to endurantism, when I persist through a period of time, I don't do it by having temporal parts. I might have a left half or a right half, but there's no such things as my "early half" and "later half." The slogan that endurantists like to use is that objects persist through time by being "wholly present"—rather than being partly there. Unlike the table, which is not wholly present in either the dining room or in the kitchen, I am wholly present right now in this moment. I do not have earlier or later temporal parts.

5.102   Does commonsense have an opinion on whether endurantism or perdurantism is correct? I'm not sure, but I'll note that the philosophical literature on persistence through time seems to presuppose that endurantism is the default, commonsense view—and given this, it has proceeded as though the fan of perdurantism has the burden of proof. In what follows, I will follow suit, although as already mentioned, it's not clear to me whether one view is the default position. So, let's consider some arguments for perdurantism.

5.103   The first argument I will discuss is called *the problem of change*. Here it is in a nutshell. Things don't merely persist through time: they also change from moment to moment. You once were very small and could easily be stored in a shoebox. Now you are comparatively much bigger, and one would have a hard time fitting you in even a very large suitcase. You've probably changed in hundreds of other ways too. But it will be enough to focus on the sort of change I've just mentioned.

5.104   Let's consider my oldest daughter, Kiddo. Kiddo was born in 2010. When she was born, she was 6 pounds 4 ounces. By 2019, she is about 52 pounds. That's a very dramatic change. But it is also philosophically puzzling. Here's one way to generate the puzzle in the form of an argument: Kiddo in 2010 weighs 6 pounds 4 ounces.; Kiddo in 2019 weighs 52 pounds; no single thing can both weigh 6 pounds 4 ounces. and 52 pounds. Conclusion: Kiddo in 2010 is not identical to Kiddo in 2019. They are different things.

5.105   The perdurantist happily accepts this argument: "Kiddo in 2010" and "Kiddo in 2019" can be thought of as names of different temporal parts of my daughter, Kiddo. And just as Kiddo's left hand is not identical with her right hand, Kiddo's temporal parts are not identical with each other either.

5.106   On the perdurantist's view, a person like Kiddo changes from moment to moment by having temporal parts that are intrinsically different from one another. Consider another spatial analogy. Suppose you have a red sweater that you just love, but one day while doing laundry, you accidentally dip the sweater in a tub of bleach. Now you have a mostly red sweater that also happens to be light pink in places. The mostly red sweater is no longer uniform with respect to its color. The sweater is qualitatively different from left to right: it has a small pinkish part, and to the right of that pinkish part is a bigger red part. For the perdurantist, qualitative change over time works in exactly the same way: you have a temporal part that doesn't last for terribly long that is very small and you have a (temporally speaking) much longer part that is adult sized. For the perdurantist, for a thing to change from moment to moment is just for that thing to have temporal parts that are not intrinsically the same.

What should the endurantist say about the problem of change? The literature on persistence is filled with answers to this question, but I'll focus on one answer: the so-called *relationalist* answer.[13] According to the relationalist, we shouldn't think when we assert sentences like "Kiddo in 2010 weighs 6 pounds 4 ounces." that we are attributing a property to a mere part of Kiddo. "Kiddo in 2010" is not a name of a temporal part that weighs 6 pounds 4 ounces. Rather, what we are doing is saying that Kiddo—the whole Kiddo, not a mere temporal part of Kiddo—stands in a particular relation to 2010, namely the *weighs 6 pounds 4 ounces* relation. Here's an analogy: When I say that the number 6 is a greater number than the number 4, I don't attribute a property to the number 6. Instead, I say that a relation obtains between 6 and 4, namely the *greater than* relation. Similarly, the endurantist who likes the relationalist answer says that Kiddo bears the weighs 6 pounds 4 ounces relation to the year 2010.

We are now in a position to see how the relationalist responds to the problem of change. Recall the argument that got us initially concerned: Kiddo in 2010 weighs 6 pounds 4 ounces; Kiddo in 2019 weighs 52 pounds; no single thing can both weigh 6 pounds 4 ounces and 52 pounds; so, Kiddo in 2010 is not identical with Kiddo in 2019. According to the relationalist, this argument is just as good as the following parody of it: Kiddo on the left

5.107

5.108

---

[13] For a critical discussion of other important answers to this question, see the excellent Haslanger, S. "Persistence through Time," in Michael J. Loux and Dean W. Zimmerman (eds), *The Oxford Handbook of Metaphysics* (Oxford: Oxford University Press, 2005), pp. 315–354. Her research page is here: http://sallyhaslanger.weebly.com/research.html

of Kris is shorter; Kiddo on the right of Babyo is taller; nothing can be both shorter and taller; so Kiddo on the left is not identical with Kiddo on the right. "Kiddo on the left" doesn't name a part of Kiddo, and there is no property of *being shorter*. Instead, we should understand this sentence as expressing the much more boring fact that Kiddo is shorter than Kris (who is standing to her left). With respect to the second sentence, we should think that Kiddo is taller than Babyo (who is sitting on her right). Hopefully the analogy is now clear: there is no part of Kiddo that deserves to be called "Kiddo in 2010" and there is no property of weighing 6 pounds 4 ounces. There is just Kiddo standing in various weights-in-pounds-and-ounces relations to various times.

5.109   Let me turn to the second argument for perdurantism, which I'll call *the problem of fission*. Metaphorically speaking, a case of fission occurs "when one thing becomes two things." The problem of fission is often illustrated in the literature using fantastical science fiction examples involving teleportation transporters that go awry, but there are actual cases of fission as well. A real-life example will help illustrate this idea, as well as set us up for the argument for perdurantism I want to talk about.

5.110   Consider a flatworm. A flatworm is a living organism, and will continue to exist as long as it is alive. They can also survive a lot of tissue damage. A flatworm can survive an accident in which half of its body is pulped. They are weird animals.

5.111   Consider a particular flatworm that I'll call "Wiggles." Wiggles is about to undergo an operation. Wiggles will be *cut* in half by a very thin blade.[14] As a result of this surgical cut, there will be two separate organisms that can now go their separate ways, never to meet again, or have any significant interaction with each other. This surgical cut results in two numerically distinct flatworms that move independently of each other.

5.112   By cutting Wiggles in two, have we caused Wiggles to go out of existence? If so, why? Wiggles could have survived the squashing of either his back half or his front half, and in the scenario we are considering, neither the front half nor the back half of Wiggles got squished. In fact, they are both perfectly preserved, although they are no longer in contact with one another. So that's a reason to think that Wiggles is still with us.

---

[14] https://www.npr.org/sections/health-shots/2018/11/06/663612981/these-flatworms-can-regrow-a-body-from-a-fragment-how-do-they-do-it-and-could-we

But now things get more puzzling. If Wiggles still exists, which of these 5.113 two worms is Wiggles? Is Wiggles the one on the left or the one on the right? Either answer seems arbitrary, especially since we perfectly cut the worm into two equal halves. Is Wiggles somehow identical to each worm? That answer seems incoherent: since neither worm is identical to the other, how could Wiggles be identical to both of them? If Wiggles is identical to both of them, and they are not identical to each other, then numerical identity is not transitive.

Is Wiggles identical to the thing composed out of the two worms? If so, 5.114 Wiggles is no longer a worm, but is rather made out of two worms. In which case, no flatworm is essentially a flatworm, because this surgery could be performed on any flatworm, at least in principle. (And since flatworms are animals, there are some animals that are not essentially an animal.) That seems kind of weird too. And according to some answers to the Special Composition Question—such as the SSTT and Life—there is no entity composed out of the two worms.

These flatworms actually generate a real conundrum! This is one actual 5.115 example of the problem of fission. Philosophers enjoy thinking about fictional ones too. Suppose you enter into the Star Trek transporter, the one that "beams you down" to a nearby planet. Suppose it malfunctions, and the end result is that two people who are perfect duplicates of each other beam down to the planet, where only one had been expected. Which one is you?

What should we say in response to the problem of fission?

The perdurantist has a nice response. To understand the response, 5.116 consider a helpful analogy. The perdurantist thinks that what happens to Wiggles is analogous to what happens to a road when it forks.

Suppose you are walking on a road called "Pleasant Road." You walk for a 5.117 while until you come to a fork. (A fork in the road, not an eating utensil.) You can go off to the left, or you can off to the right. Both options seem like equally good paths to take. There are no road signs, and no indication that one of the paths is intended to be the continuation of Pleasant Road. You might have a choice to make about where you want to end up. But you are not going to freak out about metaphysics. You aren't going to be puzzled about which path after the fork is really the continuation of the road you began walking on. Suppose you to take the left path—you aren't automatically going to think that the left path is *the* one to take if you want to *stay on the same road you started on*. What would make the left path "the" continuation of Pleasant

Road rather than the right path, other than a totally arbitrary choice on our part to label the roads one way rather than another? Suppose you are standing on one segment of Pleasant Road prior to the forking of the paths: it would be bizarre to wonder whether you should take the left fork *given that you want to stay on "the same" road*. No, the metaphysics of forking roads is clear, at least given that there are roads at all: in the case I have described, there are two roads here that share a large initial segment. Roads can share parts with other roads; this happens whenever, for example, two roads intersect. It also happens when a road "fissions," as Pleasant Road does.

5.118   To sum up, there are three road segments: the segment of road before and up to the fork (call it, "the original segment"), the segment of road that is the left path of the fork (call it "the left segment"), and the segment of road that is the right path of the fork (call it "the right segment"). In the situation you are in, there is a semantic question about what the name "Pleasant Road" refers to. Does "Pleasant Road" refer only to the original segment? If it does, then Pleasant Road terminates at the fork. Does "Pleasant Road" refer to the whole made out of the original segment and the left segment? If it does, then Pleasant Road does not terminate at the fork, but continues past it—it does not end but merely veers left. (Similar remarks apply if "Pleasant Road" refers to the whole made out of the original segment and the right segment.) Is it vague what "Pleasant Road" refers to? In which case, it is neither true nor false that Pleasant Road terminates, and it is neither true nor false that Pleasant Road veers to the left or to the right. But this semantic question is a question about what words refer to; it is not a question about what objects exist.

5.119   As I said, the perdurantist thinks that what happens to Wiggles is analogous to what happens to a road when it forks. Roads fork across space, but fission is a *temporal* case of forking. According to the perdurantist, the right thing to say is that there are two worms that share a lot of temporal parts.

5.120   Let's be a little more precise. Let's say that Wiggles hatches from his egg at time t_1. Suppose that the bisection of Wiggles occurs at t_2. After t_2, there are two separated worms that go their separate ways; call these separated flatworms "Lefty" and "Righty." Lefty is crushed by an object at t_3. Righty lives a little longer and dies at t_4. According to the perdurantist, Lefty came into existence at t_1 and went out of existence at t_3. Righty also came into existence at t_1 and went out of existence at t_4. Lefty and Righty have a lot of parts in common: all of the temporal parts of Lefty that can be found between t_1 and t_2 are also parts of Righty, and vice versa. Lefty and Righty have a common initial segment before their lives fork away from each other.

Ok, so which of Lefty and Righty is identical with Wiggles? If the perdur-   5.121
antist is correct, this a bad question to ask, since, on the perdurantist's view,
there were two worms all along, even before t_2 when the bisection occurs.
Well, it is a bad question to ask if the question is meant to be a metaphysical
question about which things are which. There is a good semantic question
to ask, namely, which of these worms is named "Wiggles"? And the answer
to that is that, in a sense, both are named "Wiggles": the name "Wiggles"
does not uniquely refer to one worm but rather ambiguously refers to both
Lefty and Righty. Suppose that when the name "Wiggles" was first used, we
didn't know what the future held; we didn't know that a worm surgery
would be performed. Suppose that it was assumed that there would be no
such surgery. But this assumption was wrong. There is an interesting question in the philosophy of language about whether names that are introduced on the basis of false assumptions nonetheless succeed in referring to
anything. My inclination is that "Wiggles" ambiguously refers to both Lefty
and Righty, but that we aren't in a position to learn this fact about the name
until later. But whatever we want to say about the earlier case involving the
name "Pleasant Road," the perdurantist will say that you should say the
same thing about the name "Wiggles."

During the times between t_1 and t_2, Lefty and Righty are located in the   5.122
same place. So, in a sense, there are two things that occupy exactly the same
space at the same time. Does this fact pose a problem for the advocate of
perdurantism? I don't think so. Keep in mind that the perdurantist believes
that objects are spread out in four dimensions—specifically, three spatial
ones plus one temporal one—and so, if we want to be precise about where
an object is located, we should talk about the *spatiotemporal* region it fills.
And, if we believe perdurantism, we don't think that Lefty and Righty are
located at the same *spatiotemporal* place, although it is true that they share
a common spatiotemporal part!

Perdurantism offers a neat and tidy solution to the problem of fission. If   5.123
endurantism can't offer a neat and tidy solution as well, then this fact counts
in favor of accepting perdurantism rather than endurantism.

How should the fan of endurantism respond to the problem of fission?   5.124
They don't believe in temporal parts, so they can't say that Lefty and Righty
share a large temporal segment and then later go their separate ways. So, the
problem of fission seems much more serious for endurantism. Perhaps the
best thing the endurantist can say about the case we are considering is that
one of Lefty or Righty is identical with Wiggles, but we have no way of figuring out which one of these two worms is Wiggles. Remember that, as I

told the story, Wiggles hatches from his egg at time t_1 and is bisected at t_2. After t_2, there are two separated worms that go their separate ways. On the theory I am now offering for you to consider, Wiggles continues to exist after t_2, but is then accompanied by a brand-new worm. Whether the worm that goes to the left or the worm that goes to the right is Wiggles is something we are not in a position to know, because there is nothing that could possibly explain why the one that moves to the left is Wiggles rather than the one that moves to the right, and vice versa. Remember that the worm I called Lefty dies at t_3. Whether Wiggles dies at t_3 is an utter mystery to us.

5.125   How should we feel about this if we are endurantists? Perhaps reflecting on one final thought experiment will help answer this question. While I describe this thought experiment, I will assume that you and I and all other human beings are physical objects in a world filled with other physical objects.

5.126   Suppose our dear friend Joshua has a serious accident and falls into a coma. Samantha and Hiro are in the hospital room when the doctor delivers the terrible news: Joshua has suffered extensive and permanent brain damage, and will never again be capable of having any kind of thoughts or feelings. Overwhelmed with sadness and grief, Samantha and Hiro do what many philosophers do in such trying circumstances, namely, argue over philosophy.

5.127   Both Samantha and Hiro believe that human persons are entirely physical creatures, but disagree over the circumstances in which they persist through time. According to Samantha, Joshua no longer exists. There is a living, breathing human body in the hospital bed in front of Samantha and Hiro, and this living, breathing human body looks a lot like how Joshua used to look. But it's not Joshua. According to Samantha, in order for a person to continue to exist from one moment to the next, it is not enough that their body continues to exist. In addition, there must be a sufficient amount of the psychology of the person preserved as well: in order for a person to continue to exist, enough of that person's beliefs, desires, plans, and so on, must also be preserved. Unfortunately, due to the extensive brain trauma caused by Joshua's accident, none of his psychological states are preserved. And this is why Samantha thinks that Joshua no longer exists. What remains is merely a living organism, but that organism is not Joshua.

5.128   Hiro disagrees. On Hiro's view, the human organism lying in the hospital bed is Joshua. Joshua has suffered a seriously debilitating injury, and as a result of this injury, he will never think or feel anything again. He will never deliver weekly reports of his activities. Joshua is now the mental equivalent of a carrot. But Joshua has not gone out of existence! The entity that is now incapable of thought is the same entity as the person who once was capable of thought. According to Hiro's theory of persistence over time, whether a human being continues to enjoy psychological states is completely irrelevant to whether that human being continues to exist. On Hiro's view, Joshua came into existence sometime prior to his birth, while he was still in the womb, and certainly sometime prior to his having any thoughts or feelings. What Joshua is most fundamentally is a living animal. There was a living animal in Joshua's mother's womb before there was a thing capable of thoughts and feelings in Joshua's mother's womb: and this living animal was Joshua! And there still is a living animal breathing and taking in nutrition (albeit intravenously) and this living animal is Joshua! On Hiro's view, Joshua still exists; it's just that Joshua is so badly damaged that his existence is of no benefit to himself.

Samantha and Hiro are having a deep debate about whether Joshua still exists. Who is right?

5.129 If endurantism is true, there is some fact of the matter about whether Joshua has continued to exist or has gone out of existence. It might be that we are never going to be in a position to decisively settle whether it is Samantha or Hiro that is correct. Maybe when it comes to philosophical questions, the best that we can hope for is to have an interesting argument in favor of an answer. But there's still a correct answer out there, even if we don't know or can't know what that answer is.

5.130 However, if perdurantism is true, it's not clear that there is a fact of the matter about whether Joshua has continued to exist or has gone out of existence. Let's be a bit more precise about the order of the relevant events in our story. Let's say that t_1 is the first moment in which a living human organism comes to exist in Joshua's mother's womb. Let's say that t_2 is the first moment in which this living human organism begins to think or feel. Let's say that t_3 is the moment of the terrible accident that irreversibly destroys Joshua's abilities to think or feel. And, finally, let's say that t_4 is the final moment in which the living human organism lying in the hospital bed dies. According to Samantha, Joshua first came into existence at t_2 and Joshua went out of existence at t_3. According to Hiro, Joshua first came into existence at t_1 and went out of existence at t_4. It seems like Samantha and Hiro are having a serious *metaphysical* disagreement about when Joshua's existence begins and ends. But if perdurantism is true, it looks like their disagreement is more of a *semantic* disagreement. Here's why. The perdurantist thinks that there is some object that comes into existence at t_1 and goes out of existence at t_2. There's also some object that comes into existence at t_1 and goes out of existence at t_3. There's also an object that comes into existence at t_1 and goes out of existence at t_4. There's also an object that comes into existence at t_2 and goes out of existence at t_3. And so on.

5.131   So, there is definitely a collection of temporal parts that starts at t_1 and ends at t_4. This collection comes into existence exactly when Hiro thinks that Joshua comes into existence. And this collection goes out of existence exactly when Hiro thinks that Joshua goes out of existence. But there's also a collection of temporal parts that starts at t_2 and ends at t_3. And that collection comes into existence exactly when Samantha thinks that Joshua comes into existence, and it goes out of existence exactly when Samantha thinks that Joshua goes out of existence. There is still a question about which of these two collections the name "Joshua" refers to, but, like before, this is a question of semantics rather than metaphysics. If perdurantism is true, there is no deeper question to ask about which of these collections really is Joshua. If "Joshua" refers to the collection of temporal parts that begins at t_1 and ends at t_4, then Hiro is right about whether Joshua still exists; if "Joshua" refers to the collection that begins at t_2 and ends at t_3, then Samantha is right about whether "Joshua" still exists. Perhaps there is even an ambiguity: perhaps Samantha refers to a different thing by "Joshua" than Hiro does, and, if this is so, Samantha and Hiro are talking past each other, rather than having a genuine disagreement. And if this is the case, then not only are Samantha and Hiro not disagreeing with each other, but both Samantha and Hiro are saying something true! This is a possibility we should take seriously if we are perdurantists.

5.132   It's also kind of a disturbing possibility. To see this, put yourself in Joshua's shoes, a few moments before the terrible accident that happens at t_3. There you are, minding your own business, thinking about philosophy as you are walking down the street, completely oblivious to the traffic cones in front of you. You stumble over one of those cones and thus begins your fall down a very deep and very dark hole. You know that this is not going to end well for you: at best, you will suffer serious brain trauma, and you probably will never be able to think or feel again. In your final moments of conscious thought, you wonder if this accident will end your existence, or if you will survive as a mindless living human being. You remember that if perdurantism is true, there is definitely something that will continue to exist after this accident, and also that there is definitely something that will cease to exist as soon as you lose the capability for thoughts and feelings. Which one of them is you? You scream out, "Will I survive?!!!" If perdurantism is true, the only question is what "I" refers to. Your metaphysical, existential crisis is reduced to a merely semantic question about which object is referred to by the word "I." Does this capture what you are afraid of?

5.7 Doing Metaphysics

As always, we'll end the chapter with some further questions to consider as well as some suggested further readings.   5.133

Must the metaphysics of time be like the metaphysics of space? Could one coherently hold a relationalist view of space and a container view of time, for example?

What other ways might the Static View change your beliefs about what emotions are reasonable?

Can it be vague whether something persists through time? If so, does either perdurantism or endurantism do a better job of making sense of how persistence over time can be vague?

Can you think of other theories of how objects might persist over time besides perdurantism or endurantism?

Is endurantism more commonsensical than perdurantism? If it is, is that a reason to believe endurantism?

Further Reading

Ben Bradley (2009) *Well-Being and Death*, Oxford: Oxford University Press.
    A comprehensive discussion of the badness of death; chapter 3 focuses on questions about existence and time.

Katherine Hawley (2004) *How Things Persist*, Oxford: Oxford University Press.
    An important book on (as the title suggests) theories of persistence over time.

Robin Le Poidevin (2005) *Travels in Four Dimensions: The Enigmas of Space and Time*, Oxford: Oxford University Press.
    This book is a good way to expose yourself to further issues in the philosophy of time.

Theodore Sider (2005) *Four Dimensionalism: an Ontology of Persistence and Time*, Oxford: Oxford University Press.
    This book provides a comprehensive defense of perdurantism.

6

FREEDOM

6.1 Freedom and Why it Might Matter

6.1 There is a freshly baked chocolate chip cookie on a plate in front of you. It smells amazing. I tell you that you can have this cookie now. But if you are willing to wait a half hour, I will give you two freshly baked chocolate chip cookies from the next batch instead. You move your left hand towards the plate. It hovers over it for a moment as the smell of caramelized sugar wafts towards you. Your mouth is watering. Your hand almost imperceptibly trembles for a moment before a decisive motion returns it to your lap. You decided to wait for two cookies, and have acted accordingly.

6.2 Your action of placing your left hand in your lap seems to be a paradigmatic example of a free action. If that action isn't a free action, then no one ever acts freely. Yet we have already encountered two possible threats to our freedom in this book. In Section 4.8, we discussed the All Limits View, which is the view that every property you have is an essential property of you. If the All Limits View is true, there is no possible situation in which you act any differently than how you in fact act. In every possible world in which you exist, you wait for the two cookies. And, in Section 5.3, we discussed the Static View, according to which future events are just as real as present events. Given the Static View, your future action of eating two cookies is just as real as the present act of refraining from eating one. In Section 6.2, we will discuss whether the Static View threatens our freedom. And, in Section 6.3, we will discuss a third potential threat to human freedom: *causal determinism*, which roughly speaking is the view that the

This Is Metaphysics: An Introduction, First Edition. Kris McDaniel.
© 2020 John Wiley & Sons, Inc. Published 2020 by John Wiley & Sons, Inc.

facts about the present and the past plus the facts about the laws of nature guarantee a unique feature. In Sections 6.4 and 6.5, we will examine *compatibilist* theories of free will, specifically, theories of free will that claim that free will is compatible with causal determinism; we will also briefly discuss the All Limits View in these sections. In Section 6.6, we will discuss whether the denial of causal determinism—that is, indeterminism—would make a difference to whether we act freely. In Section 6.7, we will briefly discuss the question of what it is to be law of nature. And, in Section 6.8, I will mention further questions to consider and additional things to read.

But before all that, I'll first talk about what is at stake. We value freedom. But why? 6.3

Let's go back to the situation with which I opened this chapter. You refrained from taking a cookie. You probably feel a little bit proud about that. After all, you wisely resisted the temptation of getting something earlier that is less good than what you would otherwise get later. But would it make sense to be proud of refraining from taking the cookie if you hadn't freely refrained from taking it? Suppose you learn that you have no free will. You might be happy, or at least relieved, that you are the kind of person who refrains in this sort of situation. But it would be inapt to still be proud of yourself for refraining. 6.4

Blame is the flip side of pride. And, for better or worse, blaming others is a big part of our lives. You are driving on the highway, and suddenly a person from the lane to your right cuts right in front of you. You slam on the brakes and narrowly avoid a collision. As you are breaking, you are also vigorously pressing the button that makes the car honk. You are pissed. Even though the other driver can't hear you, you shout angry words at the driver—words that modesty prevents me from transcribing here. You blame the driver for what he did. But suppose you learn that the driver lacks free will. You might still be angry at what happened—that is, angry that a particular situation occurs, just as one can be angry that one's house was destroyed in an earthquake—but blaming the driver for what he did is inapt. 6.5

We can distill from these two cases a general principle: blame and praise—pride is a kind of emotional praise—are appropriate only if the actions for which the actor is either praised or blamed are freely done. Losing our belief that we have free will would force us to radically rethink how we view ourselves and other people. If it isn't appropriate to praise or blame ourselves or others, this is because we are not responsible 6.6

for what we do. A lot is at stake if we never act freely. So carefully thinking about potential threats to our freedom is probably a good idea. Let's begin now.

6.2 The Static View and Freedom

6.7   This section is going to focus on whether the Static View implies that no one ever does any action freely. The initial worry is that if the Static View is true, in a very real sense, the future is "already written" in the same way that the past is "already written": just as there are truths about what did happen, there are truths about what's going to happen. Your future decisions are just as real as your current decisions, although they aren't happening now.

6.8   Since we want to see whether the Static View implies that we never act freely, we are going to temporarily assume the Static View, and then see whether it follows from it that we lack freedom. This kind of argument is called "a conditional proof," although it would be ok to also call it "a proof of a conditional." A *conditional* is a claim of the form *If P, then Q.* The first part of the conditional—the *P* part—is called *the antecedent* of the conditional; the second part of the conditional—the *Q* part—is called *the consequent* of the conditional. If you want to prove that a conditional is true, a good strategy is to temporarily assume the antecedent of the conditional, and see then whether the consequent follows from it. That's what we are going to do here.

6.9   So, we've assumed, temporarily, the Static View. Let's see whether on its basis we get to the conclusion that we lack free will. The argument that we'll discuss is *the fatalism argument*. The fatalism argument—as well as the argument to be discussed in Section 6.3—makes use of two important and initially plausible principles. The first premise is the Control Principle, which we can state as follows:

> The Control Principle: You freely perform an action only if it is under your control whether you will in fact perform that action.

6.10   Ok, but what is required for you to have control? This is a hard question, and I won't attempt to give a full answer to it. But one thing seems to be necessary for you to have control over whether you do an action: if there are any facts that guarantee that you will perform that action, then you must have control over whether those facts obtain as well. Here's what I mean by "guarantees": a fact guarantees that you perform an action if and only if, necessarily, if that fact obtains, then you perform that action. In other words, there is no possible world in which that fact obtains and you do not perform that action. This claim will be our second premise, and we will state it as follows:

> No Uncontrolled Guarantees: It is under your control whether you perform an action only if every fact that guarantees that you perform that action is also under your control.

Note that the Control Principle and No Uncontrolled Guarantees together imply the following: You freely perform an action only if every fact that guarantees that you perform that action is also under your control.

The third premise is that, for any action you perform, there are facts that 6.11 guarantee that you perform that action that are outside of your control. Note that, if the Static View is true, then whenever you are about to perform an action, it is already true right now that you will perform this action. Let's consider a specific example. It's 12:10 P.M. You are trying to decide whether to have pizza at 12:15 P.M.; it's one of the options about what to eat that you are considering. The time 12:15 P.M. is just as real as 12:10 P.M., and the action that you undertake at 12:15 P.M.—you do eat the pizza!—is just as real as the deliberations about what to eat that happen at 12:10 P.M. It's 12:10 P.M. right now, but there is a fact about what you will eat. Remember that on the Static View, the future, the past, and the present are all equally real. Just as it is true (right now) that Abraham Lincoln signed the Emancipation Proclamation in 1863, it is true (right now) that you eat the pizza at 12:15 P.M. But, if it is already true right now that you will perform this action, then there is a fact about the future that guarantees that you perform that action. According to the third premise of the fatalism argument, this future fact is no more under your control right now than past facts are under your control. Suppose that for breakfast you had oatmeal with brown sugar. There's nothing you can do right now to make the past different: what could you possibly do to make it so that you didn't eat oatmeal a few hours ago? The past is what it is. Similarly, according to the fatalist argument, there is nothing you can do right now to make a difference to what happens in the future. The future is what it is. It's already written.

These three premises logically entail that you do not freely eat the pizza 6.12 at 12:15 P.M. But this example was arbitrarily chosen—there is nothing metaphysically special about it—and so the argument's conclusion is really that no human person has ever freely done anything at all. That's a pretty radical conclusion.

6.13   This fatalist argument feels so good. But it is flawed. The fan of free will might insist that we do have control over what will happen in the future. They will grant that, given the Static View, there are facts about what I will do in the future. But they will also claim that it is up to me what those facts are. It is true that there are future facts that guarantee that I will do what I will do, but it is up to me what those future facts are. The third premise of the fatalism argument is false.

6.14   This is the big mistake that the fatalist argument makes: although the Static View of time does say that the past, future, and present are all equally real, the Static View of time is consistent with their still being other ways in which the past, present, and future are different. And one important difference between the past and the future is this: there are things we can do right now that will cause events in the future to happen. But there is nothing we can do right now that will cause events in the past to have happened. Although the past, present, and future are equally real, present events cause future events, but present events do not cause past events. This important difference between the past and the future explains why it is possible for us to have control over the future but not over the past. So even though your future actions are just as real as your present decisions, because your present decisions are the causes of your future actions, you still have control over whether those future actions happen.

6.15   It is because what we do causes the future to be a certain way rather than a different way that we have control over facts about the future—and hence, they explain why the fatalism argument is unsound. However, just as what we do now causes what happens later, what happened earlier caused what happens now. It would be ironic if causation is what gives us control over the future but at the same time strips us of control over the present. Whether it does this is what we will focus on next.

6.3 Causal Determinism and Freedom

6.16 Causal determinism is a thesis about events in time. Suppose you have a true and complete description of everything that happens at a given time t. This means that you know the location of every physical object at t, what properties these objects have at t, how these objects are related to each other at t, and so on. Let C be this complete description of everything that happens at a given time t. Let's suppose you also have a true and complete description of all the laws of nature. This means that you know all the laws of physics, all the laws of chemistry, all the laws of biology, all the laws of psychology, and so on. Let L be this complete description of all the laws of nature. Ok, now consider a complete description of what happens at a time later than t. This is E. Causal determinism is the view that the conjunction of C and L *entails* E. That is, given that C and L are true, E has to be true. It might it be useful to think of causal determinism in terms of possible worlds: causal determinism is the thesis that any possible world in which C and L are true is also a world in which E is true. In short, causal determinism is the thesis that what happens in the past in conjunction with the laws of nature guarantee what will happen in the future.

What is the relation between causal determinism and the Static View of time? The Static View of time is definitely consistent with causal determinism. But the Static View is also consistent with the denial of causal determinism. Maybe the Static View is true but future facts are not entailed by the past facts and the laws of nature. Look at it this way: The Static View says that future events are just as real as present events, even though they aren't now, just as events taking place in Bellingham, WA are just as real as those happening in Syracuse, NY even though they aren't here. But we have no expectation that the events happening in Bellingham, WA somehow guarantee the events happening in Syracuse, NY. Similarly, one could hold that although events in the past are just as real as events in the present, events in the past don't guarantee the events that happen in the present. So, we shouldn't conflate the Static View with causal determinism. They are different views. 6.17

If causal determinism is true, then every event that occurs has an in principle complete explanation. Conversely, if causal determinism is false, then there is at least one event that is not completely explained by previous facts and the laws. At most, past facts and facts about the laws might make it highly probable that this event occurs. 6.18

How plausible is causal determinism? Whenever we discover some occurrence, we look for an explanation of why that occurrence happened. Here's how we explain occurrences: we look for some other event that happened before it, and some law of nature that says that when you have an event of the first type, an event of the second type follows. 6.19

Here's an example of this idea. Suppose we go to the planet Mars. While on Mars, we discover some interesting caves of unusual shape, and decide 6.20

to enter them. Once inside, we find what looks like very old broken-down computer equipment. We discover something that looks like an old, beat-up laptop with a shattered screen, and another piece that looks eerily like a wireless router. What do you think happens next? We will immediately start to offer explanations for the events in question.

6.21   At the end of the day, whether causal determinism is true is at least as much a scientific question as it is a philosophical one. Perhaps the best quantum mechanical theory will be incompatible with causal determinism. We will focus in this section and in Section 6.4 on whether causal determinism is compatible with our ever acting freely. Later, in Section 6.6, we will explore whether the falsity of casual determinism would be enough to secure our freedom. We won't try to determine whether causal determinism is true.

6.22   So, let's temporarily assume causal determinism, just to see whether our lacking free will follows from it. We'll explore an argument that I'll call *the causal determination argument* for the conclusion that causal determinism is incompatible with our ever having free will. This argument is similar to the fatalism argument that we saw in the previous section. In fact, the first and second premises are the same: the Control Principle and the No Uncontrolled Guarantees Principle.

6.23   The third premise of the causal determination argument is that, for any action you perform, there are facts that guarantee that you perform that action that are outside of your control. These facts are not the facts about the future that the fatalism argument talked about. Rather, they are facts about the past and the laws of nature. Remember, causal determinism just is the claim that facts about the past and the laws of nature guarantee everything that happens in the future. So, the question here is whether those facts are outside of our control, not whether they guarantee what we do.

6.24   Now ask yourself the following questions: Right now, is it up to you what the laws of nature are? Is there something you can do, such that if you were to do it, the laws of nature would be different than they in fact are? Or is it completely out of your control what the laws of nature are? When I was a kid, there was a show called *Star Trek*, which featured characters like Captain Kirk and Spock, who flew in a star ship called "The Enterprise." One of these characters was named Scotty—he was Scottish—and he was the chief engineer of the star ship. Whenever things would go wrong, and Captain Kirk would demand a quick fix from Scotty, Scotty would shout (in a thick Scottish accent), "I cannot change the laws of physics!" Scotty has no control over what the laws of physics are—or for that matter any other law of nature. And if he has no control over them, despite an advanced engineering degree from a 23rd-century university, what control could any of us have? The laws of nature are not under your control.

What about facts about the past? Right now, is it up to you what hap- 6.25 pened in the year 1000 C.E.? Is there something you can do, such that if you were to do it, what happened in the year 1000 C.E. wouldn't have happened? Suppose that in the year 1000 C.E., a hermit in a cave scratched his nose. How could you have had any control over that event? What happened in the past is not under your control.

These three premises logically imply that no one ever performs an 6.26 action freely. In short, if causal determinism is true, then no one ever acts freely. Consider any allegedly free action, such as your act of refrain-ing from eating the cookie that we discussed at the start of Section 6.1. If the Control Principle is true, then you freely refrain from eating that cookie only if you have control over whether you refrain. No Uncontrolled Guarantees says that you have control over whether you refrain only if you have control over the facts that guarantee that you refrain from eating that cookie. But since the laws of nature and the facts about the past collectively guarantee that you refrain from eating the cookie, and you have no control over them, you do not have control over whether you refrain from eating the cookie, and so, you do not freely refrain from eating the cookie.

In general, it looks like, given causal determinism, no one ever performs 6.27 any action freely. The conclusion of the causal determination argument is radical. Let's see whether the argument breaks down somewhere. If it does, then, despite how things currently seem, free will and determinism might be compatible.

6.4 Compatibilism: Alternative Possibilities Compatibilism

In general, *compatibilism about X* is the theory that X is compatible with our 6.28 sometimes acting freely. We are going to focus here on compatibilism about causal determinism, and given that, in what follows, I'm just going to write, "compatibilism" instead of "compatibilism about causal determinism."

If compatibilism is true, one of the three premises of the causal determi- 6.29 nation argument is false. But which one?

Maybe the problem is the Control Principle. We'll look at two different 6.30 versions of compatibilism, both of which reject the Control Principle.

6.31   The first version is:

> Alternative Possibilities Compatibilism: A person does an action freely if and only if they do it but there is a possible world a lot like the actual world in which they don't do it.

6.32   The key notion here is the notion of a possible world a lot like the actual world. We encountered this idea in Section 4.4. We are in the actual world. There are other possible worlds, and different things happen in them. Some of those worlds are more like the actual world than others. The ones that are a lot like the actual world are realistic possibilities. They are ones that are as close to the actual world as possible given that you do not do the action in question. Alternative Possibilities Compatibilism says that an action is done freely if and only if there is a possibility like this in which you don't do that action.

6.33   Let's return to the case that we began this chapter with. In the actual world, you refrained from taking the cookie. But there are other possible worlds in which you eat the cookie. Causal determinism does not imply that there aren't these other possible worlds. Causal determinism says that any world with exactly the same laws as our world and exactly the same past as our world—which means all the same events right up until you refrain from taking the cookie—is a world in which you will refrain from eating the cookie. Causal determinism is not the thesis that you refrain from eating the cookie in all possible worlds in which you exist, that is, causal determinism is not the thesis that refraining from eating that cookie is one of your essential properties.

6.34   Causal determinism doesn't imply that there aren't other possible worlds in which you eat the cookie. But it does imply that these other possible worlds must either have different laws of nature than ours or have a different past than ours. The next question is whether these other possible worlds are a lot like the actual world. If they are, then Alternative Possibilities Compatibilism is well named, since it is a compatibilist view. If they aren't, then it's not. (And since "a lot like" is vague, maybe it is also vague whether Alternative Possibilities is a compatibilist view. Maybe it is vague whether anyone has ever acted freely.)

6.35   Let's assume that at least one of the worlds in which you eat the cookie instead of refraining are a lot like the actual world, even though either its laws or its past is different than ours. Then Alternative Possibilities Compatibilism implies that the action is freely done. According to this view, you don't need to have control over what you do in order to do it freely. You just need a possibility not too unlike actuality in which you don't do it. This is why the fan of Alternative Possibilities Compatibilism will reject the Control Principle.

Note that, although Alternative Possibilities Compatibilism seems to 6.36 imply that acting freely is compatible with causal determinism, it isn't a maximally compatibilist position. Here's what I mean by this. Recall the All Limits View, discussed in Section 4.8. The All Limits View is that every property you have is essential to you. If the All Limits View is true, there is no possible situation in which you eat the cookie. (Unlike causal determinism, the All Limits View does imply that refraining from eating that cookie is one of your essential properties.) And so, given Alternative Possibilities Compatibilism, you do not refrain from eating the cookie freely. The All Limits View and Alternative Possibilities Compatibilism together imply that no one ever acts freely. A maximalist compatibilist position would permit freedom even given the All Limits View.

Unfortunately, there is a serious problem with Alternative Possibilities 6.37 Compatibilism. I'll illustrate this problem with another case to think about. Benj is driving on the highway when another car veers out of its lane and crashes into him. This is one of those accidents that wouldn't have happened had things gone ever so slightly differently. The other driver just took his eyes off the road for a second. Had he not, the accident wouldn't have happened. But it did. Benj is trapped in his car, pinned by the other vehicle. He reaches out with his hand to open his glove compartment where his cell phone is. He strains, touches the glove compartment, but does not open it. He just can't quite reach far enough. If the other vehicle had hit him with just a little bit less force, he would have been able to reach the glove compartment.

Is Benj's not opening the glove compartment a free action just as your 6.38 refraining from eating the cookie is a free action? There is a nearby possible world in which he does open the glove compartment. All the car had to do was just hit him a little more gently. So, it seems that Alternative Possibilities Compatibilism implies that Benj freely leaves the glove compartment closed. But he doesn't freely leave it closed.

The central issue is that Benj has an ability in that other possible world 6.39 that he lacks in the actual world. Because Benj is not pinned as hard in that world, he is able to stretch further than he actually can. More generally, possibilities in which we have more abilities than we actually do are not relevant to whether the acts that we actually do are done freely. However, Alternative Possibilities Compatibilism says that these possibilities are relevant, provided that they are similar enough to actuality. This is why Alternative Possibilities Compatibilism is false.

6.40   Maybe we need to consider a revision to Alternative Possibilities Compatibilism:

> Alternative Possibilities Compatibilism*: A person does an action freely if and only if they do it but there is a possible world a lot like the actual world in which they have the same abilities that they actually do, but they don't do that action.

6.41   As before, given causal determinism, it's not clear whether there are such worlds. But set this aside. There might still be another problem to consider.

6.42   Consider Ralph. Ralph has a mood disorder. He usually takes medication for it, but his insurance has lapsed, and he is unable to afford it anymore. There doesn't seem to be a pattern to his moods. Some days he is energetic, almost dangerously so, and other days he is so low that he barely moves. Today he is low. He stays in bed. He doesn't leave. There is a nearby possible world in which he has the same abilities but he is energetic, and he does get out of bed. It isn't clear that Ralph actually acts freely. But Alternative Possibilities Compatibilism* implies that he does act freely. Is this a plausible verdict? Or is Ralph a counterexample to Alternative Possibilities Compatibilism*?

6.5 Compatibilism 2: No Constraints Compatibilism

6.43   One reason why it is unclear whether Ralph acts freely is that his actions are the result of a kind of internal compulsion caused by his mood disorder. More generally, let's say that an action is *internally compelled* if and only if the agent who performs this action does so because of a psychological disorder. In many courts of law, one can plead "not guilty by reason of insanity." Suppose that Winowa is not guilty of a crime by reason of mental insanity. If so, she did in fact do the crime, but she is not morally responsible for having done it—and, hence, she did not do the crime freely.

6.44   Let's contrast internal compulsion with *external compulsion*: a person is externally compelled to perform an action provided that there is a manifest threat of serious harm to the person if the action is not done. Both kinds of compulsion seem like they are threats to freedom because they impose serious constraints on what an agent does. Let's consider a compatibilist view that takes this into account:

> No Constraints Compatibilism: A person does an action freely if and only if they want to do that action, their action is caused by their desire to do that action, and they are under no internal or external compulsion to do that action.

No Constraints Compatibilism is another view that seems incompatible 6.45 with the Control Principle. Here's a kind of case that illustrates why.[1] Suppose you are at a party. It's a great party. There are a lot of books on shelves everywhere, and people are allowed to take them off the shelves and read them, and then talk about them with other people at the party. Some of the books are really old and rare. There's also a variety of cheese platters, so the party-goers can sample all sorts of cheese. And there's a chocolate fountain, with skewers of fresh fruit. Those are fun. It's a great party. You have no intention of leaving. On the contrary, you plan to stay until at least midnight. You actively want to stay at the party, you're loving the party, you're really into the party. Let's focus on your decision to continue to stay at the party at 11:00 P.M. You desire to stay at the party at that time, and your desire is what causes you to stay at the party then. Moreover, you aren't suffering from a psychological disorder that is causing you to stay at the party, and no one is threatening to hurt you if you leave the party. All the right boxes are checked: No Constraints Compatibilism implies that you freely stay at the party at 11:00 P.M.

Here are some things you don't know. There's only one way out of the 6.46 house—through the front door—but the last person to close the door turned the doorknob so hard that it broke. And some jackass parked his SUV on the front lawn and the back of the SUV is pressed firmly against the front door. And the storm that has been raging outside while you have been reading an original copy of *An Essay on Human Understanding* has just knocked a very large tree on top of the SUV, making it impossible for anyone to get inside it and move it. You are going nowhere. Even if you had wanted to leave the party—which you didn't—you wouldn't have succeeded

---

[1] An early presentation of this sort of case can be found in Locke, J. *An Essay Concerning Human Understanding* (first published 1689), Book 2, Chapter 21, Section 10. Here is an online version of the text: http://humanum.arts.cuhk.edu.hk/Philosophy/Locke/echu/

in leaving the party. There are factors that you have no control over that guarantee that you stay at the party.

6.47   According to No Constraints Compatibilism, these factors are irrelevant to whether you freely stayed at the party. The story I just told about the party provides an example of a free action according to No Constraints Compatibilism. And the friend of No Constraints Compatibilism would say that it also provides a counterexample to the Control Principle. If No Constraints Compatibilism is true, then the Control Principle is false.

6.48   Note that No Constraints Compatibilism not only doesn't require that you have control over whether you perform an action, it doesn't even require that there is a possible situation in which you don't perform that action. To see this, suppose that the All Limits View is true. Now return to the story where you stay at the party. Given the All Limits View, not only will you actually stay at the party at 11:00 P.M., there is no possible world where you do anything other than stay at the party at 11:00 P.M. You are an essential party stayer. Still, No Constraints Compatibilism implies that you freely stay, since the conditions for doing an action freely are still met. Even if every truth is a necessary truth—a claim even stronger than the All Limits View because it implies the All Limits View but the opposite is not the case—you still freely stay at the party at 11:00 P.M.

6.49   No Constraints Compatibilism seems like a reasonable theory. So, let's consider an argument against it. The gist of this argument is that there are possible actions that No Constraints Compatibilism implies are freely done even though the agent in question had no choice about whether he or she had the desires that led her to do the action. But actions of this sort are not free actions. So, No Constraints Compatibilism is false.

6.50   Here is one example to consider. Joshua is drinking a Kombucha tea at the local café. Perhaps his choice of beverage reflects poorly on his aesthetic standards, but it is not indicative of a mental disorder. You don't literally have to be mentally unwell to like the stuff. No one is threatening to shoot or stab or him, or even give him a paper cut, if he doesn't drink the stuff. And he does want to drink the tea, and it is his desires that cause him to drink the tea. All the boxes are checked: No Constraints Compatibilism implies that he freely drinks the tea.

6.51   But Joshua's desires also have causes. Yesterday, he (quite reasonably) hated Kombucha tea, and was completely averse to drinking even a sip of it. But his dining companion last night put a drug in the water that he was drinking, and that drug caused a radical change in his desires. He woke up this morning wanting to drink some Kombucha tea. So, he went to the local café. He ordered a Kombucha tea. And then he drank it. Do you think he freely drank the tea?

Joshua was manipulated to drink the tea. This sort of manipulation 6.52 seems incompatible with acting freely. We could add another clause to our formulation of No Constraints Compatibilism that says that an agent is not manipulated to have the desires in question. But manipulation seems to be just a special case of a more general phenomenon: namely, that there are factors outside of the actor's control that guarantee that she has the desires that in turn cause her to act. Suppose no one put the drug in Joshua's water. Instead, it's just a freak accident that it ended up in his water. In this situation, Joshua has not been manipulated, but he does not act any freer.

Moreover, if causal determinism is false, there are possible cases in which 6.53 there is no manipulation and that meet all of the conditions that No Constraints Compatibilism demands of free actions, and yet the agent does not act freely. Suppose causal determinism is false. Here's a different case. Joshua wakes up and quite reasonably does not desire Kombucha tea. But he lives in a crazy mixed-up world in which the past and the laws of nature don't guarantee how the future turns out. Random stuff just happens sometimes. Later today, for no reason whatsoever, Joshua will suddenly have a desire for Kombucha tea, and will act on it while not suffering from internal or external compulsion. In this scenario, does Joshua act freely?

6.6 Indeterminism

Perhaps causal determinism is incompatible with our ever acting freely. 6.54 Would we be better off if causal determinism were false? Is mere indeterminism enough for freedom? The last example we discussed in the previous section suggests that mere indeterminism is insufficient for freedom. But let's explore this issue further.

Suppose that causal determinism is false. The past and the laws of nature 6.55 do not guarantee a unique future. Rather, suppose that the past and the laws of nature collectively guarantee that one of two possible futures will obtain, each with a 50% probability of obtaining. More specifically, in the scenario I mentioned at the start of this chapter, the past and the laws of nature collectively guarantee a 50% chance that you will refrain from eating the cookie and a 50% chance that you will eat the cookie. As it turns out, the cosmic coin flipped heads, and you refrained from eating the cookie. Sure, you weren't guaranteed to refrain. But merely replacing determinism with indeterminism isn't enough to give you freedom.

6.56   Moreover, it is hard to see *when* the introduction of indeterminism would help secure our freedom. To see this, consider what happens when a person makes a decision. Suppose that I am in a crowded room and I see that my friend Jessica is at the opposite side of the room and is looking for me. I raise my hand high and wave it vigorously. A whole series of events had to happen first for me to successfully raise my hand. Let's walk backwards through them.

6.57   I raised my hand because I decided to raise my hand. I do not want determinism to break down during the time between deciding to raise my hand and my raising my hand. Once I have decided what to do, I want my body to comply. I would not feel relieved to learn that, after deciding, there is a chance that my body won't do what I decided it to do. I prefer a guarantee that my hand will rise after I have decided that it will rise. I am not made freer if there is a chance that I decide to do something, and my body doesn't comply.

6.58   I decided to raise my hand because I have various beliefs and wants. I want Jessica to see me. I believe that, given that I am not that tall, my best option for getting what I want—getting Jessica to see me—is to raise my hand. The combination of this belief and that desire are what caused me to decide to raise my hand. I would not feel relieved to learn that there is no guarantee that my belief and desire will cause a decision. If I learn that my belief and desire only have a 50% chance of causing the decision to raise my hand, I won't feel any freer; on the contrary, I'll feel weak-willed because the factors that would otherwise lead to making a decision don't ensure that I will decide. It's not fun to want to do so something and believe that it is the best thing to do, and still fail to decide to do it. I am not made any freer if my beliefs and desires do not ensure that a decision will be made.

6.59   I have some beliefs because of my interactions with the world and others because I have used my own abilities to think and to reason. Consider beliefs formed on the basis of interactions with the world. I believe that Jessica is at the opposite side of the room because I see her at the opposite side of the room. The time between when I see Jessica and when I form the belief that Jessica is at the opposite side of the room is not a time in which I want determinism to fail. Given that I see Jessica at the opposite side of the room, I want a guarantee that I will believe that Jessica is at the opposite side of the room. I don't want to see her there but still have a chance that I won't believe that she's there—or even worse, that there's some chance that

I will have a false belief that she isn't there. When I reason through some evidence, it is better for me if there is a guarantee that I will believe what the evidence tells me I should believe rather than it being somewhat left up to chance.

I also want at least some of my desires to be responsive to the world 6.60 too. I want to desire things because they are good things to desire, or at the very least, not bad things. Additionally, though, I want my desires, and my personality traits more generally, to have a kind of stability. I want my current personality traits—the ones I have at this moment—to be caused by the personality traits I had a few seconds ago. To sum up, I want how I think and feel now to be the result of how I thought and felt a few moments ago. That I might randomly change how I think or how I feel isn't reassuring. Think about what happens to Joshua—one minute he has sensible beverage preferences, and the next minute these unexpectedly change. I don't want this to happen to me—and I am no freer if it might.

When I think about this process of events that lead to my deciding to 6.61 raise my hand, I have a hard time seeing where it would be good for my freedom if causal determinism were to break down. I invite you to think about a situation in which you have made a decision, and then see for yourself whether there is some time during that process when you want causal determinism to break down.

If both causal determinism and causal indeterminism are incompatible 6.62 with our ever acting freely, then we never act freely. That we never act freely is a radical conclusion indeed. If we do sometimes act freely, there must be a flaw in the arguments that conclude that we don't. But what is that flaw?

6.7 Laws of Nature

Causal determinism is the thesis that the laws of nature and the past 6.63 collectively guarantee a unique future. In the previous sections, we mentioned laws of nature, but we haven't really examined what a law of nature is supposed to be. We are going to examine this here. To be clear, the question we are going to think about isn't the question of what the laws of nature are. To answer that question, we'd have to do a lot of physics, chemistry, biology, psychology, and so on. That would be a big task. Instead, the question we are going to think about is:

What is it to be a law of nature? (Recall once again the discussion of two sorts of questions in Section 1.5.)

6.64   In what follows, we will look at two types of theories of what it is to be a law of nature. These two types are *governing* theories and *regularity* theories. Let me illustrate this distinction by describing a very simple possible world. In this simple possible world, there are millions of objects in motion. Here are the regularities, that is, regular patterns of how objects are or are arranged, in this world: Objects that are a good distance from each other are darkly colored, and the further apart an object is from any other object, the darker it becomes; conversely, objects that are close to other objects are brightly colored. Objects maintain regular trajectories unless they bump into other objects, but when they do bump into other objects, they simply reverse direction.

6.65   We might wonder why there are these regularities. One explanation is that these regularities are *explained* by laws of nature. Governing theories of laws of nature say exactly that. According to governing theories, laws are what govern the patterns of the universe; they are what constrain and explain how objects change over time. The patterns are what they are because the laws are what they are. In a bit, we will examine one governing theory, namely, that laws are relations between universals.

6.66   Regularity theories deny that laws of nature explain the patterns or regularities. This is because, according to a regularity theory, laws of nature just are certain regularities. On this sort of view, all laws are regularities, but not every regularity is a law. Only regularities that satisfy certain conditions are laws, and different versions of the regularity theory disagree on what those conditions are. In a bit, we will examine one regularity theory, namely, *the best system theory*.

6.67   Here's another example to illustrate the difference between the two kinds of view. Consider a possible world in which Newtonian physics is the correct physics. One of the laws of Newtonian physics is that the force of an object is equal to its mass multiplied by its acceleration (that is, $F = ma$). And corresponding to this law is a regularity, that is, a regular pattern of how objects are or are arranged: each object is such that its force is equal to its mass times its acceleration. A governing theory of laws is a theory that says that laws of nature are what *explain* their corresponding regularities. On this sort of view, each object is such that the force of that object is equal to its mass multiplied by its acceleration *because* it is a law of nature that every object's force is equal to its mass multiplied by its acceleration. On the other hand, a regularity theory would say that the law just is this regularity.

We'll focus now on one version of the governing theory, namely the 6.68 theory that laws are special relations between universals.[2] As the name suggests, according to this view properties are universals, that is, properties are literally shared by more than one entity. (Recall the discussion of universals in Section 2.8.) A law of nature is also a universal. Specifically, it is a relation, but it is not a universal that relates objects to other objects. Instead, it is a relation that relates universals to universals. Recall the world in which Newtonian physics is true. On the view that we are considering, the law that F = ma is a relation that relates force, mass, acceleration, and maybe equality.

On this view, a law of nature is itself an entity in the metaphysics. In addi- 6.69 tion to objects and properties of objects, there are further things: the laws themselves. Let's consider an argument that this sort of entity exists. It might be useful to recall the arguments for absolute space and absolute time that we examined in Section 5.3, because the kind of argument for this theory of laws is very similar.

Here is the argument. The first premise is that there are highly general 6.70 patterns of how objects interact with each other and change over time, and these highly general patterns are not merely accidental regularities but rather the result of something that explains these patterns. The second premise is that the best candidate for being what explains these patterns is that there are entities, namely, laws of nature, and these entities govern how objects in space and time can be arranged. And so, provided that we are justified in believing that something exists when it is the best explanation for a phenomenon that needs explanation, we are justified in believing that laws of nature exist and that they govern how objects can be arranged.

Is this argument as good as the arguments for absolute space and abso- 6.71 lute time? One question you might have is how exactly a relation between universals manages to govern objects. Let's think about this question a bit.

Maybe it's clearer how absolute space and absolute time could govern the 6.72 objects within them. If absolute space exists, it is an object that has a geometric structure. For example, perhaps it is three dimensional. Objects can't be greater than three dimensional because there is no extra space, so to

---

[2] This view is defended by Armstrong, D.M., *What is a Law of Nature?* (Cambridge: Cambridge University Press, 1983). https://philpapers.org/rec/ARMWIA

speak, for that extra dimension of theirs to fit. More generally, objects in parts of space match the structure of that part of space: a spherical object is located in a spherical-shaped region of space. And the reason why things in space have the same geometrical features as the parts of space that they are located in is that things in space have those geometrical features *because* they are located in regions with those geometrical features. Similar remarks apply to absolute time: There can't be temporally circular objects if absolute time has the shape of a line. And an hour-long event takes place in—is located in—an hour of time.

6.73   But a relation between universals isn't a container that objects are in. And it doesn't seem to have a structure in the way that absolute space or time do. So how does a relation between universals govern the objects that instantiate those universals? If we can't answer this question, then it doesn't seem that relations between universals actually explain the patterns they allegedly govern. But if they don't actually explain the patterns that they allegedly govern, then the second premise of the argument for their existence is false.

6.74   Let's now discuss a regularity theory of laws, specifically, the best systems theory of laws. Remember, on a regularity theory of laws, laws of nature just are regularities that meet certain conditions. There have to be certain conditions, because not every regularity is a law of nature. Suppose it is true that no philosopher ever has more than three quarters in his or her pocket. This would be an odd regularity, but it wouldn't be a law of nature. So, if a regularity theory is true, the conditions that must be satisfied to be a law of nature need to imply that this odd regularity is not a law of nature.

6.75   According to the best systems theory of laws of nature, laws of nature are those regularities that are mentioned in the best system for the universe as a whole. The best system of a universe is the collection of descriptions of regularities that best balances being informative and being brief. Here's a way to get a handle on this idea. Suppose we want to describe what the universe is like, and we want to be as informative as we can. One maximally informative description of the universe would be a description that says of each object what features it has and how it relates to other objects. This is a maximally informative description, because it explicitly says everything that there is to say. But it is also maximally longwinded—it's not brief at all. Every object needs a name, every property or relation needs a corresponding predicate, and every fact needs a corresponding sentence. If there was some way to compress that information without significant loss, there would be a way to produce a highly informative description that was briefer. Describing regularities does just that.

Here's a really simplistic example to illustrate this idea. I'm going to give   6.76
you a longwinded description of a pretend universe. (It has way fewer things
in it in our universe. Otherwise, I'd die before finishing this book!) Here are
the objects in this pretend universe: a, b, c, d, e, f, g, h, i, j, k, l, m, n, and o.
Here is what they are like: a is red; a is a triangle; b is blue; b is a circle; c is
red; c is a triangle; d is yellow; d is a square; e is blue; e is a circle; f is red; f is
a triangle; g is yellow; g is a square; h is blue; h is a circle; i is yellow; i is a
square; j is red; j is a triangle; k is blue; k is a circle; l is yellow; l is square; m
is red; m is a triangle; n is yellow; n is a square; o is blue; o is a circle.

Man, that was tedious to write. And there are only 15 objects in this uni-   6.77
verse (forget about the question of whether the objects I mentioned compose anything!), and there are only six properties exemplified by anything
(ignore whether there are properties like being red or being green!). Here's
a way to compress that information: There are 15 objects, and an equal
number of them are red, blue, or yellow. Everything red is a triangle; everything blue is a circle; everything yellow is a square. If these propositions are
collectively the best way to balance informativeness and brevity, then these
are the laws of nature of this toy world.

Some information is lost in this compressed description. Specifically, the   6.78
compressed description doesn't say which objects have which properties.
But the compressed description is much more compact. We paid for this
compactness with the coin of information. But it was a good deal, especially
since which objects have which properties is not relevant to determining
what the laws of nature are. A law of nature, so to speak, doesn't care whether
it is Bob or it is Fred that has the negative charge; it cares only about how
negatively charged objects interact with each other and with other objects.
In the toy example, if a had been blue and a circle and b had been red and a
triangle, the regularities would be exactly the same. What is relevant aren't
the individuals that have the properties. Instead, the patterns of how properties are arranged are what matters to determining what the laws are.

If best systems theory of laws is true, then all possible worlds with the   6.79
same regularities occurring in them also have the same laws. In fact, this is
true of all regularity accounts of laws. This is an important difference
between the best system theory and governing theories of laws, such as the
relations between universals theory of laws. On a governing theory of laws,
there could be two possible worlds in which the exact same regularities
occur but that have different laws.

I'll illustrate this difference with another toy example involving two pos-   6.80
sible worlds that have the same type of objects in them. I'll call these objects

coins. In possible world w_1, there are ten coins, and they all have the property of *heads.* In possible world w_2, there ten coins and they all have the property of *heads.* There are no other objects or interesting properties in either world. If the regularity theory of laws is true, then both worlds have the same laws of nature. The regularity theory implies that w_1 and w_2 have the same laws because on that theory, laws just are regularities, and the same regularities occur at w_1 and w_2. In this case, that law is that every coin is heads. But, if a governing theory of laws is true, the worlds might have different laws. World w_1 may have the following law: every coin is heads. But world w_2 might have a different law: every coin has a 50% chance of being heads and a 50% of being tails. Given this law of nature, the pattern that occurs in w_2 is very unlikely—the chance is 1/1024 of it happening—but it could be a law that the objective probabilities are 50% for each coin.

6.81   And this points to a second difference between regularity theories and governing theories. Let's add a third world into the mix: in w_3, there are ten coins, and they all have the property of *tails.* No other objects exist in w_3, and no other interesting property is exemplified. The regularity theory implies that w_1 and w_2 have the same laws and that w_2 and w_3 have different laws. (If the best systems theory of laws is true, then the law of nature for w_3 is that every coin is tails.) But the governing theory not only allows that w_1 and w_2 might have different laws, for the reason we just discussed in the last paragraph. A governing theory also allows that w_2 and w_3 might have the same laws! This is that second difference between a regularity theory and a governing theory. Think about our toy example again. For all that has been said, given a governing theory of laws, a law of nature for w_3 might be that every coin has a 50% chance of being heads and a 50% of being tails. Given this law of nature, the pattern that occurs in w_3 is also very unlikely—the chance is also 1/1024 of it happening—but it could be a law that the objective probabilities are 50% for each coin. Worlds w_2 and w_3 might have the same laws of nature, and those laws might in turn yield very different patterns in what happens in those worlds.

6.82   In general, indeterministic laws and deterministic laws should be able to yield the same regularities. But no regularity theory can make sense of this—since if two worlds have the same regularities, then they have the same laws.

6.83   These are important metaphysical differences between governing theories and regularity theories. The friend of the best systems theory might argue that these differences provide a reason to accept her theory instead of a governing theory. The first premise is that, if the governing theory of laws is true, then there is no way for us to know what the laws of nature are, even in principle. Why might this be true? Recall that, given the governing theory, possible worlds with the same regularities can have different laws. And possible worlds with different regularities can have the same laws. So, all the facts about what regularities occur don't ensure what the laws are. We could know all the facts about what regularities occur, but still have to then make a further assumption about what the laws are. And this further assumption would be just that—an assumption, rather than knowledge.

The second premise is that there is a way for us to know what the laws of 6.84 nature are. The second premise doesn't say that it will be easy to find out what they are. It only says that there is a way to find out what they are. This way is to engage in the kind of scientific inquiry that we are currently engaged in. The more science we do, the better positioned we are to have knowledge of what the regularities actually are. And if laws of nature just are certain regularities—as a regularity theory of laws implies—then once we know what regularities occur, we will be in a position to know what the laws are.

The first and the second premise jointly imply the conclusion that no 6.85 governing theory of laws is true. Is this a good argument against the governing theory of laws? I'm going to leave you with this question.

We've spent a decent amount of time getting clearer on what a law of 6.86 nature is supposed to be. We did this not only because the topic is independently interesting—it is!—but also because we hoped that thinking about what it is to be a law of nature might help us to get clearer on whether causal determinism would threaten our freedom. I'll close this section by examining this issue a bit more.

So, let's once more temporarily assume causal determinism. Remember 6.87 that the causal determination argument began with two premises, which were the Control Principle and No Uncontrolled Guarantees. We noted (in Section 6.2) that the Control Principle and No Uncontrolled Guarantees together imply that you freely perform an action only if every fact that guarantees that you perform that action is also under your control. The third premise of the causal determination argument is that there are facts outside your control—specifically, facts about the past and the laws of nature—that collectively guarantee that you do what you do. The conclusion of the argument is that you never act freely.

If either the past or the laws of nature were at least partially under your 6.88 control, then this third premise would be false. The past is not even partially under your control, unless you have a time machine lying around the house or parked in your garage. But what about the laws of nature? If a governing theory of laws is true, it really is hard to see how you could have even partial control over the laws. But what if a regularity theory of laws is true?

6.89   If a regularity theory of laws is true, then laws of nature just are certain regularities. If you have partial control over which of those regularities occur, then you have partial control over the laws of nature. Here is an example of a regularity that seems like someone has control over whether it occurs: Whenever I teach a class, during the time that I am teaching, all the students remain sitting. All it would take for this regularity to fail to occur would be for one student to stand while I teach. This example doesn't show that the laws of nature are under our partial control. All it does is make salient that they might be. And if they are, the causal determination argument has a false third premise. I invite you to think further about whether this is the case.

6.8 Doing Metaphysics

Are there other kinds of determinism besides causal determinism? Do these other kinds also pose a potential problem for our having free will?

What is our evidence for believing that we have free will? How could we prove that we sometimes act freely?

Suppose you freely do an action. Does it follow that you are morally responsible for doing that action? Even if freely doing an action is necessary for you to be morally responsible for doing it, is freely doing that action also sufficient for you to be morally responsible for doing it? If freedom isn't sufficient for moral responsibility, what else is required?

Would a governing view of laws in which they were relations between tropes (instead of universals) make sense? Would it be a good theory?

When are we justified in believing that a pattern is a law of nature as opposed to a mere regularity?

Further Reading

Helen Beebee (2013) *Free Will: An Introduction*, New York: Palgrave Macmillan.
This is a very helpful overview of the main philosophical problems concerning free will.

John Martin Fischer (1994) *The Metaphysics of Free Will: An Essay on Control*, Oxford: Blackwell.

An important book about the nature of free will.

Peter van Inwagen (1983) *An Essay on Free Will*, Oxford: Clarendon Press.

This agenda-setting book reignited the debate over free will near the end of the 20th century.

7

META-METAPHYSICS

7.1 Getting More Meta

7.1 Every human activity generates philosophical questions. That is why philosophy is such an awesome and all-encompassing field. For each human activity, X, there either is or there could be a corresponding subfield of philosophy—*the philosophy of X*—devoted to studying the philosophical questions that come when one thinks carefully about X. The more people value a given activity, the more likely it is that there is an actually existing subfield focusing on the philosophy of that activity. This is the reason one can read about the philosophy of science, the philosophy of religion, the philosophy of sport, the philosophy of art, the philosophy of language, and so on. Every human activity generates philosophical questions, including the activity of pursuing philosophical questions!

7.2 You have *done* metaphysics as you read the previous chapters in this book and carefully thought about the arguments, questions, and theories discussed in them. We'll now turn to questions in the philosophy of metaphysics, also known as *meta-metaphysics*. Meta-metaphysics is devoted to thinking through questions raised by the activity of thinking about metaphysics. I'm going to discuss in this chapter some questions about the epistemology (in the Section 7.2), language (in Section 7.3), metaphysics (in Section 7.4), and ethics (in Section 7.5) of metaphysical inquiry. I won't give you a comprehensive overview of these topics. Rather, in each section, I will focus on one important question. I hope that this will give you a sense of the kinds of meta-metaphysical questions that one might contemplate.

This Is Metaphysics: An Introduction, First Edition. Kris McDaniel.
© 2020 John Wiley & Sons, Inc. Published 2020 by John Wiley & Sons, Inc.

Here is a more concrete overview of what we are going to talk about. In 7.3
Section 7.2, we'll focus on whether and how we know certain metaphysical
principles that can be used to constrain other metaphysical debates. In
Section 7.3, we'll examine whether some of the key metaphysical expressions, such as "exists" and "there is," have exactly one meaning or whether
they are ambiguous, and if they are ambiguous, what possible consequences
this might have for metaphysical theorizing. In Section 7.4, we will discuss
the metaphysics of doing metaphysics. More specifically, we will investigate
whether the activity of doing metaphysics makes sense only if certain metaphysical claims are true. Finally, in Section 7.5, we will discuss the ethics of
metaphysical inquiry. There, we'll think about whether metaphysical thinking is valuable or worthwhile. Given how abstract metaphysical thinking
can be, and often how far removed it can seem to be from what one might
regard as "practical" and "useful," whether engaging in metaphysical thinking is worth doing might seem like an especially challenging question to
answer.

7.2 The Epistemology of Metaphysics

Here's the overview of what happens in this section. Although metaphysi- 7.4
cians love nothing more than to disagree with each other, there is widespread agreement among metaphysicians about which answers to
metaphysical questions are genuine contenders and which are not. This
widespread agreement is tacit—it lurks in the background of metaphysical
debates. But it still requires explanation. Why is it that, despite so much
manifest disagreement, there is so much unspoken agreement? We will
explore the hypothesis that there are tacitly accepted principles that constrain metaphysical debate. We will then look at four theories about the
epistemic status of these principles. These theories say whether we know
these tacitly accepted principles and, if we do know these principles, how
we know them.

We have discussed several contentious and long-standing disputes about 7.5
metaphysics in the previous chapters. There are a lot of smart people working hard on these topics. So why is there still so much disagreement? And,
given that there is so much disagreement, how confident should we be in
our metaphysical beliefs?

Disagreement is troubling. If we have good evidence for metaphysical 7.6
theories, shouldn't we expect more agreement than we find? Consider your

evidence for the claim that there are plants. There is widespread agreement that there are plants. Most of us eat plants. Some of us eat only things that come from plants. Some of us garden. Almost no one disbelieves in plants. The evidence for the existence of plants is strong, and this is why there is so much agreement about whether there are plants. In general, when there is very good evidence for P that is publicly available for anyone who is interested in whether P, then widespread agreement about the truth of P is unsurprising. When there is very little evidence for P, it is unsurprising when there is also very little agreement about whether P is true. (Although perhaps it is surprising that people do not simply remain agnostic about the issue in question.)

7.7   That said, disagreement over metaphysical questions takes place against a background of widespread agreement. This background is, well, in the background—present, but only rarely is it explicitly talked about or consciously noticed. But we can bring it to the foreground by explicitly talking about it. Let's do that. Consider, for example, the question of when composition occurs, which we discussed in Chapter 3. We considered a number of interesting answers to this question. We considered the view that composition occurs when the putative parts are sufficiently stuck together; the view that composition occurs when the putative parts from a living being; the view that composition always occurs; and the view that composition never occurs. But we never considered any of the following theories: a bunch of objects compose a whole if and only if they are in the state of New Jersey; a bunch of objects compose a whole if and only if there are exactly 17 of those objects; a bunch of objects compose a whole if and only if they are some of my favorite things.

7.8   These alleged answers are non-starters. No one thinks otherwise. No one ever even bothers to formulate theories like them—they don't even get a chance to be refuted. Theories like these live brief lives of quiet desperation only to be crushed to death under the weight of their own absurdity. More generally, for any given metaphysical question, there is a huge variety of alleged answers for which there is widespread agreement that they are non-starters. (For a second example, consider the various views in the philosophy of time we considered: the Static View, the Growing Block View, Presentism, and so on. We never considered the view that all times are equally real except for the time that is exactly five minutes from now, which is the sole time at which nothing exists.)

7.9   Philosophical disagreement about the views on the table takes place against a massive background of unacknowledged or unspoken agreement about which views even deserve a place at the table. Here is an apparent data point: we come to philosophical disagreement already knowing that some alleged answers to philosophical questions are incorrect. If so, how do we know that they are incorrect?

Suppose that this apparent knowledge is real knowledge. Our knowledge   7.10 that these theories are false is not basic knowledge, but rather rests on more general considerations or principles that we know and that entail that these views are false. The tricky thing is to figure out what they are. There is probably more than one such consideration or principle at play when we rule out various non-starter theories. Consider the view that all times are equally real except for the moment exactly five minutes from now. This theory is incredibly arbitrary: Why is the time exactly five minutes from now the one that doesn't exist rather than exactly four minutes from now or six minutes for now, or any other fixed distance from the present moment? We know that no good answer to this question is forthcoming. If this theory were true, reality would have an inexplicable gap, and we recoil at any theory that tells us that reality is like this.

It looks like one of the background beliefs that clears the table before the   7.11 table is set is that we should prefer theories that do not imply that reality is arbitrary over those that do. Let's call this background belief *the arbitrariness constraint*. This constraint itself raises tough questions. Arbitrariness seems to be something that can come in degrees: some theories might be more arbitrary than others. Given this fact, it would be good if we had some sort of means to measure arbitrariness. Do we? In general, can we come up with a theory that will help judge when other theories are arbitrary or do we have to rely on gut intuitions about individual theories on a case by case basis? Is arbitrariness something that we recognize when we see it even if we cannot actually define it?

Let's say a *basic constraint* on which theory to believe is one that is not   7.12 justified or explained by some other constraint. That you should reject arbitrary theories in the philosophy of time is not a basic constraint, but that you should reject arbitrary theories in general might be. So, is the arbitrariness constraint a basic constraint? If it is not a basic constraint, what is the deeper constraint that justifies or explains it?

Some philosophers think that, in general, one should prefer simpler the-   7.13 ories to more complex theories other things being equal, that is, when the simpler theories explain the same data as well as the complex theories do. Let's call this constraint *the simplicity constraint*. (It is sometimes called

"Ockham's Razor.") If it is necessary that arbitrary theories are always more complex than some less arbitrary theory that explains the same data, then the arbitrariness constraint is a consequence of the simplicity constraint—and so the simplicity constraint would explain the arbitrariness constraint.

7.14   But are arbitrary theories always more complex than they need to be? Consider one of the arbitrary theories already mentioned: In what way is the theory that all times are equally real except for the moment five minutes from now more complex than the theories that are on the table? Compare this theory to Presentism. Both Presentism and the "five minutes from now theory" say that there is a metaphysically unique moment. Presentism says that everything that exists, exists at this special moment; the five minutes from now theory says that nothing exists at this special moment. They are different theories, and the five minutes from now theory is arbitrary in a way that Presentism doesn't seem to be, but is the five minutes from now theory more complex than Presentism? If it isn't more complex than Presentism, but it is more arbitrary, then the arbitrariness constraint is not explained by the simplicity constraint.

7.15   Maybe things go the other way: could the arbitrariness constraint explain the simplicity constraint? If unneeded complexity always guarantees arbitrariness, then it is plausible that the arbitrariness constraint does explain the simplicity constraint. Here's an argument for the conclusion that unneeded complexity does guarantee arbitrariness. Suppose that there is a series of theories, T_1 through T_n, each of which equally explains the data that they are supposed to explain. Each member of this series is more complex than its predecessor. So, T_n is the most complex theory, T_{n-1} is the second most complex theory, T_3 is more complex than T_2, and T_1 is the simplest theory. But suppose T_8 is the correct theory. Then reality is arbitrarily complex. In general, complexity comes in degrees, but why did reality "prefer" this degree of complexity rather than some other degree in its near neighborhood? Remember that T_1 explains the data just as well as T_8, and as well any other theory in the series of theories under consideration. And if these theories are meant to be fundamental metaphysical theories, then, by their own lights, there will be no deeper answers as to why reality is this way rather than some other way. And in this case, it would be completely unexplainable why reality is a certain degree of complexity rather than another—and so reality would be arbitrary. However, if T_1 were true, reality wouldn't be arbitrary in that way, since T_1 is an endpoint in the series rather than some arbitrary point in the middle.

This is an interesting argument. However, there is a snag: there are two 7.16
endpoints to the series we have been considering, and T_n is the other one.
Remember, T_n is the most complex theory. Perhaps we should prefer T_1 over
all the theories in the middle of the series, since otherwise reality would be
arbitrary. But why prefer one endpoint (T_1) over another (T_n)? (Why
shouldn't we prefer the most complex theory to the simplest theory?) If we
can't come up with a good answer to this question, we should worry that the
prospects for fully explaining the simplicity constraint by way of the arbitrariness constraint aren't good.

The snag assumes that there is a most complex theory. But what if there 7.17
never is a most complex theory that explains the data? What if, instead, for
any given theory, there is always a more complex but otherwise equally
explanatory theory? (If this is so, then T_n was only an apparent endpoint.) If
this is the case, then, although there is a simplest theory that explains the
data, there is no maximally complex theory that does. And if there is no
maximally complex theory that explains the data, then there is only one
endpoint to the series, namely, T_1, which is the simplest theory. And any
other theory after T_1 is such that reality would be arbitrarily complex if it
were true.

We've seen attempts to explain the arbitrariness constraint in terms of the 7.18
simplicity constraint, and vice-versa. If neither explanation works, then
either they are both explained by a third principle (but what is that principle?), or there are (at least) two independent and basic constraints that help
us eliminate possible answers to metaphysical questions.

There might be further basic constraints beyond them as well. One
important job for philosophers investigating the epistemology of metaphysics is to discover what these other constraints are. An interesting and
somewhat troubling possibility is that, if there is more than one basic constraint, then the basic constraints might in some cases pull us in different
directions. If that can happen, then a second important job for philosophers
investigating the epistemology of metaphysics is to discover how to weigh
the constraints against each other.

I've tried to get clearer on what might be basic constraints on meta- 7.19
physical theories. I'm now going to address the question of how we know
these constraints are true. For the sake of both specificity and brevity, I'll
focus on the arbitrariness constraint and the question of how we know this
constraint. I'm going to provisionally assume that what I say about it would
be equally applicable to the other basic constraints, whatever they are. But
this provisional assumption should be critically scrutinized too—maybe

knowledge of different basic constraints is explained in different ways. I'm going to focus on three theories that try to explain how we know the arbitrariness constraint: an *empiricist theory*, a *transcendental theory*, and a *default knowability* theory. We'll address these theories in that order, but prior to doing so, I will briefly mention a more skeptical response to this question that I will call *the pragmatic theory*.

7.20   According to the pragmatic theory, we don't actually know that the arbitrariness constraint is true. Rather, we have little to no evidence that it is true. Instead, we accept it for a purely practical reason. Developing and defending theories is a tough business, and for any phenomenon, there are in principle a ton of different theories—probably, infinitely many theories—that we could develop to explain the occurrence of that phenomenon. That is too many theories to assess. We need some way to make the job of developing and then assessing theories doable. So, we must have a way to whittle down a large swathe of theories before we start assessing the evidence for the remaining theories. We don't actually know that the arbitrariness constraint is true. We simply act like we know that it is true because if we didn't, we would be overwhelmed by all the options we'd have to consider.

7.21   The pragmatic theory is a skeptical theory because it denies the phenomenon that the other theories we are going to look at try to explain. This phenomenon is that we know that the arbitrary theories that we have discussed are false. This is because you can't acquire knowledge of a claim—like the claim that the "five minutes from now" theory is false—if your sole reason for believing that claim is that it follows from a more general principle that you lack evidence for believing.

7.22   Even though it is a skeptical theory, the pragmatic theory needs to be taken seriously, especially if no good explanation for how we know the arbitrariness constraint is forthcoming. That said, I am not going to discuss the pragmatic theory more in this section. The question of how we might have the knowledge that we seem to have is at least as interesting as the question of how to convince the skeptic that we do in fact have that knowledge. I'm going to focus on the former question rather than the latter.

7.23   The three answers to this question that we will discuss are *the empiricist theory*, *the transcendental theory*, and *the default knowability theory*.

7.24   According to the empiricist theory, we learn that the arbitrary constraint is true through experience. The big question for the empiricist theory is: What experiences did we have that taught us that the arbitrariness constraint is true? Experience can teach us a lot: that riding a bike to work is fun, that snarling dogs often bite, and that cookies are usually delicious. Focus on the last example. I can directly perceive cookies. I can touch, smell, and even taste them. And I can recall previous occasions in which I have tasted cookies and found that they are delicious. I have heard from the testimony of other people who have tasted cookies and reported that they are delicious. All these experiences form the basis for my knowledge that cookies are usually delicious.

But we don't have direct perceptions of reality as a whole in which we just 7.25
see that reality is not arbitrary. So, if we don't learn that reality is arbitrary directly from perception, how do we learn this? How could we learn from experience that reality is not arbitrary?

Perhaps here's how. We have a lot of scientific knowledge, that is, knowledge 7.26
about which scientific theories are either true or are at least close to being true. Much of our scientific knowledge is acquired by experience construed broadly, for example, by way of observations of lab results, computer-assisted measurements, and so on. If our most successful scientific theories tell us that the portions of reality that they study are not arbitrary, and we know that these scientific theories are true by way of experience, don't we then have some evidence gotten from experience that reality is not arbitrary?

Maybe. There are a couple of reasons to be cautious. First, when a scien- 7.27
tist tries to figure out which theory to believe, does she rely solely on her experiences alone to tell her what to believe? Or does she also appeal to principles like "pick the simplest theory among those that are equally supported by experience" or "prefer theories that minimize arbitrariness"? Probably she appeals to principles of this sort. In short, scientists also seem to make use of principles that constrain which theories to adopt. If this is the case, does the success of the theory in question help justify a presupposition of the people who ended up adopting the theory?

Second, what should we say about the fact that some of the fundamental 7.28
constants of our universe seem to be arbitrary? For example, perhaps the speed of light is a fundamental constant. But why is the speed of light the speed that it is rather than plus or minus a small difference? Perhaps the apparent arbitrariness here is a reason to think there is some (non-arbitrary) explanation for the speed of light. But if we can't find it, we might have to consider whether science can show us that some aspects of reality are arbitrary. Scientific investigation might then threaten the arbitrariness constraint rather than support it! On the other hand, some scientists are motivated by apparent arbitrariness to search for deeper theories that would explain why these values for apparently fundamental constants are not

arbitrary; perhaps this suggests that these scientists believe that reality is non-arbitrary prior to learning whether it is from experience.

7.29   Third, even if scientific investigation provides additional support for the claim that reality is not arbitrary, it is not clear that it is the only source of evidence for that claim. Suppose someone in the year 500 B.C.E. considered the question of when composition occurs, and then briefly considered the ludicrous answer that it occurs only when the objects are within exactly five feet of each other. (Presumably, they would use some other unit of measurement—such as 10 hēmipodia?) Being a sensible fellow, our ancient philosopher rejected this theory out of hand because reality would be arbitrary if it were true. Is his belief that reality is not arbitrary justified by his evidence? If it is justified by his evidence, since he knows nothing about contemporary science—and, really, he might not know anything about science period—then his justification for the arbitrariness constraint doesn't depend on the results of empirical science.

7.30   If scientists presuppose rather than prove the arbitrariness constraint, and someone in 500 B.C.E. could know that the arbitrariness constraint is true, then the arbitrariness constraint is not something that is discovered through experience. Rather, it is something that we know in some sense *prior* to experience. But even if the arbitrariness constraint is known prior to experience, the arbitrariness constraint is still something that we can use to help evaluate the data that we do get from experience, and this is why a scientist might appeal to it as she develops theories about the world.

7.31   Let's get clearer on this idea of knowing something prior to experience. Philosophers use the phrase "a priori" to stand for this idea. Here is a rough definition: A person S is *a priori justified* in believing a proposition P if and only if S has evidence for believing P but this evidence does not depend on any particular set of experiences S has.

7.32   Maybe we are a priori justified in believing the arbitrariness constraint. But if we have a priori justification for the arbitrariness constraint, the next question is, how is this possible? How can we know or be justified in believing that reality is non-arbitrary independent of experience? In general, how can we have a priori knowledge?

7.33   This is the kind of question that worried one of the most important philosophers of all time, Immanuel Kant (1724–1804), who wrote a whole book called *the Critique of Pure Reason* devoted to answering it.[1] (And then

---

[1] http://plato.stanford.edu/entries/kant/

he wrote further books designed to solidify or amplify the accomplishments of *the Critique of Pure Reason*.) Kant distinguished between two kinds of a priori beliefs, which he called *analytic a priori judgments* and *synthetic a priori judgments*. For our purposes, we can understand true analytic judgments to be those that are true by definition. Consider the judgment that all bachelors are unmarried. This judgment is true by definition: since "bachelor" just means the same thing as "adult, unmarried, eligible to be married, human male," the judgment that all bachelors are unmarried is by definition equivalent to the judgment that all adult unmarried, eligible to be married, human males are unmarried. And *that* judgment is just a truth of logic: it's an instance of the more general pattern that all As that are Bs, Cs, Ds, and Es are Bs. In general, for our purposes we can think of true analytic judgments as those judgments that reduce to truths of logic when you substitute synonyms for synonyms. (This is not Kant's own view of analytic judgments but it is good enough for our purposes.) Synthetic judgments can't be reduced to truths of logic in this way.

(There are false analytic judgments as well. These are judgments that are   7.34 false by definition; an example of a false analytic judgment is the judgment that a triangle has four angles. False synthetic judgments are those that are false, but not false by definition.)

Kant thought that there is no deep mystery in how we can have a priori   7.35 knowledge of analytic truths. We can know a judgment that is true by definition simply by thinking through the definitions employed in that judgment. No further experience is required. We don't need to spend the time or the money to survey bachelors in various countries in order to assess whether each of these bachelors is unmarried. So, we have analytic a priori knowledge.

Kant also thought that we have synthetic a priori knowledge. He thought   7.36 that mathematical judgments (such as $7/2 = 3.5$) are synthetic a priori judgments. Moreover, the kinds of synthetic judgments we can know a priori are not limited to mathematics. According to Kant, the claim that every event has a cause is not true merely by definition: you don't contradict yourself when you say that some event doesn't have a cause. So, it is a synthetic judgment, but it is one we can know a priori.[2] So, we do have synthetic a priori knowledge, but it is not clear how this is possible. Since

---

[2] This is the second analogy of Kant's *Critique of Pure Reason*. See http://staffweb. hkbu.edu.hk/ppp/cpr/toc.html

synthetic a priori judgments are not true by definition, we can't learn that they are true simply by thinking about definitions. So, how can we have synthetic a prior knowledge?

7.37   Unsurprisingly, the details of Kant's own answer to this question are a matter of intense scholarly controversy. (Do you know how many pages have been written on this since *Critique of Pure Reason* was first published? At least a million is a conservative guess!) I'm wisely not going to participate in this controversy here. Instead, I am going to explore an answer that is Kantian in spirit and leave the interpretation of Kant to the experts.

7.38   The Kantian answer is that a synthetic judgment *J* can be known a priori if and only if it is a necessary condition on our having any sort of experience at all that *J* is true. In other words, unless *J* were true, we couldn't have any experience. Since we know that we can have experiences (as we actually do have experiences), *J* must be true.

7.39   Suppose some event doesn't have a cause. Must all people fail to have experiences given that supposition? Or suppose that reality is arbitrary. Are experiences impossible in an arbitrary world? These rhetorical questions by no means show that the Kantian answer is false—how could a rhetorical question do that? Rather, they indicate that the Kantian has a lot of work to do. (Kant was more than happy to take on this job.)

7.40   Regardless, this kind of proof won't by itself answer the question of *how* we can know the arbitrariness constraint a priori. At most, it will tell us that we do in fact know it. In order to figure out *how* we could know the arbitrariness constraint, we'll need to take a detour from our discussion of the epistemology of metaphysics and instead consider the metaphysics of epistemology! The question we will look at is this: What must we be like and what must reality be like in order for us to be able to know a priori that reality is not arbitrary?

7.41   A Kantian answer to this question is that, in order for us to know a priori that reality is not arbitrary, the fact that reality is non-arbitrary must in some way depend on us. This is the transcendental theory. Kant says in the *Critique of Pure Reason* that reason has insight only to that which it produces in accordance with a plan of its own design.[3] If we buy into this Kantian idea, then we know that reality is not arbitrary because somehow we have made it non-arbitrary. Independent of us, reality is neither arbitrary nor non-arbitrary. (But how did we make reality non-arbitrary? This is the next profoundly

---

[3] He says this in B: xiii. http://staffweb.hkbu.edu.hk/ppp/cpr/toc.html (it's P 020 here).

difficult question for the Kantian to consider! We didn't make reality non-arbitrary via some choice we each made. No one woke up one morning and decided that reality should be non-arbitrary.)

The implications of the Kantian idea that we make reality non-arbitrary 7.42
are wide-ranging: there are major consequences if it is true for almost all the metaphysical questions we've talked about in this book. We might have thought that whether reality is arbitrary or not has nothing to do with us. But on the Kantian idea, somehow facts about us are what make reality non-arbitrary.

You might be concerned at this point. We are parts of reality. We aren't 7.43
things standing somehow outside of reality. So, the arbitrariness constraint applies to us too! Then how can we make reality itself non-arbitrary? Behind this question lies an objection to the Kantian idea. (The objection is similar to the one against the Mind-Dependence Theory of Composition that we discussed in Section 3.3.) Here's a statement of this objection. The first premise is that facts about us obtain only if and partly because they are not arbitrary. The second premise is that, if facts about us obtain only if and partly because they are not arbitrary, then facts about us cannot explain the arbitrariness constraint. This is because explanations can't be circular, not even partly. The conclusion is that facts about us cannot explain the arbitrariness constraint. But if facts about us can't explain the arbitrariness constraint, then the Kantian idea is not true.

Let me offer for consideration one more alternative explanation for how 7.44
we know that reality is non-arbitrary. This is the *default knowability theory*. The default knowability theory is in many ways diametrically opposed to the Kantian answer that we've been discussing. The Kantian answer is driven by the thought that synthetic a priori knowledge of the world is a cognitive achievement whose apparent difficulty is so impressive that it requires a powerful explanation. But on the default knowability theory, certain claims are actually very easy to know.

Let's say that a proposition P is *default knowable* for a person S if and 7.45
only if all that it takes for S to know that P is that (i) S believes P, (ii) P is true, and (iii) S is not aware of reasons to think that P is false. Here's an illustration of this idea. Consider the proposition that you see a book in front of you. You believe that you see a book in front of you, because you are reading this book right now, and you are aware that you are reading this book. It's true that you see a book in front of you. Unless you are aware of some reason to think that you are not seeing a book in front of you—are you aware of such a reason?—you know that you are seeing a

book in front of you. You don't have to have fancy reasons to believe that you see a book in front of you. You don't need to able to articulate a logically valid argument for the conclusion that you are seeing a book in front of you. It's not much of an achievement to know that you see a book in front of you. Propositions about what you perceive are default knowable for you.

7.46   Maybe there are other default knowable propositions besides those about what you perceive. Maybe among the default knowable beliefs are the basic synthetic a priori propositions that we use when theorizing about reality in general. The default knowability theory is the theory that the belief that reality is non-arbitrary is default knowable for us. You can know that reality is non-arbitrary simply if you believe that it is, it's true that it is, and you don't have reasons to think that it isn't.

7.47   Let's consider what can be said in favor of the default knowability theory. One way one might try to get you to accept that the arbitrariness constraint is default knowable is to point out that there are other very general claims that we know about reality, but for which it is hard to see how we know them unless these general claims are also default knowable.

7.48   Here are two possible examples. The first example is the so-called principle of induction, which is that similar causes will produce similar effects. How do we know that from similar causes will come similar effects? We either know this by experience or we know it a priori. Ok, how do we know it by experience? We could cite the fact that all the times in the past in which we have assumed that similar causes will produce similar effects, we have arrived at successful theories, and so next time we assume that similar causes produce similar effects, we also will arrive at a successful theory. But when we cite these facts, we are also assuming that similar causes will produce similar effects. (The similar cause in these cases is the common assumption we make each time and the similar effects are the purportedly successful theories.) This is what we were trying to prove! So at least on the face of it, any attempt to prove the principle of induction simply by appealing to experience will be circular. (Note that this objection is similar to the objection to the empiricist theory of how we know the non-arbitrariness constraint.) If any attempt to prove the principle of induction simply by appealing to experience will be circular, then we don't know the principle of induction via experience. And if we don't know the principle of induction via experience, then either we don't know that similar causes produce similar effects or our knowledge that similar causes will produce similar effects is justified a priori.

The second example is the claim that we discussed extensively in 7.49 Chapter 1, namely, that there are objectively better and worse ways of classifying objects. Although we need experience to tell us *which* ways are objectively better or worse, the presumption that there are ways that are objectively better or worse seems to be *a priori*. And, as we discussed in Section 1.4, we might need to assume that things do objectively belong together in order to make sense of induction.

The principle of induction, the claim that there are objectively better and 7.50 worse ways of classifying objects, and the arbitrariness constraint are each very general claims about how reality must be structured. Each claim looks, on the face of it, to be a priori. It is hard to see though how any of them could be *demonstrated* or *proved* a priori, which suggests (but does not itself prove) that we know them a priori only because they are default knowable.

These reflections have certainly generated a lot of questions. Here were 7.51 the main beats so far. First, if we do have a lot of metaphysical knowledge, the fact that we do needs to be explained in some way. Second, there are several ways to try to explain how we could have a lot of metaphysical knowledge. But, third, epistemology isn't any easier than metaphysics!

I'll conclude this section with one last question. How well will common- 7.52 sensical views about metaphysical topics survive a confrontation with the basic background constraints, once those constraints are made explicit? My suspicion is that, if we carefully inspect what common sense has to say about, for example, when some objects compose a whole, we'll see that the metaphysical theory that best fits what seems to be commonsense is itself arbitrary, overly complex, and perhaps somewhat silly as well. If this is right, then it might be that whatever principles we employ to eliminate from consideration the absurd theories discussed earlier about when composition occurs will also rule out the metaphysical theory of common sense. That might be a disquieting result.

7.3 The Philosophy of Language of Metaphysics

If you want to do philosophy with someone other than yourself, you've got 7.53 to use language to express philosophical ideas, arguments, and questions. This fact provides a sufficient reason for philosophers to be particularly careful about the words they use when engaging with each other. We are going to focus here on the word "exists," a word that has frequently appeared throughout this book. We are also going to talk here about some related phrases, such as "there is" and "being." Among the questions we are going to ask are: Are these words or phrases univocal or are they ambiguous? And do each of these words or phrases amount to the same thing, or are there important differences between them? These are important questions for metaphysicians to think about, since they are intimately concerned with the question of what exists.

7.54   Here's one view: To say that x exists is just to say that there is something that is identical to x. On this view, "exists" just means the same thing as "is identical to something." So, if someone says, "Kris exists," what she says means the same thing as "There is something identical to Kris." This view is often credited to the philosopher W.V.O. Quine. We'll call it *Quineanism* in his honor.

7.55   How plausible is this claim about the meaning of "exists"? One nice thing about Quineanism is that it provides a very simple and elegant explanation of how the meanings of "there is" and "exists" are related to each other. And this simple explanation seems to be confirmed by the fact that there doesn't seem to be a psychological difference between inquiring into whether something exists and inquiring into whether there are things of that sort. Consider a scientist trying to figure out whether she should believe in gravitons. She might ask herself, "Do gravitons exist?," but she might also ask herself, "Are there any gravitons?" Won't any evidence for the existence of gravitons also be evidence that there are gravitons, and vice versa? For a homier example, suppose you are at a party and in an existential frame of mind you plead, "Does there exist any beer here?" Surely you will be satisfied when you are told that some beer is in the fridge. You are satisfied because all that there is for beer to exist here is for some beer to be here. In general, if there is no real difference between asking whether an F exists and asking whether there are Fs, then this must be because "exists" is defined in terms of "there is" in the way suggested here.

7.56   Quineanism is a plausible semantic theory about the meaning of the word "exists." But here's a question worth considering. Are there things that don't exist? It seems that the answer is yes. Santa Claus doesn't exist. Spider-Man doesn't exist. So, there are at least two things that don't exist. That is, there is something (Santa Claus) that doesn't exist and something else (Spider-Man) that also doesn't exist, but Santa Claus and Spider-Man are not identical with each other. Spider-Man is of course self-identical, as everything is. So, Spider-Man, who doesn't exist, is identical with himself, and hence is identical with something. If "x exists" simply meant "something is identical to x," we'd have to say that Santa Claus and Spider-Man both exist.

If there are things that don't exist, then "x exists" doesn't simply mean "something is identical to x," and so Quineanism is false.

One of the most famous (among philosophers, anyway) defenders of the view that there are non-existent objects is Alexius Meinong.[4] (He also has one of the most awesome names in the history of philosophy.) Meinong argued that since thoughts about fictional objects such as Spider-Man are about something, there is something that these thoughts are about, namely, Spider-Man. He also argued that there are merely possible objects (like those discussed in Section 4.7) but they don't exist. Because Meinong was such a prominent defender of them, the view that there are non-existent objects—*Meinongianism*—was named after him.

How could the Quinean respond to the Meinongian objection that some things do not exist? One could confront this objection head-on by denying that something is identical with Santa Claus. That is, not only does Santa Claus not exist, but also there is no Santa Claus. The problem with this response is that we also seem to count non-existent objects. If there is no Santa Claus, there aren't his reindeer either. How many reindeer was Santa supposed to have anyway? There's Rudolph, and Donner and Blitzen, and I'm pretty sure that one of them is called "Dancer." There are at least four of them, right? But if there are at least four of them, then there are some things that we are counting. (If there are at least four things that are F, then there are Fs.) Similarly, if there is no Spider-Man, then there are none of the bad guys that he is depicted as fighting: no Doctor Octopus, no Green Goblin, no Morlun, and so on. But Spider-Man has a lot of enemies—including at least the three I just mentioned! So, there are some things that are Spider-Man's enemies (even if they don't exist).[5]

Denying that anything is a fictional object is tough. So, let's consider a different (and in fact completely opposite) way of defending Quineanism, namely, to flat-footedly claim that both Santa Claus and Spider-Man exist. Contrary to what Meinong might say, these are not non-existent objects. One question this defense raises is this: Why do we tell our children that Santa Claus doesn't exist? Is a parent who says this to his or her child saying something false?

7.57

7.58

7.59

---

[4] http://plato.stanford.edu/entries/meinong/

[5] According to this amusing video, there are many things that don't exist: https://www.youtube.com/watch?v=9T7ZbV-AFWo

7.60   A Quinean might answer this question in the following way: Santa Claus exists alright. But he isn't a jolly old elf who brings toys to all the good boys and girls (except for those good boys and girls whose parents are far too poor to be able to give their children toys—isn't it awful how he never gives them presents?). Instead, Santa Claus is a creature of folklore and myth, created by people long ago whose names we have long forgotten. The reason why we simply tell our kids that Santa Claus doesn't exist, even though it is true that he does exist, is that it is easier to say that he doesn't exist than it is to list all the properties that Santa Claus is depicted as having but does not in fact have. (An alternative explanation is that we are simply restricting our quantifiers to non-fictional entities.) Similarly, Spider-Man exists, but he isn't a man with great powers and the great responsibility that comes with having them. Instead, he is a fictional character, created by Stan Lee and Steve Ditko in the 1960s, who is depicted in various stories as having great power and great responsibility.

7.61   Paradigmatically existing things have certain features: they are located in space and time, they move about and bump into each other, they can cause changes in other things and in themselves, and so on. Fictional characters don't really do any of these things, though they are often depicted as doing those things. So fictional characters are not paradigmatically existing things. But the defender of Quineanism could say that they nonetheless exist. (Something can fail to be a paradigmatic F while still being an F. Penguins are not paradigmatic birds, but they are birds nonetheless.)

7.62   If Meinongianism is true, and so "exists" doesn't mean "is identical with something," then we need to rethink many of the debates discussed in the previous chapters. For example, in Section 5.4 we addressed the question of whether entities that are not, such as Abe Lincoln or dinosaurs, exist. Maybe non-present entities don't exist. But if "exists" doesn't mean the same thing as "is identical with something," there might nonetheless be (non-existent) non-present entities. On this kind of metaphysical view, even if dinosaurs do not exist, some things are dinosaurs. Maybe numbers or properties or propositions don't exist, but there might still be numbers, properties, or propositions. In general, any philosophical debate about whether there are certain things or about whether certain things exist is a lot more complicated if Meinongianism is true, because we then have to answer two metaphysical questions rather than just one.

7.63   The debate between Meinongianism and Quineanism over "exists" is important. But there is another important question about "exists" to consider even if Quineanism is true. Let's provisionally assume Quineanism, and so "exists" does mean the same thing as "is identical with something." Here is the other interesting question about "exists": Is "exists" univocal? Or is it ambiguous? (One might think that the debate between the Meinongian and the Quinean suggests that quantifiers are ambiguous, and that's why the Quinean can truthfully say that everything exists, and the Meinongian can truthfully say that something does not exist.)

A word is *univocal* if and only if it has exactly one meaning; a word is 7.64
ambiguous if and only if it has more than one meaning. The English word "bank" is ambiguous. One of the meanings is the same as "financial institution." Another meaning of "bank" is the same as "land sloping down near a river or lake." You don't want to get these meanings confused when you and your friends plan to go to the bank, because if you did, you might end up losing your checks in the water or end up in jail. Does "exist" have more than one meaning? If it does have more than one meaning, then the phrase "there is" must also have more than one meaning, given that "exists" is defined in terms of "there is."

If "exists" or "there is" are ambiguous, there might not be other expres- 7.65
sions in English that correspond to the different meanings of these phrases. In order to get around this worry, I'm going to employ a brute-force method: if "exists" or "there is" are ambiguous, we will simply use subscripts to indicate the different meanings of these expressions: "there is$_1$," "there is$_2$," and so on will each stand for a different alleged meaning of the allegedly ambiguous phrase "there is." (Recall our discussion in Section 0.1 of how it can be helpful to introduce technical terms in order to avoid speaking ambiguously. That's what we are doing here.)

If "there is" is ambiguous, perhaps what at first looked to be intractable 7.66
metaphysical debates can actually be settled simply by disambiguation. Are there numbers? Well, in some sense yes, and in some sense no. That is, there are$_1$ numbers, but there are$_2$ no numbers. Do non-present objects exist? Well, in some sense yes, and in some sense no. That is, non-present things exist$_1$ and non-present things do not exist$_2$. We thought we were having a cool debate over a hard question, but it turns out that there is really no interesting debate to be had: our only task would be to get clearer about which meaning of "there is" we had in mind.

Here's an example of a pseudo-debate: Two people are arguing over 7.67
whether you can get money from a bank. One person thinks it is obvious that you can—that's what banks are for. The other person thinks that this is really implausible. Maybe you will find some loose change lying around in the sand, but even that is unlikely. These two people aren't really debating.

They are talking past each other because they are using the same word—"bank"—but they mean different things by it.

7.68   Are metaphysical debates about what exists pseudo-debates? Maybe they aren't, if "exists" is univocal. Maybe they are, if "exists" is ambiguous. But maybe metaphysical debates are not pseudo-debates even if "exists" is ambiguous. This is an intriguing possibility, and we will explore it more in a bit at the end of this section.

7.69   As a test case, let's focus on the apparent debate between the presentist and the friend of the Static Universe View. (Recall, we discussed both of these views in Section 5.4.) Let's focus on their apparent disagreement over what there is; if the debate between them is merely semantic, their disagreement is merely apparent. The presentist says that there are no dinosaurs. When the presentist says this, he intends to be speaking absolutely unrestrictedly: among absolutely everything that there is, there are no dinosaurs to be found. The proponent of the Static Universe View seems to disagree: on her view, when we speak unrestrictedly about what there is, we can truly say that dinosaurs exist. This feels like a real debate, rather than a pseudo-debate consisting of people who are just talking past each other.

7.70   But notice that the friend of the Static Universe will claim that we often speak truly when we say that there are no dinosaurs, because we are not speaking absolutely unrestrictedly but instead are just talking about objects that presently exist. And, unless things are getting really weird in some secret biology lab right now, there are no presently existing dinosaurs. So, the friend of the Static Universe can say that what the presentist says is true—provided that the presentist is restricting her quantifiers.

7.71   And, on the other side, the presentist can accommodate what the friend of Static Universe says: although there are no dinosaurs, there *were* dinosaurs. If what the friend of the Static Universe means by "there is" is what the presentist means by "there was or there is or there will be," then the presentist can concede that, in this sense, there "are" dinosaurs. (And that there "are" intelligent robots, for example.) If both sides of the debate can interpret the opposing side as saying something true, then it looks like the debate is merely a semantic one rather than an interesting one over how the world is.

7.72   So, is the debate merely semantic? The friend of the Static Universe interprets the presentist as speaking only about some of what there is. The presentist might demand to be interpreted as trying to speak about absolutely everything, and if she is interpreted in this way, then, according to the friend of the Static Universe, what she says is false.

The fact that "there is" can be used more or less restrictedly doesn't 7.73 imply that "there is" has more than one meaning. Remember in Sections 3.8 and 4.4, when we talked about quantifier domain restriction? Here was the kind of example I used: Shamik is hosting a party in Manhattan and tells his friend Shieva that all the beer is in the fridge. Shieva protests that some beer is in Michigan that is not in the fridge. Of course, what Shieva said was true, but what Shamik said was also true. That's because Shamik was using "all" restrictedly, in order to talk only about a certain subset of what there is, while Shieva decided to use "some" less restrictedly, to talk about more things than what Shamik wanted to talk about. "All" and "some" can be used more or less restrictedly, but this doesn't mean that they are ambiguous. Here's an analogy to consider. The word "this" can be used to refer to different things in different circumstances. I can say, "This is a poached egg" and say something true and then later say, "This is my favorite city" and say something true as well. I'm using the word "this" to talk about different things in these cases. But this doesn't mean that "this" is ambiguous. If "this" were ambiguous, I guess we'd have to say that "this" has infinitely many different meanings, since anything can be referred to by the word "this." But while "this" just has one meaning, what it refers to is determined by the context in which it is used, and in a similar way "exists," "some," and "there is" are sensitive to context.

"There is" and "exists" can be used absolutely unrestrictedly, and when a 7.74 speaker uses them in this way, she intends to be talking about absolutely everything that there is. When conducting metaphysical debates, philosophers intend to talk about absolutely everything, and we will follow their lead here. So, with all this in mind, let's return to the question of whether "exists" or "there is" are ambiguous.

In order for the debate between the presentist and the advocate of the 7.75 Static Universe View to be a merely semantic debate, there must be a sense of "there are" that can be used absolutely unrestrictedly and for which "there are only present objects" says something true. And there must also be a distinct sense of "there are" that can be used absolutely unrestrictedly and for which "there are non-present objects as well as present objects" says something true. We haven't yet seen a reason to think that there are these different senses of "there are."

But suppose, just for the sake of argument, that "there are" is ambiguous. 7.76 Let's even suppose that the presentist and the proponent of the Static Universe View mean different things by that phrase, and so, they are talking past each other. Let's suppose that "there is$_1$" can be used absolutely unrestrictedly to say truthfully that there are$_1$ no non-present objects and let's suppose that "there is$_2$" can be used absolutely unrestrictedly to say truthfully that there are$_2$ non-present objects. Maybe even granting all this, there still could be a way for them to have an interesting metaphysical debate (rather than a semantic pseudo-debate).

7.77   That's because there is still the question of which of these meanings of "there is" is the better meaning to use in metaphysical debates. And this question might itself be a metaphysical question! To see this, we need to go all the way back to the discussions we had in Chapters 1 and 2 about classification and natural properties.

7.78   Remember that, in those chapters, we discussed the idea that some properties carve nature at the joints closer than others: those that do carve closer are the properties that explain why things objectively belong together. We called these properties "natural properties." If we want to figure out how the world objectively is, we should formulate theories about the most natural properties. This is what physicists, chemists, biologists, and so forth do. They search for better ways to objectively classify objects by figuring which are the more natural properties, and they strive to formulate laws that explain how these natural properties interact with each other. (Maybe the laws themselves just are natural relations that relate natural properties; this idea was discussed in Section 6.7.)

7.79   Maybe metaphysicians should do this too. If expressions like "there is" and "exist" correspond to properties, we can try to figure out how natural these properties are. And if "there is" is ambiguous and has two meanings that correspond to two different properties, then we can compare those two properties to see which one is more natural. And then we can choose to always mean the more natural property when we conduct metaphysical debates.

7.80   So, do expressions like "there is" correspond to properties? Initially, it might seem that the answer is no. Recall the simple semantic theory we discussed in Section 2.4. According to that theory, properties are what predicates refer to. And "there is" is not a predicate. Think about the sentence, "There are dogs." In that sentence, "dogs" is the predicate, not "there are."

7.81   Nonetheless, many philosophers of language think that quantifiers like "there is," "some," "all," "most," and so on, stand for properties or relations. However, they stand for properties or relations that are themselves exemplified by properties or relations. (Remember, properties or relations can themselves have properties or stand in relations: the property of being red has the property of being a color, the property of being a dog has the property of being awesome, the relation of being taller than has the property of being transitive, and so on.) On this view, "some dogs are fat" has the same meaning as "The property of being a dog and the property of being of being fat are co-instantiated" and "There are dogs" has the same meaning as "The property of being a dog is instantiated."[6]

If this theory in the philosophy of language is correct, then "there is" 7.82 corresponds to at least one property. It corresponds to exactly one if "there is" is univocal, and to more than one if it is ambiguous. "There is" might be ambiguous. It might be that when doing metaphysics we should carefully distinguish between "there is$_1$" and "there is$_2$." But corresponding to "there is$_1$" and "there is$_2$" are two properties of properties. And so, we can take the debate one level up and fight over which of these properties is more natural. The most natural of them is the one that we could use when conducting our metaphysical debates, and if we do so, our debates will be genuine debates.

But what if they are both equally natural?   7.83

7.4 The Metaphysics of Metaphysics

We are now going to discuss the metaphysics of metaphysics. This might 7.84 sound initially kind of odd, but it turns out that pretty much every subfield of philosophy reflects on itself in a similar way. We might study the philosophy of language of philosophy of language. Some of the important questions we'd study are about the semantics of key philosophy of language vocabulary—what do "language," "meaning," and "reference" mean, for example? We might study the epistemology of epistemology, and in the course of our study, we'd consider the question of how we can know which epistemological principles are correct. Are they known by experience? Are they a priori? We might study the ethics of ethics, and perhaps we'd consider the question of whether pursuing ethical questions is itself ethically questionable—what if, for example, seriously studying ethics makes us

---

[6] For more sophisticated discussions, see: http://www.linguistics.ucla.edu/people/keenan/Papers/quantifiers%20semantics.pdf http://plato.stanford.edu/entries/generalized-quantifiers/

worse people? That one can think about the metaphysics of metaphysics turns out to be not that surprising after all.

7.85   The question we are going to focus on here is the question of whether the practice of thinking about questions in metaphysics itself presupposes a metaphysical view.

7.86   Some activities make sense only if some propositions are true. Consider this conversation between Ryan and Michaeala:

Ryan: "I failed to find a present for my brother."
Michaeala: "Oh, you couldn't find anything he likes?"
Ryan: "I don't have a brother."

This conversation is bizarre, and it's all Ryan's fault: the activity of shopping for a present for your brother doesn't make sense if it isn't true that you have a brother. Here is a second example; this one involves a theoretical activity. Consider theology, which is the study of God's nature. The activity of theology doesn't make sense if there is no God.

7.87   In general, any sort of investigation makes sense only if there are some propositions that are true. If every proposition is false, you can never learn anything via investigation—and so there would be no point in investigating. It would be an activity that makes no sense. In a way, this is kind of a silly example, since logic alone guarantees that there are some true propositions. But the reason I used this example is to show that sometimes the presuppositions of an activity—that is, what has to be true in order for that activity to make sense—can be very general. And when these presuppositions are very general, they can fade into the background. When the background presuppositions of an activity are more questionable, philosophers who think about that activity can bring them into the foreground so that they can be explicitly questioned.

7.88   Investigation in general presupposes that not everything is false. Specific kinds of investigation have correspondingly more specific presuppositions. I mentioned theology a minute ago. Theology makes sense only if there are truths about the nature of God. If there is no God, there are no such truths. Similarly, doing physics makes sense only if there are truths about physical objects.

7.89   Similar remarks apply to metaphysics. Considering, deliberating about, and engaging in debate with others about metaphysical questions are some of the things you do when you do metaphysics. You've been doing metaphysics as you've worked through this book. Since metaphysics is an investigation into metaphysical claims, it makes sense only if there are truths about its subject matter. If we can get clearer on the subject matter of metaphysics, we will thereby get clearer on the presuppositions of doing metaphysics.

But that's a big task, and it's too big to tackle here. So, instead, I am going to focus on a specific kind of investigation that metaphysicians pursue, and see whether this investigation itself presupposes a metaphysical theory. It might help you get a feel for what I am interested in if I first briefly revisit some of the metaphysical investigations we have already discussed. 7.90

So, here's a quick review. In Section 2.6, I discussed one of the branches of metaphysics, ontology. I there described ontology as the branch of metaphysics whose job is to figure out the correct list of ontological categories. A list of ontological categories is meant to be a list of fundamental and highly general kinds of things that is both comprehensive (everything is either a member of one of the kinds or composed of members of those kinds) and exhaustive (nothing is a member of more than one kind). A kind of thing is a fundamental kind only if the members of that kind objectively belong together. 7.91

Trying to figure out the correct list of ontological categories makes sense only if some things do objectively belong together. If the idea of things objectively belonging together is just a big mistake—if things that are not violins objectively belong together to the same degree as electrons, because both groups do not objectively belong together to any degree at all—then ontology is a pointless enterprise. So, ontological investigation is an activity that has a metaphysical presupposition. 7.92

Figuring out the correct list of ontological categories is an important part of metaphysics. In general, figuring out what exists is one of the jobs of the metaphysician. Here are some places in this book where we tried to figure out whether something exists. Chapter 3 largely focused on the question of when composite objects exist. Various sections in Chapter 4 contained arguments about the existence of merely possible things, such as possible worlds, possible objects, or possible states of affairs. Chapter 5 discussed whether objects that aren't located in the present moment exist. In Section 7.3, we discussed whether fictional objects, like Spider-Man, exist. Figuring out what exists is an important part of metaphysics. 7.93

But, in Section 7.3, we discussed a potential reason to be concerned about this part of metaphysics: what if "exists" itself is ambiguous? If it is, are metaphysical debates merely semantic debates? At the end of Section 7.3, we discussed how a metaphysician might respond to this potential 7.94

concern: she might recommend that we use the meaning of "exists" that corresponds to the most natural property, and then conduct our debates about what exists using that meaning alone. If the worry about the ambiguity of "exists" is legitimate, and if the only satisfactory way to respond to this worry is to say that some meanings of "exist" are more natural than others, then there is a second presupposition of metaphysical inquiry: that some properties are more natural than others. This presupposition is closely tied to the presupposition of ontology, since some properties are more natural than others only if some things objectively belong together more than other things do.

7.95   We've discussed two examples of metaphysical inquiry that seem to presuppose the truth of a metaphysical claim. In the remainder of this section, I am going to focus on another kind of activity metaphysicians engage in, namely, the activity of asking questions of the form "What is it to be X?."

7.96   We've seen instances of this type of question throughout the book. Here are some of them: in Section 1.5, we discussed the question of what it is for some things to objectively belong together; in Section 2.8, we discussed the questions of what it is for things to be duplicates and what it is for a property to be intrinsic; in Section 3.4, we briefly discussed what it is to be alive; and, finally, in Section 6.7, we discussed the question of what it is for something to be a law of nature. Asking and trying to answer this sort of question is an important metaphysical activity. This is a different sort of question than questions about what there is. Let's call questions of this sort *"what is"* *questions*.

7.97   Let me make a brief observation about "what is" questions. Answers to "what is" questions imply necessary *biconditionals*. A biconditional is a statement of the form "P if and only if Q"; they are so-called because they are equivalent to a conjunction of two conditionals: "If P, then Q" and "If Q, then P." Suppose the correct answer to the question, "What is it to be alive?" is this: To be alive is to be capable of reproduction. It follows from this answer that, necessarily, something is alive if and only if it is capable of reproduction. But a necessarily true biconditional is not by itself the correct answer to a "what is" question. Necessary biconditionals can contain information that is not relevant to answering a "what is" question. Here is an example to show this: Necessarily, something is alive if and only if it is capable of reproduction and $2 + 5 = 7$. This biconditional is true if the other biconditional just mentioned is true. But it doesn't answer the question, "What is it to be alive?" because, even though $2 + 5 = 7$, it isn't relevant information.

The metaphysical presuppositions of the activity of trying to answer "what 7.98 is" questions might be different than the presuppositions of ontology. What might these presuppositions be? We can't answer this question without answering a prior question: What is it to be an answer to a "what is" question? (Note that this question is itself a "what is" question!)

In the remainder of this section, we are going to look at three different 7.99 theories that answer this prior question: *the semantic view, the identity view,* and *the real essence view.*

The semantic view says that "what is" questions are questions about the 7.100 definitions of words. According to the semantic view, the question "What is it to be alive?" is answered by a definition of the word "alive." One bit of evidence that favors the semantic view is that sometimes "what is" questions do feel like requests for definitions. If someone asks, "What is it to be a bachelor?" then telling that person the definition of "bachelor" is plausibly the right way to respond.

The semantic view explains why answers to "what is" questions imply 7.101 necessary biconditionals. They do this because in general definitions imply necessary biconditionals, and, according to the semantic view, answers to "what is" questions are definitions. Here's an example. Suppose that the definition of "bachelor" is "eligible to be married adult human male." Given this definition, necessarily, something is a bachelor if and only if it is an eligible to be married adult human male.

The semantic view also explains why not every necessary biconditional is 7.102 an answer to a "what is" question. Consider the claim that, necessarily, something is a bachelor if and only if it is an eligible to be married adult human male and $7 + 5 = 12$. This claim doesn't answer the question "What is it to be a bachelor?" because, although $7 + 5$ does equal 12, that information is not part of the definition of "bachelor."

If the semantic view is true, then the activity of asking "what is" questions 7.103 doesn't presuppose much heavy-duty metaphysics: there must be words and expressions, and some of them must have definitions.

Let's consider an argument against the semantic view. Consider the 7.104 question "What is it to be a sample of water?" This is a plausible answer: "To be a sample of water is to be a sample of H_2O." But this plausible answer does not provide a definition of the word "water." Chemists rather than readers of dictionaries discovered that samples of water are samples of H_2O, and what they discovered wasn't the definition of a word but rather something about the property of being a sample of water. The semantic view gets this wrong.

7.105   So, let's consider a second view, one that says that answers to "what is" questions are about things rather than words. According to the identity view, a "what is" question is correctly answered by a true identity statement about properties. For example, the question, "What is to be alive?" is answered by filling in the blank, "The property of being alive is identical with _____." According to the identity view, there are properties—a metaphysical claim!—and one and the same property can be referred to by different expressions.

7.106   In general, we can refer to one and the same entity with different expressions. My kids use the expression "Papa" to refer to me, while most of my friends use "Kris." But my friends from graduate school use the name "McX." I am one person with three names. That's why this sentence expressing identity is true: "Kris is McX."

7.107   Here's an example of the identity theory in action. Consider the question "What is it to be a sample of water?." Now consider a purported answer to this question, which is expressed by the sentence "What it is to be a sample of water is to be a sample of H_2O." According to the identity theory, this purported answer is really a claim about the identity of "two" properties, which can be explicitly stated as "The property of being a sample of water is identical with the property of being a sample of H_2O." The property of being a sample of water is one property with two names. The identity of these "two" properties is a chemical discovery rather than a lexicographical discovery.

7.108   The identity theory explains why answers to "what is" questions imply necessary biconditionals. If the property of being a sample of water just is the property of being a sample of H_2O, it follows that, necessarily, something is a sample of water if and only if it is a sample of H_2O.

7.109   If the identity theory is true, then one metaphysical presupposition of trying to answer "what is" questions is that there are properties. But, unlike the activity of doing ontology, the identity theory doesn't say that trying to answer "what is" questions presupposes that some properties are more natural than other properties.

7.110   The main problem with the identity view is that certain identity claims are more relevant than others to answering "what is" questions. Here is a silly example to illustrate the problem. Suppose that Chris has given a name to the property of being a sample of water. Suppose he has named this property "Heathwood." Chris can now truthfully say, "The property of being a sample of water is identical with Heathwood." But he hasn't successfully answered the question, "What is it to be water?". It's not enough to correctly identify "two" properties to answer a "what is" question. At the very least, some ways of referring to properties are more relevant to answering a "what is" question. The identity theorist needs a way to explain why this is the case, and she needs to give a theory of when a way of referring to a property is more relevant than another way.

Let's turn to a third theory of what it is to be an answer to a "what is" question. This is the real essence view. In order to understand this view, we need to first get clearer on what a *real essence* is supposed to be. The idea of real essence is really old, but it has recently gotten a lot of attention in metaphysics, largely because of the work of a philosopher named Kit Fine.[7] One of the things that Fine argues is that a thing's real essence is not simply the properties that it must have if it is to exist at all. {.marginnote 7.111}

We discussed these sort of properties in Section 4.8, and there we did use the expression "essential property" to mean a property that a thing must have if it is to exist at all. So, unfortunately, there are two similar-sounding names for two different ideas. In order to avoid making things even more confusing in this section, I am going to henceforth use the expression "necessary property" to mean a property that a thing must have in order to even exist at all. Sorry about this! If you are going to read further on these topics, you are going to encounter both of these expressions: "essential property" (with the meaning I gave it in Section 4.8) and "real essence" (with the meaning Fine gives to it). {.marginnote 7.112}

A real essence of a thing is supposed to be what that thing most fundamentally is. And not every necessary feature of an object is what an object fundamentally is. Consider a kitchen table that I'll call "Ted." One of the necessary features of Ted is that it is either a physical object or a number; there is no possible world in which Ted exists, but it is not either a physical object or a number. (If there were such a possible world, it would be a world in which Ted is not a physical object. But no table could be a non-physical object.) But this necessary feature of Ted is not a part of Ted's real essence. When you learn that Ted is necessarily either a physical object or a number, you do not learn what Ted fundamentally is. If Ted has a real essence, it is plausible that Ted's real essence is simply that Ted is a table. {.marginnote 7.113}

---

[7] Kit Fine is a professor of philosophy at NYU. His homepage is here: http://as.nyu.edu/content/nyu-as/as/faculty/kit-fine.html

7.114   Here's a second example, one that Fine uses. Consider you and your singleton set—that is, the set whose sole member is you. Fine claims that, in every possible world in which you exist, your singleton set exists, and vice versa. In other words, one of your necessary properties is that you are a member of this singleton set. But this necessary property is not part of your real essence—it is not part of "what it is to be you." Maybe your real essence is that you are a living human animal. Maybe your real essence is that you are a conscious being. (These are both plausible claims, even though they are not equivalent.) But you are not defined by the fact that you are a member of your singleton set.

7.115   According to the real essence view, an answer to a "what is" question is one that states the real essence of the thing in question. Consider the question "What is it to be alive?". According to the real essence view, an answer to this question will state the real essence of being alive. Similarly, an answer to the question "What is it to be a law of nature?" will state the real essence of being a law of nature. The idea is that real essences provide definitions not of words, but of things themselves.

7.116   The real essence view might be able to explain why certain ways of referring to properties are more relevant when answering "what is" questions. Consider again the following sentence: "What it is to be a sample of water is to be a sample of H_2O." If being a sample of water has a real essence, it is plausible that the real essence of a sample of water is that it is made of H_2O.

7.117   It is not clear that the real essence view implies that answers to "what is" questions imply corresponding necessary biconditionals. Suppose that there are two different properties, F and G, that have the same real essence, which is the property X. Suppose that something could exemplify F without exemplifying G, and vice versa. Then one of the following can't be true: (i) necessarily, something is F if and only if it is X; (ii) necessarily, something is G if and only if it is X. You can derive a contradiction from our two suppositions plus (i) and (ii). The key supposition here is that two different properties could have the same real essence. However, if two properties cannot have the same essence, then the real essence view does imply that answers to "what is" questions imply corresponding necessary biconditionals.

7.118   Out of the three views we have talked about, the real essence view is the most metaphysically committal: it is neck deep in real essences. If the real essence view is right, then one serious metaphysical presupposition of trying to answer "what is" questions is that some things—things like knowledge or laws of nature—have real essences.

7.5 The Ethics of Metaphysics

You've made it through a lot of text to get here. It is likely that you've had to 7.119
work pretty hard at times. You might reasonably wonder whether it was
worth it. It probably won't surprise you to hear that philosophers are pretty
used to hearing people question whether philosophy is worthwhile.
Philosophy is awfully difficult and abstract, and its concerns can sometimes
seem very distant from the concerns of the ordinary person on the street.
And metaphysical questions are among the most abstract of philosophical
questions. So, what's the point of trying to figure out the answers to these
questions?

   This is a question that itself requires a lot of thought. Unsurprisingly, the 7.120
question about the value of philosophy is itself a philosophical question.
This is why it is depressing when someone simply prejudges that philosophy is without value: they are unreflectively endorsing a philosophical
claim in their very attempt to dismiss the value of philosophy. At the very
least, if someone is going to offer a quick dismissal of philosophy as a useless enterprise, that person should be willing to explain what he or she
means by "useless" and "useful."

   By "useful," some people just mean "conducive to making money." 7.121
Philosophy actually is useful in this sense. Philosophy majors earn
good money upon graduation; they do better on the LSATs than any
other major, and rock other entrance examinations for professional
schools as well; and they are increasingly sought after by major players
in business.[8]

   I've been talking about philosophy in general rather than metaphysics. 7.122
That's partly because, while there are well-documented stats on the usefulness of philosophy, there are not well-documented stats on the usefulness of
metaphysics per se. I'd be surprised though if metaphysicians did worse on
average on standardized tests or made less money than, for example, episte-
mologists upon graduation.

   But usefulness in this sense is not the only kind of value, and it isn't the 7.123
most important kind either. Caring for your children or elderly grandparents,

---

[8] https://criticalthinkeracademy.com/courses/special-topics/lectures/51628
https://www.forbes.com/sites/noodleeducation/2017/03/01/a-case-for-majoring-
in-philosophy/#64b0838c5315

or making music, or working through some abstract mathematical question, are not clearly useful in the sense of being conducive to making money. That doesn't make these activities any less valuable or important. In general, focusing on whether something will make your bank account happy is a bad opening move when thinking deeply about whether something is useful. So, let's explore a better definition of "useful."

7.124   Here's one: An activity is *useful* if and only if engaging in it is likely to make one's life go better than it would have otherwise. And let's say that an *intrinsically* useful activity is an activity that, when you engage in it, makes a life be *intrinsically* better than it would have otherwise been in virtue of engaging in that activity. Making money might be a useful activity, but it is not an intrinsically useful activity: you should care about making money not because money in itself makes one's life go better but rather because having money typically allows one the freedom to pursue activities that can make a life be a better life.

7.125   The definition of "useful" we are going to focus on is only one of many possible meanings for that word. Another reasonable definition is "conducive to helping us get what we care about." Doing metaphysics might be useful in this sense too. As I mentioned in Section 6.1, one of the things we care about is whether we have freedom, and because we care about whether we have freedom, we might also care about what it is to be free—and what it is to be free is a metaphysical question. Religion is important to many people, and religions make metaphysical claims. Perhaps getting clearer on the metaphysics underlying political disputes might help us too. So, although I am going to focus on the sense of "useful" that I explicitly defined earlier, this isn't because it's not worth thinking about whether doing metaphysics is useful in other senses of "useful."

7.126   Is thinking through metaphysical problems a useful activity in my sense of "useful"? This is the question I will talk about in the final section of this chapter. I'm going to focus primarily on whether thinking through metaphysical problems is an intrinsically useful activity or directly produces something intrinsically valuable.

7.127   I said that an *intrinsically useful activity* is an activity that, when you engage in it, makes a life be *intrinsically* better than it would have otherwise been in virtue of engaging in that activity. Our first step will be to get clearer on the idea of a good life, since this is the central idea that I used in my definition of "useful." One of the central questions of value theory—a sub-discipline of ethics—is the question of what makes a life go better or worse for the person who lives it.

I am going to discuss a couple of ways to get a handle on the concept of a 7.128
life worth living.[9] Here's the first way. Suppose you are looking down at a
newborn child sleeping in her crib. Maybe she's your child, or a younger
sibling, but whoever she is, she is someone for whom you feel a tremendous
amount of love. You look down at her as she sleeps, and you think about the
ways her life might turn out. However her life turns out, you hope that it
will be a good life for her, rather than a life that goes poorly for her. As you
feel this hope, you also begin to feel fear because you feel the tremendous
weight of your responsibility to make sure she has a good life. When you
have this hope and this fear, you are using the concept of a life that is good
or bad for the person who lives it.

Here's a second example to consider. Suppose you are nearing the end 7.129
of your life. Your chapter will soon come to a close. You reflect on all the
things that you have done and all the things that have happened to you;
you conclude that your life has been a good one for you. You are glad that
you were born. You do feel a pang of guilt as you reflect also on the fact
that many other people in the world lived lives that were so bad for them
that arguably they would have been better off never having been born.
When you give a thumbs up to your own life, you are using the good concept of a life that is good or bad for the one who lives it. You are also using
this concept when you feel guilty for insufficiently helping improve the
lives of others.

Now that we have focused in on the concept of a good or bad life for the 7.130
one who lives it, we can now ask an important question: What are the factors that make a life a good life or a bad life?

Some philosophers think that the answer to this question is very simple: 7.131
A life is a good life to the extent that it is filled with pleasant sensations and
lacks unpleasant ones. On this view, which we can call "simple hedonism,"
every episode of pleasure a person experiences intrinsically makes her life
better, and every episode of pain a person experiences intrinsically makes
her life worse. How good or bad an episode of pleasure or pain is for a person is simply a function of how intense and long-lasting that episode of
pleasure or pain is.

---

[9] These ways of getting clearer on the concept of a life worth living for the one who
lives it are proposed by Feldman, F. *Pleasure and the Good Life* (Oxford: Oxford
University Press, 2004). Professor Feldman's research page is here: http://people.
umass.edu/ffeldman/

7.132   A simple hedonist will grant that a given episode of pleasure experienced by a person might be *extrinsically* bad for that person, or that a given episode of pain experienced by a person might be *extrinsically* good for that person. Something is *extrinsically* bad for a person if and only if it leads to something that is intrinsically bad for that person. Similarly, something is extrinsically good for a person if and only if it leads to something that is intrinsically good for that person. Suppose you make a crazy bet and the excitement feels so pleasant. Things work out for you, luckily enough, and you get even more pleasure as a result. All that pleasure, which (according to simple hedonism) is itself intrinsically good for you, leads you to make yet another crazy bet. But this second crazy bet costs you your house, your car, most of your stuff, and now gangsters are breaking your legs with baseball bats. All that pain you are now experiencing is intrinsically bad for you. Because the earlier pleasure led you to have all this later pain, the earlier pleasure, despite being intrinsically good for you, is very extrinsically bad for you. In this case, the extrinsic badness of this pleasure—which (according to the simple hedonist) is measured by the intrinsic disvalue of the pain it led to—is probably greater than its intrinsic goodness.

7.133   If simple hedonism is true, thinking through metaphysical problems is not intrinsically useful. It is extrinsically useful only to the extent that it makes people happy. Some people are made happy by thinking through metaphysical problems. A lot of philosophers seem to enjoy it anyway. Other people might not enjoy thinking through them. That's fine, though. There are other things they can do instead. Probably thinking through metaphysical problems doesn't result in as many people being happy as thinking through other problems. This isn't a reason to think thinking through metaphysical problems is extrinsically useless though, even given simple hedonism. It is a reason to think that it is less extrinsically useful than other activities one could do instead. That said, most of what people do is less extrinsically useful than much of what they could do instead. (How much time did you spend goofing off on the internet today?) And if simple hedonism is true, no activity is intrinsically useful.

7.134   Simple hedonism is a straightforward and initially plausible answer to the question of what makes a life worth living. It delivers clear verdicts about whether doing metaphysics is intrinsically or extrinsically useful. Simple hedonism implies that it is definitely not intrinsically useful, and it is extrinsically useful only to the extent that it makes you feel pleasure. If thinking through the metaphysical topics in this book caused you more pain than pleasure, then simple hedonism implies that thinking through the topics in this book was worse than extrinsically useless—it was extrinsically bad for you.

Here's an argument against simple hedonism. Let's return to the first 7.135 example I talked about. Suppose you are in the hospital room, looking down at that newborn baby who you love. You feel that hope and fear. The doctor comes into your room and tells you that she has some wonderful news for you. A new medical procedure has just been developed. If it is administered to your baby, she will live a very long life, and this life will be filled with pleasant experiences and very close to zero unpleasant ones. Here's how the procedure works: the doctor will take your baby and put her in an Isocube, which is a cubical container that your baby will remain in for the rest of her life. Inside the Isocube, she will be hooked up to machines that will stimulate the pleasure centers of her brain. Other machines will take care of her digestive needs. Your baby will never make friends or love anyone else, your baby will never accomplish anything of significance, and your baby will never acquire any interesting knowledge about herself or the world. But your baby will almost never feel any pain and she will feel continuous high levels of pleasure.[10]

Probably a life in the Isocube is not the worst life possible for your baby. 7.136 If the only alternative to life in the Isocube is a life of unending excruciating pain, probably a life in the Isocube is better for the baby. But this is to set a very low bar. If simple hedonism is true, a life in the Isocube is one of the best lives possible for your baby. There's just no way to secure that high level of pleasure and low level of pain outside of an Isocube. If simple hedonism is true, a life in the Isocube is an excellent life for the one who lives it. But life in an Isocube is not an excellent life. So simple hedonism is not true.

Think about how few people at the end of their lives would sigh and say, 7.137 "If only I had spent my whole life in an Isocube. How much better for me that would have been." There are people whose lives are arguably bad enough that they would have been better off having lived in an Isocube. Life in an Isocube is probably a better choice for some people. But if simple hedonism is true, pretty much *everyone* would have been better off had they lived in an Isocube rather than having lived the life they in fact lived. However, a lot of

---

[10] Compare life in the Isocube to the life of the shelled water creatures described in Plato's *Philebus*. http://classics.mit.edu/Plato/philebus.html (use your find function to locate "oyster").

us would not have been better off had we lived in the Isocube instead of lived our actual life, contrary to what simple hedonism implies.

7.138   When I think about a life in the Isocube, what stands out for me are the intrinsically valuable things that life is missing: knowledge of reality, genuine achievements, and love. Contrary to simple hedonism, each of these things are intrinsically valuable for people to have, and the best lives we can live are ones in which each of these things are present. (Pleasure is good to have too.) That said, I don't know how to prove this—it's much easier to argue that simple hedonism is false than it is to argue for whatever theory we are going to put in its place.

7.139   Rather than a proof, I'll suggest a procedure you can follow for figuring out what things are intrinsically useful. Think about something that you think would make your life better. Now ask yourself why it would make your life better. Would it make it better only because of what it leads to? Or would it make it better simply because of what it is? (Having money can make one's life better only because of what it leads to; having money does not intrinsically make one's life better.) One thing that is awesome about philosophy is that it can get you to really sit down and question what it is you value and why. So now I'm asking you to do this.

7.140   When I follow this procedure and I then contemplate knowledge, achievement, and love, I find myself thinking that these things make lives better not simply because of what they lead to but also because of what they are. I find myself thinking that they make our lives intrinsically better just in virtue of having them. Perhaps you think this too.

7.141   I haven't proven that knowledge, achievement, and love are intrinsically useful—I haven't even argued that they are. I just gave you a procedure to follow so that you can check whether you think this too. In what follows, I am going to presuppose that these things are intrinsically useful, and then see whether given that they are, doing metaphysics might be intrinsically useful. We already know that, given simple hedonism, doing metaphysics is not intrinsically useful. So now we are going to try to figure out whether it might be given this different and more complicated theory of what is intrinsically useful. Even if the more complicated theory is not true, it will be interesting to see what it implies about doing metaphysics.

7.142   We'll start with knowledge. Suppose that having knowledge is intrinsically valuable for a person. How intrinsically valuable is it? Is every instance of knowledge that a person has equally intrinsically good for that person? Not everything that is intrinsically valuable is equally intrinsically valuable. For example, not every pleasure is equally intrinsically valuable; the value of an episode of pleasure is a function of its duration and intensity. If not every instance of knowledge is equally intrinsically valuable, what determines how valuable an instance of knowledge is?

Franz Brentano, a really interesting 19th-century philosopher, defended 7.143 the following theory about what makes an instance of knowledge more or less intrinsically valuable:

> And it [knowledge] is a proportionately greater good the more important it is, the more general and penetrating, the greater the range of things it illuminates, the more difficult the questions that it clarifies, and the richer the springs that it opens up for the discovery of new truths. Fundamental principles, such as Newton's law of gravitation, are more valuable than the knowledge of the char- acteristics of a particular variety of plant or mineral. Yet these latter are, in turn, more valuable than completely concrete pieces of information. The value also varies according to the quality of knowledge—whether it is affirmative or negative. ... Just as knowledge is a good, error is as an evil as such, and the magnitude of the evil varies in proportion to the goodness of the knowledge cor- responding to it and to its distance from the truth.[11]

Here's an example to help illustrate Brentano's theory. Suppose you learn 7.144 how many bricks there are in the biology building of the closest college campus. What you have learned is not that important or intrinsically inter- esting. This bit of knowledge might still intrinsically benefit you a little bit, just as the miniscule pleasure you get from momentarily scratching your nose might be just barely intrinsically good for you. Brentano's theory explains why: knowing how many bricks are in the biology building of the closest college campus is highly concrete knowledge in the sense that you can't deduce or infer much about the world from just that bit of informa- tion. This is why, according Brentano's theory, it isn't very intrinsically valu- able knowledge. That said, it's better to know this though than it is to know that exact number of bricks is *not* 10,012, because this provides you with even less information. On Brentano's view, the intrinsically best kind of knowledge to have is general, positive knowledge of fundamental truths. Among those fundamental truths are truths of physics, of religion, of ethics, and metaphysics. If knowledge is intrinsically good for us to have, and

---

[11] This comes from Brentano, F. *Foundations and Construction of Ethics* (London: Routledge, 1973), pp. 168–169. For more on Brentano, go here: http://plato.stanford. edu/entries/brentano/

Brentano is right about how to determine the value of instances of knowledge, then knowledge of metaphysical truths would be highly intrinsically useful.

7.145   How else are we going to acquire knowledge that would be intrinsically good for us to have without thinking through metaphysical problems? Granted, in Section 7.2, we did discuss the idea that some metaphysical knowledge might be easy knowledge to acquire. But even supposing that this view is correct, a lot of metaphysical knowledge is not easy to acquire. And it might be that the metaphysical knowledge that is easy to acquire is not as intrinsically good for us as much of the harder to acquire metaphysical knowledge would be.

7.146   On Brentano's view, thinking through certain metaphysical questions is necessary for us to acquire something intrinsically useful, and if we successfully think through these metaphysical questions—if we acquire knowledge of the answers to these metaphysical questions—we will get something that is intrinsically good for us.

7.147   Suppose all this is correct. Does it follow that the activity of doing metaphysics is useful? Not yet—we need the additional premise that it is likely that doing metaphysics will probably to lead to metaphysical knowledge. How likely is this?

7.148   Here are some things to keep in mind when trying to answer this question. First, metaphysicians have acquired a lot of metaphysical knowledge over the past decades. Metaphysical questions are not independent: the answer to one impacts what the answers to others will be. This deep connectivity was something I noted way back in Section 0.4, where I said that, in general, metaphysical claims connect in intricate and important ways with other metaphysical claims. And you have seen some of this connectivity displayed in this very book. We might not know the answers to the big questions in metaphysics, but we have learned a lot about how these answers are connected to each other. This is genuine metaphysical knowledge.

7.149   Moreover, as we learn more about these connections, it might be that we get closer to actually answering the big questions themselves. There are more philosophers than ever before. Moreover, philosophers are able today to share results, and to read and comment on each other's work, with a speed that would have been unimaginable as little as thirty years ago. As our community continues to become more inclusive and as technology enables further ways in which philosophers can interact with one another, who knows what the future holds? But perhaps cautious optimism is reasonable.

We've talked about knowledge. We'll talk about achievement next. 7.150 Suppose that achievement is itself intrinsically valuable. Are all achievements equally valuable? If not, how is the value of achievement to be measured?

One possible answer to this question is that the intrinsic value of an 7.151 achievement is proportionate to how significant the achievement is. For an illustration of this idea, consider someone who tirelessly works to find a cure for a devastating disease in order to save thousands upon thousands of lives. Suppose this person does discover the cure to this disease, but dies before the scientific community confirms that she did in fact discover the cure. She never sees her cure administered to the suffering population. She achieved what she fervently wanted to achieve, even though she did not live to see her achievement take place. She did not feel the pleasant feelings one typically feels when one knows that one has achieved something of significance. Nonetheless, if achievement is itself intrinsically valuable, her life is a better life than it otherwise would have been simply because of that achievement.

In many cases, acquiring knowledge is an achievement. But there are 7.152 other cognitive achievements besides acquiring knowledge. One of these is acquiring reasons to believe something. The stronger the reason to believe that you acquire, the more impressive the cognitive achievement is, at least if the thing believed is itself an important thing to believe. This is one reason why new arguments for old views are prized among philosophers. We love to consider new considerations! Even if knowledge of metaphysical answers is out of our reach, having better reasons for believing them is not.

Working through metaphysical problems also provides the opportunities 7.153 to hone one's intellectual skills. There's a weird disparity in how a lot of people think about intellectual and physical skills. Some people are really good at climbing mountains. They develop an almost single-minded obsession for climbing, and they seek harder and harder mountains to conquer. When they succeed, the typical reaction is to marvel at their achievements. But often even impressive failures—those that come close to succeeding but don't quite make it—are greeted with acclaim. One might wonder, what could be more useless than climbing a mountain simply because it is there to climb? But it isn't useless if the skills developed and displayed are themselves of intrinsic value, because both the development and the displaying of the skills in question are themselves achievements.

Metaphysicians are mountain climbers of the mind. They wrestle with 7.154 metaphysical questions because they are there to be wrestled with. Maybe they will always fall short of reaching the top. Often times, they will fall hard. But honing and displaying one's intellectual skills are achievements in themselves, just as much as honing and displaying one's mountain climbing skills. What could justify treating mental achievements as less important than physical ones?

7.155   Another respect in which metaphysical theorizing can result in achievements is that the products of such theorizing are often beautiful. Physical objects like mountains and sunsets are not the only objects that are beautiful. Theories can also be objects of beauty, especially when they are elegant and powerful.[12] For example, the conjunction of the Static Universe View and perdurantism is a remarkably elegant and powerful theory: it is intellectually beautiful regardless of whether it is true. Producing an object of beauty is an achievement.[13]

7.156   We've talked about knowledge and achievement. In the final part of this section, we will discuss love. What's love got to do with it? (Metaphysics, that is.) Well, first, metaphysics might enable you to make friends and win you love. That's probably true of a lot of things though. Second, metaphysics might help you to understand what love is.[14] But rather than discussing the metaphysics of love, I'm going to focus on the love of metaphysics.

7.157   Since we are nearing the end of the book, I am going to lay my cards on the table. Maybe this will sound hokey or cheesy to you, but I'm willing to take that risk. In a certain sense, love is the most important thing for you to have in your life. Here are some theses about the value of love: First, although a life might be worth living even if the individual whose life it is feels no love throughout that life, the very best of lives will be lives in which love is experienced. (I concede that a life in the Isocube might be better than no life at all. But it is a life without love, and so it cannot be an excellent life.) And so, the value of some instances of love must be greater than the value of any possible amount of pleasure. I say "some" here rather than "all" because it is not obvious that all instances of love are of equal value. Let me say a bit more about this.

---

[12] For interesting reflections about whether scientific theories are beautiful see: http://blogs.scientificamerican.com/the-curious-wavefunction/2014/05/21/truth-and-beauty-in-science/

[13] In an interesting unpublished paper, Robert Pasnau argues that philosophers do in fact care a lot about beauty, perhaps even more than truth. http://spot.colorado.edu/~pasnau/inprint/pasnau.beauty.pdf

[14] See, for example: http://www.themetaphysicsoflove.com/

Many different sorts of things can be loved. You can love yourself or 7.158 other people. You can love animals, some of whom might also be (non-human) people. You can love particular natural objects, such as forests or streams, or works of art, or even your material possessions. And you can love activities, such as hiking, running, or working through metaphysical problems. A wide variety of different kinds of things can be loved; I've barely scratched the surface here. Given the wide range of things that can be loved, we should consider whether every instance of love has the same value, or rather if love is like pleasure, knowledge, and achievement, each of which can have instances that differ in value.

According to the theories we have examined, the value of an item of 7.159 knowledge is measured by the importance of what is known, and the value of an achievement is measured by how impressive that achievement is. An analogous theory of the value of love is that the value of an instance of love is proportionate to how worthy of love the beloved is. Consider the difference between a Scrooge-like character who loves only the act of acquiring money, but loves it intensely, and a doctor who loves just as intensely practicing medicine. On the analogous theory we are considering, the doctor is benefited more by her love than the Scrooge-like character is by his love simply because the practice of medicine is more worthy of love than the act of acquiring money.

Since I am laying down my cards, I'll once again say that I don't know how 7.160 to prove that the analogous theory is the case. I invite you to use the procedure I suggested a little while back to think about whether you agree with it. When I think about the lives my young children might one day live, I hope for their own sakes that they love more in their lives than merely grubbing money. A life spent loving only the acquisition of money is a hollow and pathetic life.

I also hope for their own sakes that they love more in their lives than just 7.161 the activity of doing metaphysics, since such a life would also be too one dimensional. But even a one-dimensional life would be a better life for each of them to live than the life of a mere money grubber, because it is a more meaningful life in which love is directed to something worthier.[15]

We have discussed knowledge, achievement, and love, because each of 7.162 these is plausibly intrinsically useful. We have also discussed how the activity

---

[15] It's worth comparing what I say here to what is claimed in the final chapter of the excellent Russell, B. *Problems of Philosophy* (Charlotte, N.C.: IAP, 2019): http://www.ditext.com/russell/rus15.html

of doing metaphysics might be useful given that knowledge, achievement, and friendship and love are intrinsically useful.

7.163   You have gone through the previous chapters working through some of the main puzzles, problems, and arguments in metaphysics. I hope this has made you realize how much weirder the world is than you previously thought. There are puzzles hiding behind every aspect of our world, which we can find if we only look carefully enough. This is important knowledge to have. Realizing how puzzling the world is can cause a feeling of being profoundly not at home in the world. The feeling often passes but the sense of wonder remains, and this sense of wonder is what leads many of us to feel a love for the discipline of metaphysics.

7.164   But even if you have not come to share this love, I am grateful that you have shared your time. Thanks for reading this book.

7.6 Doing Metaphysics

In Section 7.2, we discussed how we have a lot of "negative metaphysical knowledge," such as the knowledge that certain theories are false. We also seem to have a lot of positive metaphysical knowledge, for example, that something exists, that some truths are contingent, and that some features are essential. What explains the fact that we have this positive knowledge?

We've asked this question before, but this a good place to ask it again: how reliable is common sense as a guide to metaphysical questions?

Suppose there are things that don't exist. Are there things that don't exist that no one else has ever even thought of? Or are the only things that don't exist creatures of fiction (like Spider-Man) or mythology (like Santa Claus)?

If there are things that don't exist, how can I tell whether I exist?

How can we tell which things are intrinsically valuable? What is the epistemology of value? If metaphysical speculation is not intrinsically valuable, in what ways might it be extrinsically valuable?

Further Reading

Berit Brogaard (2015) *On Romantic Love: Simple Truths about a Complex Emotion*, Oxford: Oxford University Press.
    A philosophical examination of one variety of love (among many).

Carrie Jenkins (2017) *What Love Is and What It Could Be*, New York: Basic Books.
    An accessible book on the metaphysis of love.

David Chalmers, David Manley, and Ryan Wasserman (editors) (2009) *Metametaphysics: New Essays on the Foundation of Ontology*, Oxford: Oxford University Press.
    This collection contains classic papers on questions about being, existence, and quantification.

Richard Feldman and Ted Warfield (editors) (2010) *Disagreement*, Oxford: Oxford University Press.
    An important anthology on the epistemological consequences of disagreement.

Tarmara Horowitz (2005) *The Epistemology of A Priori Knowledge*, Oxford: Oxford University Press.
    A collection of papers, most of which focus on the philosophical problem of *a priori* knowledge.

Gwen Bradford (2017) *Achievement*, Oxford: Oxford University Press.
    A book length exploration of the nature and value of achievements.

Theodore Sider (2011) *Writing the Book of the World*, Oxford: Oxford University Press.
    An in-depth defense of a metaphysically privileged notion of existence.

GLOSSARY

For the convenience of the reader, I have created a glossary of important technical terms and key theories. But the reader should use this glossary with caution. One of the things that philosophers do is start with rough and simple definitions and then gradually refine them into something more precise and complicated. Some of the entries in this glossary are the preliminary definitions rather than the final ones. And sometimes philosophers argue about how best to define a technical notion or characterize a view. So, you should think of what follows as a guide to help you if you need it—but you should also use the index to read again how and why terms or theories are defined or characterized in the way that they are.

A Theory of Time. The theory that time itself changes from moment to moment.

Accidental properties. A property of an object is an accidental property of that object if and only if it is possible for that object to exist without having that property.

All limits view. This is the theory that every property that you have is an essential property.

Alternative Possibilities Compatibilism. This is the theory that a person does an action freely if and only if they do it but there is a possible world a lot like the actual world in which they don't do it.

Analytic Truth. A truth is analytic if and only if it is true by definition.

A priori truth. A truth that can known independently of particular experiences that justify believing it.

This Is Metaphysics: An Introduction, First Edition. Kris McDaniel.
© 2020 John Wiley & Sons, Inc. Published 2020 by John Wiley & Sons, Inc.

The arbitrariness constraint. The theory that we should prefer theories that do not imply that reality is arbitrary over those that do.

Argument. An argument is a sequence of claims, the last of which is supposed to follow from the previous ones. The last claim in an argument is the conclusion of that argument, and the claims that are supposed to provide support for that conclusion are the premises of that argument.

Basic constraint (on theory choice). A basic constraint on which theory to believe is one that is not justified or explained by some other constraint.

The best systems theory of laws of nature. This is the theory that laws of nature are those regularities that are mentioned in the best system for the universe as a whole. The best system of a universe is the collection of descriptions of regularities that best balances being informative and being brief.

Biconditional. A biconditional is a statement of the form "P if and only if Q"; they are so-called because they are equivalent to a conjunction of two conditionals: "If P, then Q" and "If Q, then P".

Bundle theory of particulars. This is the view that particulars are nothing more than bundles of the various properties that they have.

Causal determinism. Let C be this complete description of everything that happens at a given time t. Let's suppose you also have a true and complete description of all the laws of nature. This means that you know all of the laws of physics, all the laws of chemistry, all the laws of biology, all the laws of psychology, and so on. Let L be this complete description of all the laws of nature. Ok, now consider a complete description of what happens at a time later than T. This is E. Causal determinism is the view that the conjunction of C and L entails E. That is, given that C and L are true, E has to be true. In other words, causal determinism is the thesis that any possible world in which C and L are true is also a world in which E is true.

Composition. The relation that parts stand in to a whole that they make up.

Composition as identity. This is the theory that the parts of a whole just are the whole; the whole is literally identical to its parts.

Compositional nihilism. This is the theory that composition never occurs, that is, in no possible situation do some objects make up a whole.

Compositional universalism. This is the theory that composition always occurs, that is, whenever you have some things, there is a whole made out of them.

The container view (of time). This is the theory that time itself is a whole that is made out of smaller bits, which are called "times." On the container view, times belong to their own distinctive ontological category.

The constituency view. This is the theory that an object, such as a table, has two very different sorts of constituents: the table's shape, size, color, and so on, and the table's substance.

The control principle. This is the theory that you freely perform an action only if it is under your control whether you will in fact perform that action.

Counterfactual. Counterfactuals are claims about what would happen if something else were to happen. They are instances of the form "If P were the case, then Q would be the case."

Counterpart theory. Counterpart theory says that something x could have been F if and only if there is a possible object y that is a counterpart of x and y is F.

Default knowable. A proposition P is default knowable for a person S if and only if all that it takes for S to know that P is that (i) S believes P, (ii) P is true, and (iii) S is not aware of reasons to think that P is false.

Dispositional property. A dispositional property is a tendency or liability to bring about some effect in the appropriate circumstances.

Endurantism. This is the theory that objects persist through time but not by having temporalo parts. Objects persist through time by being "wholly present"—rather than being partly there.

Epistemology. Epistemology is the subfield of philosophy that studies what makes knowledge different from mere true belief, what it is for something to be evidence for a belief, what kinds of evidence we have, and where those kinds of evidence come from.

Epistemic possibility. A proposition is epistemically possible for a person if and only if that person's evidence does not rule out that the proposition is true.

The epistemic theory of vagueness. This is the theory that vague expressions do have sharp cut-offs. Vagueness is simply our unfixable ignorance of where in a given spectrum the sharp cut-off happens to be. Something is definitely F if and only if it is F and it is a clear case of being F.

Essential property. A property of an object is an essential property of that object if and only if it is not possible for that object to exist without having that property.

Ethics. Ethics is the subfield of philosophy that is concerned with (among other things) the questions of what makes an action right or wrong, what makes a life a life worth living, and what character traits are admirable or despicable.

Factually correct. An argument is factually correct when all of its premises are true.

Facts/states of affairs. Combinations are properties and objects that make propositions true.

General Composition Question. This is the question *What is composition?*

Governing theories of laws. A theory that says that laws are what govern the patterns of the universe; they are what constrain and explain how objects change over time.

The Growing Block View. This is the theory that there are both past and present objects, but there are no future objects.

Hedonism. The theory that a person's life is worth living if and only if that person experiences a greater amount of pleasure than pain throughout the course of her life, and that a life is better or worse for the person who lives it to the extent that the balance of pleasure over pain is higher or lower.

Ideology. The ideology of a theory consists in the primitive expressions of the theory.

The identity view of "what is" questions. This is the theory that a "what is" question is correctly answered by a true identity statement about properties.

Intrinsic properties. Intrinsic properties are those properties that objects can in principle have independently of how those objects relate to other things. Extrinsic properties are properties that objects have because of how they are related to other things.

Lewisian Modal Realism. This is the theory that possible worlds are entire physical universes that are completely disconnected from our own, but otherwise are fundamentally the same kind of thing as our own universe. It is named after David Lewis.

Life (theory of composition). This is the theory that, in all possible cases, some objects make up a whole if and only if the activities of those objects constitute a life.

Logic. Logic is the subfield of philosophy that studies what makes an argument a good argument.

Meinongianism. The theory that there are non-existent objects. It is named after Alexius Meinong.

Metaphysical possibility, impossibility, and necessity. Every kind of genuine possibility implies metaphysical possibility: if something is genuinely possible in any way whatsoever, it is metaphysically possible.

Metaphysical impossibility is the strongest kind of genuine impossibility: what is metaphysically impossible is in no way genuinely possible. Similarly for metaphysical necessity: what is metaphysically necessary is absolutely guaranteed to happen.

Metaphysics. This is the philosophical study of reality.

Metaphysically dependent. One thing is metaphysically dependent on another if the dependent thing can't exist without the other thing existing.

Metaphysical vagueness. This is (alleged) vagueness that would remain even if all representational vagueness were eliminated.

Mind-dependence theory of composition (MDTC). This is the theory that, in all possible cases, some objects make up a whole if and only if those objects are arranged in a way that is interesting to us.

Necessary equivalence. Two propositions P and Q are necessarily equivalent if and only if (i) any possible situation in which P is true is also a situation in which Q is true, and vice versa, and (ii) any possible situation in which P is false is also a situation in which Q is false, and vice versa.

No constraints compatibilism. This is the theory that a person does an action freely if and only if they want to do that action, their action is caused by their desire to do that action, and they are under no internal or external compulsion to do that action.

No limits view. This is the theory that no object has an essential property that is not also an essential property of everything else.

No uncontrolled guarantees. This is the theory that it is under your control whether you perform an action only if every fact that guarantees that you perform that action is also under your control.

Ockham's Razor. This is the theory that, when trying to explain some phenomenon, we should prefer simpler theories to more complex ones. (Also called the Simplicity Constraint.)

Ontological commitment. A sentence is ontologically committed to some things if and only if the only way for that sentence to be true is for those things to exist.

Ontology. Ontology is the study of being, or what there is. An ontology is a theory of what there is. An ontology differs from other theories of what there is because it aims to provide a comprehensive and exclusive list of fundamental categories of what there is.

Particular. A particular is a non-repeatable entity.

Perdurantism. This is the theory that an object persists through time in the same way that it is spread out in space. Just as an object has spatial parts, it has temporal parts.

Possible objects first view. The theory that *possible object* is an ontological category, and that possible worlds are built up out of possible objects.

Possible worlds. A possible world is a maximal way that all of reality could have been. There is one possible world that corresponds to exactly how the world actually is. Metaphysicians call this unique world the actual world.

Predicates. A predicate is a part of a sentence that is used to say something about what is named by the subject (or subjects) of the sentence.

Presentism. Presentism is the theory that the only things that exist are the things that exist now.

Primitive. Philosophers call the activity of introducing a new technical expression without defining it "taking an expression as primitive." An expression is primitive if and only if it cannot be explicitly defined.

The primitive possible worlds theory. This is the theory that *possible world* is an ontological category.

Projectible. An expression is projectable if and only if it stands for a feature that we can justifiably make inductive inferences about.

Propositions. Propositions are the contents of beliefs and are what are expressed by declarative sentences. Propositions can be true or false, and a sentence is true (or false) because it expresses a true (or false) proposition. Similarly, a belief is true (or false) because the content of that belief—the proposition believed—is true (or false).

The propositions first theory. This is the theory that possible worlds are maximally consistent sets of propositions.

Quantifier. A quantifier is a linguistic expression that indicates quantity. Four examples of quantifiers are "some", "all", "most", and "none".

Quineanism. A theory about existence. According to Quineanism, to say that x exists is just to say that there is something that is identical to x. Named after Willard Van Orman Quine, who believed something like Quineanism.

Race eliminativism. The theory that there are no races.

Ranger. My dog.

Real essence. A real essence of a thing is supposed to be what that thing most fundamentally is.

The real essence view of "what is" questions. This is the theory that an answer to a "what is" question is one that states the real essence of the thing in question.

A reductio ad absurdum argument. Also known as "a reductio". One begins a reductio by initially assuming the opposite of what one actually wants to prove, and one then proceeds to demonstrate that this assumption generates an absurd conclusion.

Regularity theories (of laws of nature). These are theories that deny that laws of nature explain the patterns or regularities found in the world. This is because, according to a regularity theory, laws of nature just are certain regularities.

The relationalist view (of change). This the theory that an object undergoes change by bearing different relations to different times. An example: my t-shirt bears the white at relation to noon and the red at relation to 12:30 (when I dye it).

The relationalist view (of objects). This is the theory that an object (e.g., a dog or a table) doesn't have properties as components; instead, the only components of a substance like a table are other substances, such as the legs of the table. Relationalists believe that objects stand in a relation to their properties: objects have their properties, they exemplify their properties; but the properties are not parts or components of the objects in question.

The relationalist view (of time). According to the relationalist view of time, strictly speaking there aren't any times. There are, however, temporal relations between physical objects and events.

Semantic theory. A semantic theory is a theory about what the expressions of a given language mean or refer to.

The semantic theory of vagueness. This is the theory that vagueness is the result of our failing to make decisions about how our words are to be used. Something is definitely F if and only if our implicit decisions about how words are to be used classify that thing as an F.

The semantic view of "what is" questions. This is the theory that "what is" questions are questions about the definitions of words.

Set. A set is a collection or ensemble of things, which are called the members of the set.

The simplicity constraint. See Ockham's Razor.

Sound. An argument is sound when it is both valid and factually correct.

The Special Composition Question. This is the Special Composition Question: What are the necessary and jointly sufficient conditions a bunch of things must meet in order to compose a single thing?

The Static View. This is the theory that things in time change, but time itself doesn't change. According to the Static View, past objects and future objects and events are just as real as present ones.

Sufficiently stuck together theory (SSTT). This is the theory of composition that says that, in all possible cases, some objects make up a whole if and only if those objects are sufficiently stuck together.

Theoretical posit. A theoretical posit is something that we believe in on the basis of indirect evidence rather than direct observation. We posit its existence in order to explain certain things that we can directly observe.

The transcendental theory. This is the theory that we know that the world is non-arbitrary because we have (somehow) made it be non-arbitrary.

Transitive. A relation R is transitive if and only if it has the following feature: necessarily, if x bears R to y and y bears R to z, then x bears R to z.

Tropes. An entity that is both a property and a particular.

The truth-maker principle. This is the theory that, whenever some proposition C is true, there is something that makes it true. An entity x makes proposition C true if and only if it is impossible for x to exist without C's being true. That is, an entity x makes a proposition C true provided that the existence of x guarantees the truth of C.

Universals. A property that many things can literally share.

Useful. An activity is useful if and only if engaging in it is likely to make one's life go better than it would have otherwise. An intrinsically useful activity is an activity that, when you engage in it, makes a life be intrinsically better than it would have otherwise been in virtue of engaging in that activity.

Vagueness. An expression is vague if and only if there is a spectrum of possible cases such that (i) in some of the cases, the expression definitely applies, (ii) in some of the cases, the expression definitely does not apply, and (iii) in the remainder of the cases, the expression neither definitely applies nor definitely doesn't apply.

Valid. Logicians call an argument valid (this is a technical term!) when it is not possible for the argument to have all true premises and a false conclusion.

"What is" question. This is a question of the form "what is it to be X?" or even more simply, "What is X?". Some examples include: "What is knowledge?"; "What is freedom?"; "What is it to be a law of nature?"

INDEX

This Is Metaphysics: An Introduction, First Edition. Kris McDaniel.
© 2020 John Wiley & Sons, Inc. Published 2020 by John Wiley & Sons, Inc.

INDEX

This Is Metaphysics: An Introduction, First Edition. Kris McDaniel.
© 2020 John Wiley & Sons, Inc. Published 2020 by John Wiley & Sons, Inc.

Printed in Poland
by Amazon Fulfillment
Poland Sp. z o.o., Wrocław